PRAYERS OF THE AGES

COMPILED BY

CAROLINE S. WHITMARSH

"I believe in the communion of saints." — *Creed.*

BOSTON
TICKNOR AND FIELDS
1868

University Press: Welch, Bigelow, & Co.,
Cambridge.

THIS BOOK IS DEDICATED TO

A. E. G.,

MY INVALUABLE HELPER IN MAKING FORMER COMPILATIONS; THE FRIEND WHO "MAKES MY HAPPY LIFE A PRAYER."

C. S. W.

PREFACE.

THE disciples of Christ asked how his great works of healing had been wrought; and he answered, "This kind can come forth by nothing but by prayer and fasting." To show how the great healers and helpers of the world have prayed, has been my aim in compiling this volume.

It may seem contradictory to omit from such a work those noble Hebrew Prayers with which the Scriptures abound, and that central Prayer of the Church, the liturgy which has come down from Apostolic times; but they are already to be found in every home; and wishing to make a useful rather than a curious book, I have abandoned my original purpose of giving these with their changes, as used in different times and by different churches.

From Müller's Sanscrit Literature, from Bright's collection of Ancient Collects, from the Visitatio Infirmorum, the Confessions of St.

Augustine, and other works not in print in this country, I have made large selections; and also from the memoirs and private diaries of such men and women as were great in goodness;—from Fénelon and Oberlin and Madame Guyon, from Arnold of Rugby and Wilberforce and Channing and Sir Thomas Browne and Jeremy Taylor and Wilson and Andrewes and Luther; from the countless saints and martyrs of the Romish Church; from saints of heathen times, like Socrates and Epictetus; from Mahomet, Saadi, and the Hindoo Vedas; from modern books of prayer in various denominations; and from those excellent manuals of devotion in which the Roman Church abounds, and which are fitted to every shade of character and every emergency of life, through that fine tact which the disciples of Loyola so wisely cultivate.

The prayers are given without alterations,—except, in a very few instances, some necessary abridgment. A religious rather than a literary genius has been my test in making the selections. I have sought for records of the "conversation in heaven," the "heavenly places" of the soul, which the saints enjoyed while on earth,—the ladders of light whereby they have drawn earth closer to heaven.

C. S. W.

Roxbury, Oct. 1, 1867.

CONTENTS.

PART I.

Heathen and Mohammedan Prayers.

PART II.

Opinions and Instructions Concerning Prayer.

PART III.

COMMUNION WITH GOD.

PART IV.

Praise.

PART V.

Self-Renunciation.

PART VI.

For Spiritual Quickening.

PART VII.

For a Benevolent Spirit.

PART VIII.

Confession.

PART IX.

In Trouble.

PART X.

Old Age and Sickness.

PART XI.

Death.

PART XII.

Collects.

PART XIII.

Times and Seasons.

PART XIV.

Working Prayers.

PART XV.

Pater-Noster, Liturgical, &c.

PART I.

HEATHEN AND MOHAMMEDAN PRAYERS.

IF we traverse the world, it is possible to find cities without walls, without letters, without kings, without wealth, without coin, without schools and theatres; but a city without a temple, or that practiseth not worship, prayers, and the like, no one ever saw.

PLUTARCH. (A. D. 50–120.)

NOT with fond shekels of the tested gold,
  Nor gems whose rates are either rich or poor,
As fancy values them: but with true prayers,
That shall be up at heaven, and enter there
Ere sunrise; prayers from preserved souls,
From fasting maids, whose minds are dedicate
To nothing temporal.

SHAKESPEARE.

THE Pythagoreans bid us in the morning look to the heavens that we may be reminded of those bodies which continually do the same things, and in the same manner perform their work, and also be reminded of their purity and nudity. For there is no veil over a star.

M. ANTONINUS. (Born A. D. 121.)

The Contemplation of God.

SOCRATES. And to know one's self we acknowledge to be wisdom.

Alcibiades. By all means.

Socrates. As mirrors, then, are more clear and more pure and more brilliant than the mirror in the eye, so the Deity is more pure and more brilliant than that which is best in our soul.

Alcibiades. It is likely, Socrates.

Socrates. Looking, therefore, at the Deity, we should make use of him as the most beautiful mirror: but of things belonging to man, to the virtue of the soul; and shall we not thus especially see and know our very selves?

PLATO, *First Alcibiades.* (B. C. 429-348.)

That Men should praise God.

WHAT words can proportionably express our applauses and praise? For if we had any understanding, ought we not, both in public and private, incessantly to sing hymns and speak well of the Deity, and rehearse his benefits? Ought we not, whether we are digging or ploughing or eating, to sing the hymn due to God? Great is God, who has supplied us with these instruments to till the ground. Great is God, who has given us hands, a power of swallowing, a stomach: who has given us to grow insensibly, to breathe in sleep. Even these things we ought upon every occasion to celebrate; but to make it the subject of the greatest and most divine hymn, that he has given us the faculty of apprehending them, and using them in a proper way. Well, then, because the most of you are blind and insensible, was it not necessary that there should be some one to fill this station, and give out for all men the hymn to God?

What else can I, a lame old man, do but sing hymns to God? If I was a nightingale, I would act the part of a nightingale; if a swan, the part of a swan; but since I am a reasonable creature, it is my duty to praise God. This is my business. I do it. Nor will I ever desert this post, as long as it is vouchsafed me: and I exhort you to join in the same song.

EPICTETUS. (Born A. D. 90.)

How a Man should Pray.

EITHER the gods have no power, or they have power. If they have no power, why dost thou pray to them? But if they have power, why dost thou not pray for them to give thee the faculty of not fearing any of the things which thou fearest, or of not desiring any of the things which thou desirest, or not being pained at anything, rather than pray that any of these things should not happen or happen? for certainly if they can co-operate with men, they can co-operate for these purposes.

But perhaps thou wilt say the gods have placed them in thy power. Well, then, is it not better to use what is in thy power like a free man, than to desire in a slavish and abject way what is not in thy power? Begin, then, to pray for such things, and thou wilt see. One man prays thus: How shall I be able to attain that object? Do thou pray thus: How shall I not desire to attain it? Another prays thus: How shall I be released from this? Another prays: How shall I not desire to be released? Another thus: How shall I not lose my little son? Thou thus: How shall I not be afraid to lose him? In fine, turn thy prayers this way, and see what comes.

M. ANTONINUS. (Born A. D. 121.)

Directness in Prayer.

A Prayer of the Athenians.

"RAIN, rain, O dear Zeus, down on the ploughed fields of the Athenians and on the plains."

In truth, we ought not to pray at all, or we ought to pray in this simple and noble fashion.

M. ANTONINUS.

The Balanced Soul.

EVERYTHING harmonizes with me, which is harmonious to Thee, O Universe. Nothing for me is too early nor too late, which is in due time for Thee. Everything is fruit to me which Thy seasons bring, O Nature; from Thee are all things, to Thee all things return.

The poet says, Dear city of Cecrops; and wilt not thou say, Dear city of Zeus?

M. ANTONINUS.

The Prayer of Socrates.

O BELOVED Pan, and all ye other gods of this place, grant me to become beautiful in the inner man, and that whatever outward things I have may be at peace with those within.

May I deem the wise man rich, and may I have such a portion of gold as none but a prudent man can either bear or employ.

Do we need anything else, Phædrus? for myself I have prayed enough.

PLATO. (Phædrus.)

Harmony with God.

BOLDLY make a desperate push, man, as the saying is, for prosperity, for freedom, for magnanimity. Lift up your head, at last, as free from slavery. Dare to look up to God, and say,

Make use of me for the future as Thou wilt. I am of the same mind: I am equal with Thee. I refuse nothing which seems good to Thee. Lead me whither Thou wilt. Clothe me in whatever dress Thou wilt. Is it Thy will that I should be in a public or private condition; dwell here, or be banished; be poor, or rich? Under all these circumstances I will make Thy defence to men. I will show what the nature of everything is.

EPICTETUS. (Born A. D. 90.)

The Final Prayer.

IF death overtakes me in such a situation, it is enough for me if I can stretch out my hands and say, "The opportunities which Thou hast given me, of comprehending and following (the rules) of Thy administration, I have not neglected. As far as in me lay, I have not dishonored Thee. See how I have used my perceptions, how my preconceptions. Have I at any time found fault with Thee? Have I been discontented at Thy dispensations? or wished them otherwise? Have I transgressed the relations of life? I thank Thee that Thou hast brought me into being. I am satisfied with the time that I have enjoyed the things which Thou hast given me. Receive them back again, and assign them to whatever place Thou wilt; for they were all Thine, and Thou gavest them to me.

EPICTETUS.

The Wise Prayer.

SOCRATES. That poet was near to being a sensible person, who, when connected with some friends void of understanding, and observing them to do and pray for things which it were better for them not to have, but which appeared to them to be good, thought proper to use in common a prayer, which he expresses somehow to this effect: —

> O Zeus, our king, whate'er is good vouchsafe
> To us, if prayers we offer or do not;
> But evil, when we pray thee to avert,
> Do thou ordain.

To me, indeed, the poet appears to speak safely and correctly.

The Lacedemonians, having admired this very poet, or having so considered themselves the matter, put up on every occasion, in private and in public, a similar prayer, by requesting the gods to grant them ever things honorable in addition to what are good; and no one has ever heard them pray for anything more.

PLATO, *Second Alcibiades.* (B. C. 429–348.)

For Light.

THOU God of all! infuse light into the souls of men, whereby they may be enabled to know what is the root from whence all their evils spring, and by what means they may avoid them.

EURIPIDES.

That the Spirit is more important than Forms.

THE Lacedemonians were highly favored by the gods, while the Athenians were unfortunate. Whereupon the latter consulted the oracles, saying that they brought the gods solemn processions and costly sacrifices, while the Lacedemonians were careless of ceremonies, and offered even maimed animals at the altar. The oracle replied that he preferred the "good omened address" of the Lacedemonians, before all the sacrifices of the rest of the Greeks. "For it would be a dreadful thing indeed, if the gods looked to gifts and sacrifices, and not the soul, should a person happen to be holy and just."

It seems, then, that justice and prudence are near to being honored above all things by the gods, and by men too, that have any sense.

PLATO.

PAUSANIAS, a general of Aristides's army, perceiving that the tide of fortune was against him, and extremely afflicted thereby, while the priest offered sacrifice upon sacrifice, turning toward the temple of Juno, and with tears trickling from his eyes, and uplifted hands, prayed to that goddess, the protectress of Cithæron, and to the other tutelar deities of the Platæans, "That if the fates had not decreed that the Grecians should conquer, they might at least be permitted to sell their lives dear, and show the enemy by their deeds that they had brave men and experienced soldiers to deal with." The very moment that Pausanias was uttering this prayer, the tokens so much desired appeared in the victim, and the diviners announced him victory.

PLUTARCH.

THE city thus taken by the Romans sword in hand, while they were busy in plundering it, and carrying off its immense riches, Camillus, beholding from the citadel what was done, at first burst into tears: and when those about him began to magnify his happiness, he lifted up his hands towards heaven, and uttered this prayer: "Great Jupiter, and ye gods that have the inspection of our good and evil actions, ye know that the Romans, not without just cause, but in their own defence, and constrained by necessity, have made war against this city, and their enemies, its unjust inhabitants. If we must have some misfortune in lieu of this success, I entreat that it may fall, not upon Rome or the Roman army, but upon myself: yet lay not, ye gods, a heavy hand upon me."

PLUTARCH.

GRANT, we beseech Thee, O Lord, the Giver and Guide of all reason, that we may always be mindful of the nature, of the dignity, and of the privileges Thou hast honored us with, that we may act in all things as becomes free agents, to the subduing and governing of our passions, to the refining them from flesh and sense, and to the rendering them subservient to excellent purposes. Grant us also Thy favorable assistance in the forming and directing our judgment, and enlighten us with Thy truth, that we may discern those things which are really good, and having discovered them, may love and cleave steadfastly to the same. And, finally, disperse, we pray Thee, those mists which darken the eyes of our mind, that so we may have a perfect understanding, and know both God and man, and what to each is due.

Simplicius.
(Translated by George Stanhope, Dean of Canterbury, 1704.)

To Jupiter.

O THOU who hast many names, but whose power is infinite and uncommunicated! O Jupiter, first of immortals, sovereign of nature, who governest all, who subjectest all to thy law, I worship thee; for man is permitted to invoke thee. Everything that lives or creeps, everything mortal on earth is from thee, and of thee but an imperfect image. I will address to thee my hymns, and will never cease to celebrate thee.

This universe expanded over our heads, and which seems to roll around the earth, is obedient to thee alone; and at thy command are its motions in silence performed. Thunder, the executioner of thy will, is launched by thy invincible arm. Endowed with immortal life, it strikes, and nature is appalled.

Thou directest the universal mind that animates the whole, and that exists in all thy creatures; so unlimited and supreme is thy power, O king! Nothing in heaven, on the earth, or in the sea, is produced without thee, except the evil that proceeds from the heart of the wicked.

Thou bringest order out of confusion, and by thee is the jarring of the elements composed. Thou hast so mingled good and evil, that general and universal harmony is established. The wicked alone, amongst all thy creatures, disturb this general harmony.

Wretched men! they seek for happiness, but do not comprehend thy universal law that by making them wise would make them good, and consequently happy; but declining from the path of what is beautiful and just, they run headlong to the object that attracts them; they pant after fame, they grasp at sordid treasures, they lust after pleasures that entice but to deceive them.

O God! from whom all blessings descend, whom the storm and the thunder obey, preserve us from error; deign to inform our minds; attach us to that eternal reason by which thou art guided and supported in the government of the world; that being ourselves honored we may also honor thee, as becomes feeble and mortal beings, by celebrating thy works in an uninterrupted hymn; for neither the inhabitant of earth, nor the inhabitant of heaven can be engaged in a service more noble than that of celebrating the divine mind which presides over Nature.

HYMN OF CLEANTHES. (About 210 B. C.)

Hindoo Prayer.

LET me not yet, O Varuna, enter into the house of clay; have mercy, almighty, have mercy!

If I go along trembling, like a cloud driven by the wind; have mercy, almighty, have mercy!

Through want of strength, thou strong and bright god, have I gone to the wrong shore; have mercy, almighty, have mercy!

Thirst came upon the worshipper, though he stood in the midst of the waters; have mercy, almighty, have mercy!

Whenever we men, O Varuna, commit an offence before the heavenly host; whenever we break thy law through thoughtlessness; have mercy, almighty, have mercy.

VEDA. (1000 to 800 B. C.)

To Varuna.

HOWEVER we break thy laws from day to day, men as we are, O god, Varuna,

Do not deliver us unto death, nor to the blow of the furious; nor the anger of the spiteful!

To propitiate thee, O Varuna, we bind thy mind with songs, as the charioteer a weary steed.

Away from me they fly dispirited, intent only on gaining wealth; as birds to their nests.

When shall we bring hither the man who is victory to the warriors, when shall we bring Varuna, the wide-seeing, to be propitiated?

He who knows the place of the birds that fly through the sky, who, on the waters, knows the ships, —

He, the upholder of order, who knows the twelve

months, with the offspring of each, and knows the month that is engendered afterwards, —

He who knows the track of the wind, of the wide, the bright, the mighty; and knows those who reside on high, —

He, the upholder of order, Varuna, sits down among his people; he, the wise, sits there to govern.

From thence, perceiving all wondrous things, he sees what has been and what will be done.

May he, the wise son of time, make our paths straight all our days; may he prolong our lives!

Varuna, wearing golden mail, has put on his shining cloak: the spies sat down around him.

The god, whom the scoffers do not provoke, nor the tormentors of men, nor the plotters of mischief, —

He, who gives to men glory, and not half glory, who gives it even to our own bodies, —

Yearning for him, the far-seeing, my thoughts move onwards, as kine move to their pastures.

Let us speak together again, because my honey has been brought: thou eatest what thou likest, like a friend.

Now I saw the god who is to be seen by all. I saw the chariot above the earth: he must have accepted my prayers.

O hear this my calling, Varuna, be gracious now; longing for help, I have called upon thee.

Thou, O wise god, art lord of all, of heaven and earth: listen on thy way.

That I may live, take from me the upper rope, loose the middle, and remove the lowest.

[Ascribed to *Śunahśepha*, according to the legend of the later Brâhmanas, the victim offered to Varuna by his own father.]

HINDOO VEDA. (From Müller's Sanscrit Literature.)

To the Dawn.

SHE shines upon us, like a young wife, rousing every living being to go to his work. The fire had to be kindled by men; she brought light by striking down darkness.

She rose up, spreading far and wide, and moving towards every one. She grew in brightness, wearing her brilliant garment. The mother of the cows [of the morning clouds], the leader of the days, she shone gold-colored, lovely to behold.

She, the fortunate, who brings the eye of the god, who leads the white and lovely steed (of the sun), the Dawn was seen, revealed by her rays, with brilliant treasures she follows every one.

Thou, who art a blessing where thou art near, drive far away the unfriendly; make the pastures wide, give us safety! Remove the haters, bring treasures! Raise up wealth to the worshipper, thou mighty Dawn.

Shine for us with thy best rays, thou bright Dawn, thou who lengthenest our life, thou the love of all, who givest us food, who givest us wealth in cows, horses, and chariots.

Thou, daughter of the sky, thou high-born Dawn, whom the Vasishthas magnify with songs, give us riches high and wide: all ye gods, protect us always with your blessings!

VEDA. (Müller's Sanscrit Literature.)

To God.

IN the beginning there arose the Source of golden light. He was the only born Lord of all that is. He stablished the earth and this sky; — Who is the God to whom we shall offer our sacrifice?

He who gives life, He who gives strength; whose blessing all the bright gods desire; whose shadow is immortality; whose shadow is death; — Who is the God to whom we shall offer our sacrifice?

He who through His power is the only king of the breathing and awakening world; He who governs all, man and beast; — Who is the God to whom we shall offer our sacrifice?

He through whom the sky is bright and the earth firm. He through whom the heaven was stablished, — nay, the highest heaven. He who measured out the light in the air; — Who is the God to whom we shall offer our sacrifice?

He to whom heaven and earth, standing firm by His will, look up, trembling inwardly. He over whom the rising sun shines forth; — Who is the God to whom we shall offer our sacrifice?

Wherever the mighty water clouds went, where they placed the seed and lit the fire, thence arose

He who is the only life of the bright gods;—Who is the God to whom we shall offer our sacrifice?

He who by His might looked even over the water-clouds, the clouds which gave strength and lit the sacrifice, He who is God above all gods;—Who is the God to whom we shall offer our sacrifice?

May He not destroy us,—He the creator of the earth; or He, the righteous, who created the heaven; He who also created the bright and mighty waters;—Who is the God to whom we shall offer our sacrifice?

VEDA. (1000 to 800 B. C. Müller's Translation.)

Prayer to Indra.

LET no one, not even those who worship thee, delay thee far from us! Even from afar come to our feast! Or, if thou art here, listen to us!

For these here who make prayers for thee sit together near the libation like flies round the honey. The worshippers, anxious for wealth, have placed their desire upon Indra, as we put our foot upon a chariot.

Desirous of riches, I call him who holds the thunderbolt with his arm, and who is a good giver, like as a son calls his father.

These libations of Soma, mixed with milk, have been prepared for Indra: thou, armed with the thunderbolt, come with the steeds to drink of them for thy delight; come to the house!

May he hear us, for he has ears to hear. He

is asked for riches; will he despise our prayers? He could soon give hundreds and thousands;—no one could check him if he wishes to give.

He who prepares for thee, O Vitra-Killer, deep libations, and pours them out before thee, that hero thrives with Indra, never scorned of men.

Be thou, O mighty! the shield of the mighty when thou drivest together the fighting men. Let us share the wealth of him whom thou hast slain; bring us the household of him who is hard to vanquish.

Offer Soma to the drinker of Soma; give strength to the great god, make him to give wealth! He alone who perseveres, conquers, abides, and flourishes: the gods are not to be trifled with.

No one surrounds the chariot of the liberal worshipper, no one stops it. He whom Indra protects and the Maruts, he will come into stables full of cattle.

He will, when fighting, obtain spoil, O Indra, the mortal whose protection thou shouldst be. O hero, be thou the protection of our chariots and of our men.

His share is exceedingly great, like the wealth of a winner. He who is Indra with his steeds, him no enemies can subdue; may he give strength to the sacrificer!

Make for the sacred gods a hymn that is not small, that is well set and beautiful! Many snares pass by him who abides with Indra through his sacrifice.

What mortal dares to attack him who is rich in thee? Through faith in thee, O mighty, the strong acquires spoil in the day of battle.

Stir us mighty Vasishthas in the slaughter of the enemies, stir us who give their dearest treasures. Under thy guidance, O Haryaśva, we shall with our wise counsellors overcome all hardships.

To thee belongs the lowest treasure; thou rearest the middle treasure; thou art king always of all the highest treasure; no one withstands thee in the flock.

Thou art well known as the benefactor of every one, whatever battles there be. Every one of these kings of the earth implores thy name, when wishing for help.

If I were lord of as much as thou, I should support the sacred bard, thou scatterer of wealth, I should not abandon him to misery.

I should award wealth day by day to him who magnifies, I should award it to whosoever it be. We have no other friend but thee, no other happiness, no other father, O mighty!

He who perseveres acquires spoil with his wife as his mate; I bend Indra, who is invoked by many, for you, as a wheelwright bends a wheel made of strong wood.

A mortal does not get richer by scant praise: no wealth comes to the grudger. The strong man it is, O mighty, who in the day of battle is a precious gift to thee like as to me.

We call for thee, O hero, like cows that have not been milked; we praise thee as ruler of all that moves, O Indra, as ruler of all that is immovable.

There is no one like thee in heaven or earth; he is not born, and will not be born. O mighty Indra, we call upon thee as we go fighting for cows and horses.

Bring all this to those who are good, O Indra, be they old or young; for thou, O mighty, art the rich of old, and to be called in every battle.

Push away the unfriendly, O mighty; make us treasures easy to get! Be the protector of ourselves in the fight, be the cherisher of our friends!

Indra, give wisdom to us, as a father to his sons. Teach us in this path, let us living see the sun!

Let not unknown wretches, evil-disposed and unhallowed, tread us down. Through thy help, O hero, let us step over the rushing eternal waters!

VASISHTHA. HINDOO VEDA.
(Müller's History of Sanscrit Literature.)

Gratitude.

I SAW on the seashore a holy man, who had been torn by a tiger; and could get no salve to heal his wound. For a length of time he suffered much pain, and was all along offering thanks to the Most High. They asked him, saying, "Why are you so grateful?" He answered, "God be praised that I am overtaken with misfortune and not with sin."

SAADI. (A. D. 1175-1292.)

THE bad fortune of the good turns their faces up to heaven; and the good fortune of the bad bows their heads down to the earth.

The Wicked.

GREAT God, have pity on the wicked, for thou didst everything for the good when thou madest them good!

SAADI.

The Caliph's Prayer.

O THOU whose kingdom never passes away, pity one whose dignity is so transient!

CALIPH WACIC. (A. D. 845.)

Prayer of Mahomet.

MAHOMET was strenuous in enforcing the importance and efficacy of prayer. "Angels," said he, "come among you both by night and day; after which those of the night ascend to heaven, and God asks them how they left his creatures. We found them, say they, at their prayers, and we left them at their prayers."

Prayers were enjoined at certain hours of the day and night; they were simple in form and phrase, addressed directly to the Deity, with certain inflections, or at times a total prostration of the body, and with the face turned towards the Kebla.

At the end of each prayer the following verse from the second chapter of the Koran was recited.

It is said to have great beauty in the original Arabic, and is engraved on gold and silver ornaments, and on precious stones worn as amulets.

"God! There is no God but He, the living, the ever living; he sleepeth not, neither doth he slumber. To him belongeth the heavens, and the earth, and all that they contain. Who shall intercede with him unless by his permission? He knoweth the past and the future, but no one can comprehend anything of his knowledge but that which he revealeth. His sway extendeth over the heavens and the earth, and to sustain them both is no burden to him. He is the High, the Mighty!"

IRVING'S LIFE OF MAHOMET. (Born A. D. 569.)

The Call to Prayer.

HE was for some time at a loss in what manner his followers should be summoned to their devotions; whether with the sound of trumpets, as among the Jews, or by lighting fires on high places, or by the striking of timbrels. While in this perplexity, a form of words to be cried aloud was suggested by Abdallah, the son of Teid, who declared that it was revealed to him in a vision. It was instantly adopted by Mahomet, and such is given as the origin of the following summons, which is to this day heard from the lofty minarets throughout the East, calling the Moslems to the place of worship: —

"God is great! God is great! There is no God

but God. Mahomet is the apostle of God. Come to prayers! Come to prayers! God is great! God is great! There is no God but God." To which at dawn of day is added the exhortation, "Prayer is better than sleep! Prayer is better than sleep!"

IRVING.

The Prayer of Abraham.

FEELING his end draw near, Mahomet resolved to expend his remaining strength in a final pilgrimage to Mecca.

After praying in the mosque, he mounted his camel Al Aswa, and entering the plains of Baïda, uttered the prayer or invocation called in Arabic Talbijah, in which he was joined by all his followers. The following is the import of this solemn invocation:—

"Here am I in Thy service, O God! Here am I in Thy service! Thou hast no companion. To Thee alone belongeth worship. From Thee cometh all good. Thine alone is the kingdom. There is none to share it with Thee."

This prayer, according to Moslem tradition, was uttered by the patriarch Abraham, when, from the top of the hill of Kubeis, near Mecca, he preached the true faith to the whole human race, and so wonderful was the power of his voice, that it was heard by every living being throughout the world; insomuch that the very child in the womb responded, "Here am I in Thy service, O God!"

IRVING'S LIFE OF MAHOMET.

PART II.

OPINIONS AND INSTRUCTIONS CONCERNING PRAYER.

A Distinction.

THERE is a wider division of men than that into Christian and Pagan; before we ask what a man worships, we have to ask whether he worships at all.

RUSKIN.

Consistency.

AURELIUS painted all the faces of his pictures to the air and resemblance of the woman whom he loved; and every one painteth Devotion according to his passion and fancy. He that is given to fasting, thinks himself very devout if he fast often, be his heart never so full of rancor; and though he does not dare to moisten his tongue with wine and water, for sobriety's sake, yet makes no difficulty to drink deep of the blood of his neighbor by slander and calumny. Another will account himself full of devotion for huddling over a multitude of prayers every morning, though afterwards he give his tongue a liberty to utter offensive, arrogant, and reproachful speeches amongst his neighbors and family. One willingly draws an alms out of his purse to give the poor, but cannot draw clemency out of his heart to pardon his enemies. Another forgiveth his enemies, yet cares not to satisfy his creditors, but by constraint. All these people are devout in the rote of the vulgar, yet indeed they are not so at all.

De Sales. (1567-1622.)

That Men should Pray.

WE go to God by prayers, not by steps.

Bishop Andrews.

GOD commandeth thee to ask, and teacheth thee how to ask, and promiseth that which thou askest, and is angry if thou askest not; and yet askest thou not?

Ibid.

IF He prayed who was without sin, how much more it becometh a sinner to pray!

St. Cyprian.

WE, ignorant of ourselves,
Beg often our own harm which the wise Powers
Deny us for our good; so find we profit
By losing of our prayers.

Shakespeare. Antony and Cleopatra.

Dr. Martin Luther's Simple Method how to Pray.

DEAR MASTER PETER. I give you as good as I have, and will show you how I manage myself with prayer. Our Lord God grant unto you and every one to manage better. Amen.

First, when I feel that I am become cold and indisposed to prayer, by reason of other business and thoughts, I take my psalter and run into my chamber, or, if day and reason serve, into the church to the multitude, and begin to repeat to myself — just as children use — the ten commandments, the creed, and, according as I have time, some sayings of Christ or of Paul, or some psalms. Therefore it is well to let prayer be the first employment in the early morning, and the last in the evening. Avoid diligently those false and deceptive thoughts which say, Wait a little, I will pray an hour hence; I must first perform this or that. For, with such thoughts, a man quits prayer for business, which lays hold of and entangles him, so that he comes not to pray the whole day long.

Howbeit works may sometimes occur which are as good or better than prayer, especially if necessity require them. There is a saying to this effect, which goes under the name of St. Jerome: "All the works of the faithful are prayer." And there is a proverb: "Whoso labors faithfully he prays twice." The meaning of which saying must be, that a believer fears and honors God in his labor, and thinks of his commandment, to do wrong to no man, not to steal nor take advantage, nor to betray. And, doubtless, such thoughts and such faith make his work a prayer and an offering of praise. On the other hand, it must be equally true that the works of the unbelieving are mere curses, and that he who labors unfaithfully curses twice. For the thoughts of his heart in his employment must lead him to despise God and to trangress his law, to do wrong to his neighbor, to steal, and to betray. What are such thoughts but mere curses against God and man? . . . . Of constant prayer, Christ indeed says, men ought always to pray. For men ought always to guard against sin and wrong, which no man can do except he fear God and set his commandment before his eyes. Nevertheless, we must take heed that we do not disuse ourselves to actual prayer, and interpret works to be necessary which are not necessary, and by that means become at last negligent and indolent, and cold and reluctant to pray. For the Devil is not indolent nor negligent around us. And our flesh is alive and fresh toward sin and averse from the spirit of prayer.

Now when the heart is warmed by this oral communion and has come to itself, then kneel down or stand with folded hands and eyes toward heaven, and say or think in as few words as possible, &c., &c.*

* Here follows, in the original, after a brief invocation, a paraphrase of the Lord's Prayer.

Finally, observe that thou must ever make the "amen" strong, and not doubt but that God assuredly heareth thee with all his grace, and saith "yea" to thy prayer. And think that thou kneelest or standest not alone, but the whole Christendom, or all pious Christians, with thee, and thou among them, in consenting unanimous supplication which God cannot despise. And quit not thy prayer until thou hast said or thought, "Go to now, this prayer hath been heard with God; that know I surely and of a truth." That is the meaning of Amen.

Also, thou must know that I would not have thee to repeat all these words in thy prayer, for that would make it, at last, a babble and a vain empty gossip, — a reading from the book and after the letter, such as the rosaries of the laity and the prayers of priests and monks have been. My purpose is to awaken the heart and instruct it what kind of thoughts to connect with the Lord's prayer. If the heart be rightly warmed and eager for prayer, it can express these thoughts with very different words, perhaps with fewer, perhaps with more. For I myself do not bind myself to precisely these words and syllables, but say the words to-day after this fashion, to-morrow otherwise, according as I feel warm and free. I keep as nearly as I can to the same thoughts and meaning. But it will sometimes happen that, while engaged with some single article or petition, I walk into such rich thoughts that I leave the other six.* And when these rich and good thoughts come, one ought to give place to them and let other prayers go, and listen in silence, and on no account offer any hindrance; for then the Holy Ghost himself preaches, and one word of his preaching is better than a thousand of our prayers. And so I have often learned more in one prayer than I could have got from much reading and composing.

Wherefore, it is of the greatest importance that the heart be disengaged and disposed to prayer; as saith the Preacher (cap. iv. 17), "Prepare thy heart before prayer, that thou mayest not tempt God."† What else is it but tempting God, when the mouth babbles while the heart is distracted with other things? Like that priest who prayed after this fashion: "*Deus in auditorium meum intende;* Fellow, hast thou unharnessed the horses? *Domine adjuvandum me festina;* Maid, go and milk the cows! *Gloria Patri et Filio et Spiritui Sancto;* Run, boy, as if the Devil were after thee!" &c. Of such prayers I have heard and experienced much in Popedom, in my day. . . . . But now, God be praised, I see well that that is not prayer, in which one forgets what one has said. For a true prayer is conscious of all its words and thoughts, from the beginning to the end of the prayer.

* Luther divides the Lord's Prayer into seven petitions.

† The text here quoted is probably the first verse of the fifth chapter of Ecclesiastes; but it differs widely from the common English version.

This is briefly said of the "Our Father" or of prayer, as I myself am wont to pray. For, to this day, I suck still at the *Pater-noster*, like a child. I eat and drink thereof like a full-grown man; and can never have enough. It is to me, even more than the psalter (which, notwithstanding, I dearly love), the best of all prayers. Assuredly, it will be found that the right master hath ordained and taught it. And it is a pity upon pities that such a prayer of such a master should be babbled and rattled over by all the world, so entirely without devotion. Many pray, it may be, some thousand *Pater-nosters* a year; and if they should pray a thousand years, after that fashion, they would not have tasted or prayed one letter or tittle thereof. In fine, the *Pater-noster* (as well as the name and word of God) is the greatest martyr upon earth, for every one tortures and abuses; few comfort and make it glad by a true use of it.

Dr. F. H. Hedge's Prose Writers of Germany.

The Pater-Noster.

TO distort one's eyes in prayer does not seem to me necessary; I hold it better to be natural. But then one must not blame a man on that account, provided he is no hypocrite. But that a man should make himself great and broad in prayer, — that, it seems to me deserves reproach, and is not to be endured. One may have courage and confidence, but he must not be conceited and wise in his own conceit; for if one knows how to counsel and help himself, the shortest way is to do it. Folding the hands is a fine external decorum, and looks as if one surrendered himself without capitulation, and laid down his arms. But the inward, secret yearning, billow-heaving, and wishing of the heart, — that, in my opinion, is the chief thing in prayer; and therefore I cannot understand what people mean who will not have us pray. It is just as if they said one should not wish, or one should have no beard and no ears. That must be a blockhead of a boy who should have nothing to ask of his father, and who should deliberate the whole day whether he will let it come to that extremity. When the wish within you concerns you nearly, and is of a warm complexion, it will not question long; it will overpower you like a strong and armed man. It will just hurry on a few rags of words, and knock at the door of heaven.

Whether the prayer of a moved soul can accomplish or effect anything, or whether the *Nexus Rerum* does not allow of that, as some learned gentlemen think, — on that point I shall enter into no controversy. I have great respect for the *Nexus Rerum*, but I cannot help thinking of Samson, who left the *Nexus* of the gate-leaves uninjured and carried the whole gate, as every one knows, to the top of the hill. And, in short, I believe that the rain comes when it is dry, and that the heart does not cry in vain after fresh water, if we pray *aright* and are *rightly disposed.*

"Our Father" is once for all the best prayer, for you know who made it. But no man on God's earth can pray it after him, precisely as he meant it. We cripple it with a distant imitation; and each more miserably than the other. But that matters not if we only mean well; the dear God must do the best part at any rate, and he knows how it ought to be. Because you desire it, I will tell you sincerely how I manage with "Our Father." But it seems to me a very poor way, and I would gladly be taught a better.

Do you see, when I am going to pray, I think first of my late father, how he was so good and loved so well to give to me. And then I picture to myself the whole world as my Father's house, and all the people in Europe, Asia, Africa, and America are then, in my thoughts, my brothers and sisters; and God is sitting in heaven on a golden chair, and has his right hand stretched out over the sea to the end of the world, and his left full of blessing and good; and all around the mountain-tops smoke; and then I begin:—

Our Father who art in Heaven, hallowed be thy name.—Here I am already at fault. The Jews are said to have known special mysteries respecting the name of God. But I let all that be, and only wish that the thought of God, and every trace by which we can recognize him, may be great and holy above all things, to me and all men.

Thy kingdom come. — Here I think of myself, how it drives hither and thither within me, and now this governs, and now that; and that all is sorrow of heart, and I can light on no green branch. And then I think how good it would be for me, if God would put an end to all discord, and govern me himself.

Thy will be done as in heaven so on earth. — Here I picture to myself heaven and the holy angels who do his will with joy, and no sorrow touches them, and they know not what to do for love and blessedness, and frolic night and day; and then I think if it were only so here on the earth!

Give us this day our daily bread. — Everybody knows what daily bread means, and that one must eat as long as one is in the world, and also that it tastes good. I think of that. Perhaps, too, my children occur to me, how they love to eat and are so lively and joyful at table. And then I pray that the dear God would only give us something to eat.

Forgive us our debts as we forgive our debtors. — It hurts when one receives an affront; and revenge is sweet to man. It seems so to me, too, and my inclination leads that way. But then the wicked servant in the Gospel passes before my eyes and my heart fails, and I resolve that I will forgive my fellow-servant and not say a word to him about the *hundred pence.*

And lead us not into temptation. — Here I think

of various instances where people in such and such circumstances have strayed from the good and have fallen; and that it would be no better with me.

But deliver us from evil. — Here I still think of temptations, and that man is so easily seduced and may stray from the straight path. But at the same time I think of all the troubles of life, of consumption and of old age, of the pains of childbirth, of gangrene and insanity and the thousand-fold misery and heart-sorrow that is in the world and that plagues and tortures poor mortals, and there is none to help. And you will find, if tears have not come before, they will be sure to come here; and one can feel such a hearty yearning to be away, and can be so sad and cast down in one's self, as if there were really no help at all. But then one must pluck up courage again, lay the hand upon the mouth and continue, as it were, in triumph.

For thine is the kingdom and the power and the glory forever. Amen.

MATTHIAS CLAUDIUS. (A. D. 1740-1815.)
Hedge's Prose Writers of Germany.

Injunction on Praying the Lord's Prayer.

WHEN ye pray be ye not as the hypocrites, but as the Lord hath appointed us in the Gospel, so pray ye: Our Father which art in heaven; hallowed be Thy name; Thy kingdom come; Thy will be done as in heaven so on earth; give us this day our daily bread; and forgive us our debts as we forgive our debtors; and lead us not into temptation, but deliver us from evil; for Thine is the kingdom forever. Amen. Pray thus thrice in a day, preparing yourselves beforehand, that ye may be worthy of the adoption of the Father; lest when ye call him Father unworthily, ye be reproached by him, as Israel his first-born son was once told: *If I be a Father, where is my glory? and if I be a Lord, where is my fear?* For the glory of Fathers is the holiness of their children, and the honor of masters is the fear of their servants, as the contrary is dishonor and confusion: for, saith he, *Through you my name is blasphemed among the Gentiles.*

GREEK CONSTITUTIONS.

Sincerity in Prayer.

A MAN may pray according to his ability and knowledge, with every language, and in every place. Now here is a confession and a prayer in English; but whoever will sing this, let him say no more in the confession, than he has [actually] committed; for our Saviour will not have a man lie on himself: neither do all men sin in one wise.

Rubric of the early Saxon Church, by
Aelfric, Archbishop of Canterbury. Died 1005.

To pray Frequently.

THERE is much need that, in addition to set seasons, we shall often and unseldom praise God, and cry to God for many needs; as the

Apostle says: "Be aye incessantly praying." And again the Apostle says: "If ye eat or drink or elsewhat work, whatsoever ye do, do all thanking and praising God. Be the thing what it may be, that the man will work to profit, let him pray God for aid: ever and aye he will speed the better; as David says: "My Lord, be my help." And again he says: "Our help is God, who shaped and wrought heavens and earth, and all creatures." God assist us at our need, so his will be. Amen.

Benedictine Liturgy of the Tenth Century.
Offices of the Canonical Hours.

Seasons of Prayer.

IN one sense prayer may be considered a duty. It is a duty to pray, just as it is a duty to live on terms of affectionate intimacy and intercourse with our father and our mother, our wife and children. But it is not a duty in the sense in which it is our duty to tell the truth or to pay our debts. In other words, it does not belong to that class of duties in which the outward act is the principal thing. A man ought to tell the truth, he ought to pay his debts, no matter in what frame of mind he does it. But what would you think of a child who should make it a rule to go to its father so many times a day, and express gratitude to him in a formal manner for his love and paternal care? The moment that the expression of affection was made a duty, in this sense of the word, it would become a cold and difficult matter enough. But in the same way we often freeze our religious affections, by making it a mere matter of duty to pray so much and so often every day, instead of regarding prayer in its true light, as the highest joy, the freest and happiest privilege allotted to us here below.

In describing the true way to cultivate the spirit of prayer, we must say that to pray *merely* as a duty, rather hinders than helps it. But let the mind and heart be pervaded with the conviction of those great truths which constitute the Gospel, — and being filled with a spirit of trust, never to be shaken, in God as our tenderest friend, we shall always be ready to come boldly to the throne of grace, to find help in time of need. We shall have that sense of a Divine Presence which shall cause us to pray without ceasing, — though our prayers will be often only a throb of gratitude, or a sudden aspiration of love, or the soul falling down in humility, and bowing itself before God. And then, too, we shall find a place and a use for times of prayer, and for a certain degree of method and system in prayer. . . . . It does not prove my friendship insincere, that I say to my friend when we part, "Let us write to each other at least twice a week," or "Let us look every evening, at a certain hour, at a particular star, and think of one another." If the letter-writing and star-looking are done *merely* as a duty, it will be bad, and if the method of prayer be retained when its life is gone, this is also bad. But every pious heart must feel that God, in the very arrangements of nature, and in the ordinances of the heavens, says to us, "In the morning think of me, in that calm hour which I send you before the din and toil of life commences; and in the evening think of me; after it is over, when the holy stars pour quiet upon the earth, then remember me." And so, too, on the Sabbath day, we shall have opportunity for a closer walk with God.

J. F. CLARKE.

Nature of Prayer.

THE great thing needed for moral development is more vital power. Love will make all things new. A profound influence in the centre of the soul will cause all parts of life to bud and blossom, and bear fruit.

But what can we do when the door of the heart is closed to God by sin, and the soul is left barren, cold, empty, incapable of any true virtue? We cannot, by an act of the will, create within the heart Christian sentiments and graces; we cannot by moral effort create within the soul generosity or love. What *can* we do? We can open the door; we can let God's influence come into the heart to lead us to Christ, to give us a sense of his pardoning love, to lift us to a higher plane of conviction. And this is *prayer* in its most essential nature.

J. F. CLARKE.

HE that has learned to pray as he ought, has got the secret of an holy life.

IT is of greater advantage to us than we imagine, that God does not grant our petitions immediately. We learn by that, that whereunto we have already attained, it was the gift of God.

THE lukewarmness of our prayers is the source of all our infidelities.

IT is a rudeness amongst men to ask for a favor and not stay for an answer. And do we count it no fault to pray for blessings, and never to think of them afterwards, — never to wait for them, never to give God thanks for them?

IT was the saying of a learned man, saith Dr. Lightfoot, that he got more knowledge by his prayers than by all his studies.

SACRA PRIVATA. (Bp. Wilson, 1722.)

"BEFORE thou prayest," says the wise man, "prepare thyself." Let the mind, as much as may be, be solemnized, calmed, toned down, by taking in the thought of the presence of God, and the sublime idea of coming to Him.

GOULBURN.

PRAYER is an act of homage done to the majesty of God. Accordingly, it is to be performed with the utmost reverence and solemnity; there is to be no babbling in it, no familiar glibness of the tongue, no running of words to waste, but simple, grave, short, sound, well-considered speech. So had King Solomon said long centuries ago: Be not rash with thy mouth, and let not thine heart be hasty to utter anything before God: for God is in heaven, and thou upon earth: therefore let thy words be few." And so says one greater and wiser than Solomon, even Christ. "But when ye pray, use not vain repetitions as the heathen do: for they think that they shall be heard for their much speaking. Be not ye therefore like unto them."

WILL petitions that do not move the heart of the suppliant, move the heart of Omnipotence?

THOMPSON.

PRAYER is a closing of the eyes on things seen, and opening them on things unseen. It is penitence vocal, faith making its profession, and love kindling into a flame. It is a heart brought to the altar, a flower opening to the benignant eye of Heaven; it is a putting off the shoes at Horeb; it is a walk to Emmaus; it is to be present in the upper chamber; to sit quietly by the Saviour's side, lean the head on his bosom, and feel the beating of Immanuel's heart.

REV. A. C. THOMPSON. (1860.)

IT will sometimes seem to you in prayer that your soul is not in the presence of God, and that your body alone is in the church, like the statues and chandeliers that ornament the altar: on such occasions, think that it shares with these inanimate objects in the honor of adorning the house of God, and that this humble occupation should seem glorious and honorable to you.

David Brainerd.

WE enjoyed not only the benefit of his conversation, but had the comfort and advantage of hearing him pray in the family, from time to time. His manner of praying was very agreeable; most becoming a worm of the dust, and a disciple of Christ, addressing an infinitely great and holy God, and Father of mercies; not with fluid expressions, or a studied eloquence; not with any intemperate vehemence, or indecent boldness; at the greatest distance from any appearance of ostentation, and from everything that might look as though he meant to recommend himself to those that were about him, or set himself off to their acceptance; free, too, from vain repetitions, without impertinent excursions, or needless multiplying of words. He expressed himself with the strictest propriety, with weight and pungency; and yet what his lips uttered seemed to flow from the *fulness of his heart*, as deeply impressed with a great and solemn sense of our necessities, unworthiness, and dependence, and of God's infinite greatness, excellency, and sufficiency, rather than merely from a warm and fruitful brain, pouring out good expressions. And I know not, that ever I heard him so much as ask a blessing or return thanks at table, but there was something remarkable to be observed both in the matter and manner of the performance. In his prayers he insisted much on the prosperity of Zion, the advancement of Christ's kingdom in the world, and the flourishing and propagation of religion among the Indians. And he generally made it one petition in his prayer, that we might not outlive our usefulness.

JONATHAN EDWARDS, Life of David Brainerd. (1747.)

A LAYMAN of rare spirituality, in the seventeenth century, wrote thus: "As all ordinances are the galleries of intercourse between God and his people in Christ, so prayer hath this work in an eminency. It is the very intercession of God's own spirit in them; it is the private retirement in which the soul is brought into the presence chamber, and hath private conference with Christ, and the Father in him. The very nature of prayer is a thirst after the living God. It is the very breathing of the soul's union with God, and the means whereby it is preserved, fortified, carried on, and confirmed; and whereby the sweetness and nourishing virtue of it to the soul is improved, enjoyed, and increased. Let thy prayers, then, be inward and single-hearted, chiefly aiming at and prizing this union; and refer all other things of a remote nature to the wisdom of Him to whom thou art united. Speak to him as one who is in his bosom, and consider him as thy only helper and thy most sure friend. Come reverently, believingly, with resignation of thy heart to his, and so creep forward into an humble intimacy and familiarity with thy God. This union only begets the true cry of Abba, Father, and nourisheth it."

REV. A. C. THOMPSON.

"RESOLVED," wrote President Edwards, at twenty years of age, — "Resolved, very much to exercise myself in this all my life long, namely: With the greatest openness of which I am capable, to declare my ways to God, and lay open my soul to him, all my sins, temptations, difficulties, sorrows, fears, hopes, desires, and everything, and every circumstance."

PIOUS Icelanders, on waking in the morning, do not salute any one in the house, till, after hastening to the door, they have lifted up their eyes in silent prayer. Returning into the house, they greet every one with, "God grant you a good day!" Before and after crossing a river the devout Icelander will raise his hat in token of the sense he entertains of his dependence on God.

REV. A. C. THOMPSON.

Efficacy of Prayer.

IT was said of Luther, that he could have what he would of God; and Queen Mary confessed that she feared the prayers of John Knox more than an army of ten thousand men. In reference to the defeat of the Emperor Julian's designs, Nanzianzen exclaims, "How many myriads and squadrons of men were there whom we, only praying, and God willing, discomfited."

REV. A. C. THOMPSON.

GOOD prayers never come creeping home. I am sure I shall receive either what I ask or what I should ask.

BISHOP HALL.

WHEN Job looked on himself as an outcast, the Infinite spirit and the Wicked spirit were holding a dialogue on his case!

CECIL.

New-Year's Meditation.

GOD will give his holy spirit to them that ask him. O then pray, — pray, — be earnest, — press forward and follow on to know the Lord. Without watchfulness, humiliation, and prayer, the sense of divine things must languish, as much as the grass withers for want of refreshing rains and dews. Heaven is not to be won without labor. O then press forward; whatever else is neglected, let this one thing needful be attended to: then will God bless thee. Let me every evening give half an hour or an hour to secret exercises, endeavoring to raise my mind more, and that it may be more warmed with heavenly fire. Help me, O Lord; without Thee I can do nothing.

W. WILBERFORCE.

WE should give God, if needful, our best time. O Lord, Thy blessing can render far more than a day's time as nothing even in my worldly business, and if the mainspring's force be strengthened, and its working improved (cleansed from dust and foulness), surely the machine will go better.

WILBERFORCE.

ALMIGHTY prayer, I am made to say, and why not? For that it is almighty, is only through the gracious ordination of the God of love and truth. O then pray, pray, pray, my dearest;—but then remember to estimate your state, on self-examination, not by your prayers, but by what you find to be the effects of them on your character, temper, and life.

WILBERFORCE.

Persistency in Prayer.

THERE was a parable that men ought *always* to pray and not to faint. Prayer with some is a mere jet or explosion, and then the spirit of prayer dies out.

The true scriptural idea of prayer is, that it is calm, earnest, steady to its purpose. Perhaps the most beautiful representation we have of this quality is found in the narrative of the Canaanitish woman (Matt. xv. 22, 28). She came to Christ in great anguish, and said: "Have mercy on me, O Lord, thou Son of David, my daughter is grievously vexed with a devil." Now Christ had often answered similar applications immediately, but now he seemed strangely altered and insensible; "he answered her not a word." Heedless of her cry, he passed on as one deaf. In such circumstances, most persons would have concluded that he could not or would not aid; or perhaps they would have resented this cold, contemptuous treatment. But she persisted; she repeated and reiterated her requests, till the disciples, apparently irritated by her importunity, following them, as we may suppose, through the street, interposed, they begged Jesus to comply and dismiss her. He, though not directly refusing, replied with a remark which seemed like a refusal: "I am not sent but unto the lost sheep of the house of *Israel*." Now as this woman was a Canaanite and not an Israelite, this reply seemed to cut off all hope.

But hers was no fair-weather purpose. So she came nearer and fell down at his feet, saying: "Lord, help me." Grief, faith, changeless importunity, condensed into three words. His answer was still discouraging, apparently contemptuous:

"It is not meet to take the children's bread and cast it to the dogs!" Dogs! was she thus insulted? Hear her answer: "Truth, Lord, yet the dogs eat of the crumbs which fall from the master's table." You have called me a dog, which means a worthless sinner, undeserving of notice or favor. I *am* such a sinner. I know it and confess it, and as such I still beg for a favor which I have not deserved. "Her daughter was made whole from that very hour."

REV. G. W. PERKINS.

The Greatest of these is Charity.

I COULD never hear the Ave Mary bell without an elevation; or think it a sufficient warrant, because they erred in one circumstance, for me to err in all, that is, in silence and dumb contempt: whilst therefore they directed their devotions to her, I offered mine to God, and rectified the errors of their prayers, by rightly ordering mine own. At a solemn procession I have wept abundantly, while my consorts, blind with opposition and prejudice, have fallen into an access of scorn and laughter.

I CANNOT contentedly frame a prayer for myself in particular, without a catalogue for my friends; nor request a happiness wherein my sociable disposition doth not desire the fellowship of my neighbor. I never hear the toll of a passing bell, though in my mirth, without my prayers and best wishes for the departing spirit: I cannot go to cure the body of my patient but I forget my profession, and call unto God for his soul: I cannot see one say his prayers, but instead of imitating him, I fall into a supplication for him, who perhaps is no more to me than a common nature: and if God hath vouchsafed an ear to my supplications, there are surely many happy that never saw me, and enjoy the blessing of mine unknown devotions.

SIR THOMAS BROWNE. (Religio Medici. 1605-1682.)

A Sailor's Confession.

"HE stood with one arm akimbo, and looked steadily all round on his fellow-seamen. He was a large and powerful man, and had a face as bold as a lion. He began, 'Shipmates,'—and he paused a moment,—'I suppose you know what *I* have been,—a ringleader in everything that was wrong,—in every kind of deviltry. I confess what I *was*. I stand up here to tell you what I *am*. By the grace of God I am what I am,'—and here his voice choked with emotion, while the stillness of death prevailed all around. 'I had a praying mother; and when the minister said, "Perhaps some of you have had praying mothers," a shot went clean through me. I was in agony. As soon as the meeting was over I ran down into the hold, hid in the coal-bunkers to get away all alone in the dark, and I kneeled down and cried, "O God, my mother's God, have mercy on me, mercy on *me!*

Can you have mercy on such a wretch as *me?*" And there I kept praying, till all at once I felt as if a fifty-six pound weight was taken right off my heart; and when I came out of the coal-bunker that night I felt as if all my sins were washed away in the blood of Christ. O shipmates,' — and the tears were falling all around, — 'I tell you, Jesus Christ is able to forgive sins. O how I want some of you should try it. Come to Jesus right off. Knock off your old ways; knock right off, and come to Jesus, and try Him once, and see if the load of sin won't soon be gone. You know what I was. Nothing but the power and mercy of God could make me what I hope I am. I thank God I had a praying mother,' and he sat down weeping like a child."

PRIME'S "Five Years of Prayer."

The Sailor's Closet.

"I WAS chief mate of a ship; a great sinner, cursing at everything and everybody; but the Spirit of God got foul of me and showed me my sins. I was distressed and discouraged; it went on so for two weeks. But I resolved to make just one more effort. I knew God was true. I threw down the block and strap, and started aloft for the main-topsail yard, and then I leaned over that yard and prayed, 'O Lord! if there is mercy for a poor sinner, let me have it now, here on this topsail yard, before I go down on deck. Thou art able:

O come now.' Just at that moment, when I felt, 'I can do nothing; O God, help me!' then the answer came; then the light broke on my soul; then I knew that *God is love.*"

PRIME'S "Five Years of Prayer."

Prayer in High Places.

LORD BURLEIGH coming in from prayers, Sir Francis Walsingham, who had been waiting, said to him jocularly (which in the cant of the present day would be styled quizzingly), "that he wished himself so good a servant of God as Lord Burleigh, but that he had not been at church for a week past." To which Lord Burleigh thus gravely replied: "I hold it meet for us to ask God's grace to keep *us* sound of heart, who have so much in our power; and to direct us to our well-doing for all the people, whom it is easy for us to injure and ruin; and herein, my good friend, the special blessing seemeth meet to be discreetly asked and wisely worn."

LORD MUNCASTER. (1805.)

Necessity for Public Prayer.

The Prophecy of Franklin.

HE (Franklin) was elected one of the delegates from Pennsylvania to the convention for forming the Constitution of the United States, which met at Philadelphia in May, 1787, and continued in session four months. Although he was now in the eighty-second year of his age, and at the same time discharged the duties of President of the State, yet he attended faithfully to the business of the convention, and entered actively and heartily into the proceedings.

After the members of the convention had been together four or five weeks, and made very little progress in the important work they had in hand, on account of their unfortunate differences of opinion and disagreements on essential points, Dr. Franklin introduced a motion for daily prayers. "In the beginning of the contest with Britain," said he, "when we were sensible of danger, we had daily prayers in this room for the Divine protection. Our prayers, sir, were heard; and they were graciously answered. All of us who were engaged in the struggle must have observed frequent instances of a superintending Providence in our favor. To that kind Providence we owe this happy opportunity of consulting in peace on the means of establishing our future national felicity. And have we now forgotten that powerful Friend? or do we imagine we no longer need his assistance? I have lived, sir, a long time; and the longer I live, the more convincing proofs I see of this truth, *that* GOD *governs in the affairs of men.* And, if a sparrow cannot fall to the ground without his notice, is it probable that an empire can rise without his aid? We have been assured, sir, in the Sacred Writings, that, 'except the Lord build the house, they labor in vain that build it.' I firmly believe this; and I also believe that, without his concurring aid, we shall succeed in this political building no better than the builders of Babel; we shall be divided by our little, partial, local interests, our projects will be confounded, and we ourselves shall become a reproach and a by-word down to future ages. And, what is worse, mankind may hereafter, from this unfortunate instance, despair of establishing government by human wisdom, and leave it to chance, war, and conquest. I therefore beg leave to move, that henceforth prayers, imploring the assistance of Heaven and its blessing on our deliberation, be held in this assembly every morning before we proceed to business; and that one or more of the clergy of this city be requested to officiate in that service."

The motion was not adopted, as "the convention, except three or four persons, thought prayers unnecessary."

SPARKS's Life of Benjamin Franklin.

PART III.

COMMUNION WITH GOD.

Communion with God.

O HOW shall I call upon God, my God and Lord, since, when I call for Him, I shall be calling Him into myself? and what room is there within me, whither my God can come into me? Whither can God come into me, God who made heaven and earth? Is there, indeed, O Lord my God, aught in me that can contain Thee? Do, then, heaven and earth, which Thou hast made, and wherein Thou hast made me, contain Thee? or, because nothing which exists could exist without Thee, doth therefore whatever exists contain Thee? Since, then, I too exist, why do I seek that Thou shouldest enter into me, who were not, wert Thou not in me? Why? Because I am not gone down in hell, and yet Thou art there also. For if I go down into hell, Thou art there. I could not be, then, O my God, could not be at all, wert Thou not in me; or rather, unless I were in Thee, of whom are all things, by whom are all things, in whom are all things! Even so, Lord, even so. Whither do I call Thee, since I am in Thee? or whence canst Thou enter into me? For whither can I go beyond heaven and earth, that thence my God should come into me, who hath said, "I fill the heaven and the earth"?

O God, the vessels which Thou fillest uphold Thee not, since, though they were broken, Thou wert not poured out. And when Thou art poured out on us, Thou art not cast down, but Thou upliftest us; Thou art not dissipated, but Thou gatherest us.

The house of my soul is too straight for Thee to come into; but let it, O Lord, be enlarged, that Thou mayest enter in. It is ruinous: repair Thou it. It has that within which must offend Thine eyes; I confess and know it. But who shall cleanse it? or to whom should I cry out, save Thee? Cleanse me from my secret faults, O Lord, and forgive those offences to Thy servant which he has caused in others. I contend not in judgment with Thee, who art Truth; I fear to deceive myself; lest my sin should make me think that I am not sinful. Therefore I contend not in judgment with Thee; for if Thou, Lord, shouldst mark iniquities, O Lord, who shall abide it?

St. Augustine. (A. D. 354-403.)

Intimate Presence of God.

O LORD my God, Light of the blind, and Strength of the weak; yea also light of those that see, and strength of the strong: hearken unto my soul, and hear it crying out of the depths.

Woe is me! how high art Thou in the highest, and how deep in the deepest! and Thou never departest from us, and we scarcely return to Thee. For whither fly we when we fly from Thy presence, or where dost not Thou find us out? We fly that we may not see Thee looking upon us, but blinded may stumble against Thee (because Thou forsaketh nothing Thou hast made). We stumble upon Thee, and justly are hurt; withdrawing ourselves from Thy gentleness, and stumbling at Thy uprightness, and falling upon our ruggedness. We forget that Thou art everywhere, whom no place encompasseth! that Thou alone art near even to those that remove far from Thee. O Lord, help us to turn and seek Thee; for not as we have forsaken our Creator hast Thou forsaken Thy creation. Let us turn and seek Thee, for we know Thou art here in our heart, when we confess to Thee, when we cast ourselves upon Thee, and weep in Thy bosom, after all our rugged ways; and Thou dost gently wipe away our tears, and we weep the more for joy; because Thou, Lord, — not man of flesh and blood, — but Thou, Lord, who madest us, remakest and comfortest us.

O God, we thank Thee for Thy chastisements

which begin with the master's ferula and go on to the martyr's torments, tempering for us a wholesome bitter, recalling us to Thyself from that deadly pleasure which lures us from Thee. Thy face, Lord, will we seek. For darkened affection is removal from Thee. For it is not by our feet or change of place that we leave Thee, or return unto Thee. Nor did that younger son of Thine look out for horses, or chariots, or ships, and fly with visible wings, or journey by the motion of his limbs, that he might in a far country waste in riotous living all Thou gavest at his departure. A loving Father Thou wert when Thou gavest; but more loving unto him wert Thou when he returned empty.

Hear, Lord, my prayer; let not my soul faint under Thy discipline, nor let me faint in confessing unto Thee all Thy mercies, whereby Thou hast drawn me out of all my most evil ways, that Thou mightest become a delight to me, above all the allurements which I once pursued; that I may most entirely love Thee, and clasp Thy hand with all the roots of my heart, and Thou mayest yet rescue me from every temptation, even unto the end.

O Lord our God, under the shadow of Thy wings is our hope; protect us, and carry us, both when we are little, and even in hoar hairs wilt Thou carry us; for our firmness only when it is in Thee is firmness; when it is our own, it is infirmity. Our good only lives with Thee; when we turn away from Thee we are perverted. Let us, then, O Lord, return, that we may not be overturned; because with Thee good lives without any decay, for Thou art good; nor need we fear lest there be no place whither to return, because we fell from it; for our mansion — Thy eternity — fell not when we left Thee.

O Lord God, give peace unto us (for Thou hast given us all things): the peace of rest, the peace of the Sabbath, which hath no evening: yea, give us rest in Thee, the Sabbath of eternal life. For Thou shalt rest in us, as now Thou workest in us; and Thy rest shall be through us, as Thy works are through us. Amen.

St. Augustine.

Eternal Joy in God.

O GOD, Thou light of my heart, Thou bread of my inmost soul, Thou power who givest vigor to my mind, who quickenest my thoughts, let my soul praise Thee that it may love Thee; and let it confess Thy own mercies to Thee that it may praise Thee. Thy whole creation ceases not to praise Thee; neither my spirit, whose voice is towards Thee, nor creation animate or inanimate, by the voice of those who meditate thereon; when our souls from their own weariness arise towards Thee, leaning on those things which Thou hast created, and by them passing on to Thyself, who madest them wonderfully; whereby cometh refreshment and true strength.

Not with doubting, but with assured consciousness, do I love Thee, Lord. But what do I love, when I love Thee? Not the beauty of bodies, nor the fair harmony of time, nor the brightness of the light, so gladsome to our eyes, nor sweet melodies of varied songs, nor the fragrant smell of flowers, and ointments, and spices, not manna and honey, not limbs acceptable to embracements of flesh. None of these I love, when I love my God; and yet I love a kind of light, a kind of melody, a kind of fragrance, a kind of meat, and a kind of embracement, when I love my God, the light, the melody, the fragrance, meat, the embracement of the inner man: where there shineth unto my soul what space cannot contain, and there soundeth what time beareth not away, and there smelleth what breathing disperseth not, and there tasteth what eating diminisheth not, and there clingeth what satiety divorceth not. This is it which I love, when I love my God.

Too late loved I Thee, O Thou Beauty of ancient days, yet ever new! too late loved I Thee! And behold Thou wert within, and I abroad, and there I searched for Thee; plunging deformed amid those fair forms, which Thou hadst made. Thou wert with me, but I was not with Thee. Things held me far from Thee, which, unless they were in Thee, were not at all. Thou didst call, and shout, and burst my deafness. Thou didst flash, shine, and scatter my blindness. Thou didst breathe odors, and I drew in breath, and pant for Thee. I tasted, and I hunger and thirst for Thee. When I shall with my whole self cleave to Thee, I shall nowhere have sorrow, or labor; and my life shall wholly live, as wholly full of Thee. But because I am not full of Thee I am a burden to myself. Woe is me! Lord, have pity on me. My evil sorrows strive with my good joys; and on which side is the victory I know not. Woe is me! Lord, have pity on me. Woe is me! lo! I hide not my wounds; Thou art the Physician, I the sick; Thou merciful, I miserable. And all my hope is in Thy exceeding great mercy. Give what Thou enjoinest, and enjoin what Thou wilt. For too little doth he love Thee, who loves anything with Thee, which he loveth not for Thee. O love, who ever burnest and never consumest! O charity, my God! Kindle me. Give me what Thou enjoinest, and enjoin what Thou wilt.

St. Augustine. (A. D. 354–403.)

For Repose in God.

WHAT art Thou, O my God? What but the Lord God, — most hidden, yet most present; most beautiful, yet most strong; stable, yet incomprehensible; unchangeable, yet all-changing; never new, never old; all-renewing, and bringing age unto the proud, and they know it not: ever working, ever at rest; still gathering, yet not lacking; supporting, filling, and overspreading; creating, nourishing, and maturing; seeking, yea, having all things. Thou changest Thy works, Thy purpose unchanged; receivest again what thou findest, yet didst never lose; never in need, yet rejoicing in gains; never covetous, yet exacting usury. Thou receivest over and above, that Thou mayest owe; and who hath aught that is not Thine? Thou payest debts, owing nothing; remittest debts, losing nothing. And what have I now said, my God, my life, my holy joy? or what saith any man when he speaks of Thee? Yet woe to him that speaketh not, since mute are even the most eloquent.

O that I might repose in Thee! O that Thou wouldst enter into my heart and inebriate it, that I may forget my ills, and embrace Thee, my sole good! What art Thou to me, O Lord? Have mercy on me, that I may ask. Or what am I to Thee, that Thou shouldst command me to love Thee, yea, and to be angry with me, and threaten to lay huge miseries upon me, if I love Thee not? Is it, then, a slight woe to love Thee not? O for Thy mercies' sake tell me, O Lord my God, what Thou art unto me. Say unto my soul, I am thy salvation; but say it so that I may hear Thee. Behold, Lord, my heart is before Thee; open Thou the ears thereof, and say unto my soul, I am thy salvation. Let me know Thee, O Lord, who knowest me: let me know Thee, as I am known. Power of my soul, enter into it, and fit it for Thee, that Thou mayest enjoy it without spot or wrinkle.

St. Augustine.

God All-in-All.

O THOU Good omnipotent, who so carest for every one of us, as if Thou caredst for him alone; and so for all, as if all were but one! Better and more certain is the life of the bodies than the bodies, but Thou art the life of lives, having life in Thyself; and Thou changest not, O life of my soul! Blessed is the man who loveth Thee, and his friend in Thee, and his enemy for Thee. For he only loses none dear to him, to whom all are dear, in Him who cannot be lost. And who is that but our God, the God that made heaven and earth, and *filleth them*, even by filling them creating them. None loseth but he who leaveth Thee. And who leaveth Thee, whither goeth or whither fleeth he, but from Thee pleased, to Thee displeased? For doth he not find Thy law in his own punishment? And Thy law is truth, and truth is Thyself.

The Word itself calleth me to return to that place of rest where love is not forsaken, if it forsaketh not to love. I behold how some things pass away, that others may replace them, and so this lower universe be completed by all his parts. But Thou dost never depart, O God, my Father supremely good, Beauty of all things beautiful! With Thee will I fix my dwelling, for now I am tired out with vanities. To Thee will I intrust whatsoever I have received from Thee, so shall I lose nothing; and my decay shall bloom again, and all my diseases be healed. Thou madest me for Thyself, and my heart is restless until it repose in Thee.

St. Augustine.

Relation to God.

BEING admonished to reflect upon myself, I entered into the very inward parts of my soul, by Thy conduct; and I was able to do it, because now Thou wert become my helper. I entered and discerned with the eye of my soul (such as it was) even beyond my soul and mind itself the Light unchangeable. Not this vulgar light which all flesh may look upon, nor as it were a greater of the same kind, as though the brightness of this should be manifold greater, and with its greatness take up all space. Not such was this light, but other, yea, far other from all these. Neither was it so above my understanding, as oil swims above water, or as the heaven is above the earth. But it is above me, because it made me; and I am under it, because I was made by it. He that knows truth or verity, knows what that Light is, and he that knows it knows eternity, and it is known by Charity. O eternal Verity! and true Charity! and dear Eternity! Thou art my God, to Thee do I sigh day and night. Thee when I first knew, Thou liftedst me up that I might see there was what I might see, and that I was not yet such as to see. And Thou didst beat back my weak sight upon myself, shooting out beams upon me after a vehement manner, and I even trembled between love and horror, and I found myself to be far off, and even in the very region of dissimilitude from Thee.

St. Augustine.

Hope of Heaven.

SWEET Jesus, the word of the Father, the brightness of paternal glory, whom angels delight to view, teach me to do Thy will; that, led by Thy good Spirit, I may come to that blessed city where day is eternal, where there is certain security, and secure eternity; and eternal peace, and peaceful happiness; and happy sweetness, and sweet pleasure; . . . . where is light without darkness; joy without grief; desire without punishment; love without sadness; satiety without loathing; safety without fear; health without disease; and life without death; . . . . where Thou, O God, with the Father and the Holy Spirit, livest and reignest world without end. Amen.

St. Gregory. (1731. Translated by Francis Quarles.)

Dependence upon God.

I STAND astonished, when I consider that the heavens are not clean in Thy sight. If Thou hast found folly and impurity in angels, and hast not spared even them, what will become of me? If the stars have "fallen from heaven; if Lucifer, son of the morning," hath not kept his place; shall I, that am but dust, dare to presume upon my own stability? Many whose holiness had raised them to exalted honor, have been degraded by sin to infamy; and those that have fed upon the bread of angels, I have seen delighted with the husks of swine.

There is no holiness if Thou, Lord, withdraw Thy presence; no wisdom profiteth if Thy Spirit cease to direct; no strength availeth without Thy support; no chastity is safe without Thy protection; no watchfulness effectual when Thy holy vigilance is not on guard. No sooner are we left to ourselves, than the waves of corruption rush upon us, and we sink; but if Thou reach forth Thy omnipotent hand, we walk upon the sea. In our own nature we are unsettled as the sand upon the mountain; but in Thee we have the stability of the throne of heaven. We are cold and insensible as darkness and death; but are kindled into light and life by the fire of Thy love.

How worthless and vain should I deem the good that appears to be mine! With what profound humility, O Lord, ought I to cast myself into the abyss of Thy judgments, where I continually find myself to be nothing! O depth immense! Where, now, is the lurking-place of human glory; where the confidence of human virtue? In the awful deep of Thy judgments which cover me, all self-confidence and self-glory are swallowed up forever.

Lord, what is all flesh in Thy sight? Shall the clay glory against Him that formed it? Can that heart be elated by the vain applause of men, that has felt the blessing of submission to the will of God? The whole world has not power to exalt that which truth has subjected to himself; nor can the united praise of every tongue move him, whose hope is established in Thee: for those that utter praise, behold they also are nothing, like those that hear it! They shall both pass away and be lost, as the sound of their own words; but "the truth of the Lord endureth forever."

THOMAS À KEMPIS. (1388-1471.)

Love of God.

I WILL now speak again unto my Lord, and will not be silent; I will say to my King, and my God, who sitteth in the highest heaven, O how great and manifold are the treasures of Thy goodness, which Thou hast laid up for them that fear Thee! But what art Thou, O Lord, to those that love Thee with all their heart? Truly, the exquisite delight derived from that privilege of pure contemplation with which Thou hast invested them, surpasseth the power of every creature to express. How free, and how exalted above all blessing and praise, is that goodness which Thou hast manifested toward Thy poor servant; which not only called him into being, but when he had wandered far from Thee, by its redeeming virtue brought him back to Thee again, and with the command to love Thee, conferred the power to fulfil it! O source of everlasting love! what shall I say concerning Thee! How can I forget Thee, who hast condescended to remember me, pining away and perishing in the poverty of sinful nature, and to restore me to the divine life! Beyond all hope Thou hast shown mercy to Thy servant, and beyond all thought hast made him capable of Thy friendship, and dignified and blessed him with it.

O Lord, my God, who hast mercifully numbered me among the objects of Thy redeeming love, Thou art my glory and my joy, my hope and refuge in the day of my distress. But my love is yet feeble, and my holy resolutions imperfect: do Thou, therefore, visit me continually, and instruct me out of Thy law; deliver me from malignant passions and sensual desires, that, being healed and purified, I may love with more ardor, suffer with more patience, and persevere with more constancy.

Expand my heart with love, that I may feel its transforming power, and may even be dissolved in its holy fire! Let me be possessed by Thy love, and ravished from myself! Let the lover's song be mine, "I will follow my beloved on high!" Let my soul rejoice exceedingly, and lose itself in Thy praise! Let me love Thee more than myself; let me love myself only for Thy sake; and in Thee love all others, as that perfect law requireth, which is a ray of the infinite love that shines in Thee!

THOMAS À KEMPIS.

Repose in Christ.

O MOST lovely, and most loving Jesus! grant me the will and power, above all created beings, to rest in Thee: above all health and beauty, all glory and honor, all power and dignity, all knowledge and wisdom, all riches and all arts; above all promise and hope, all holy desires and actions, all gifts and graces which Thou thyself canst bestow, all rapture and transport which the heart is able to receive; above angels and archangels, and all the hosts of heaven; above all that is visible and invisible; and finally above everything, which Thou, my God, art not! For Thou, O Lord God! art above all, in all perfection! Thou art most high, most powerful, most sufficient, and most full! Thou art most sweet, and most abundantly comforting! Thou art most lovely, and most loving; most noble and most glorious! In Thee all good centres, from eternity to eternity! Therefore, whatever Thou bestowest on me, that is not Thyself; whatever Thou revealest or promisest, while I am not permitted truly to behold and enjoy Thee, is insufficient to fill the boundless desires of my soul, which, stretching beyond all creatures, and even beyond all Thy gifts, can only be satisfied in union with Thy all-perfect Spirit.

Dearest Jesus, spouse of my soul, supreme source of light and love, and sovereign Lord of universal nature! O that I had the wings of true liberty, that I might take my flight to Thee, and be at rest! When will it be granted me, in silent and peaceful abstraction from all created being, to "taste and see how good" Thou art, O Lord, my God! When shall I be fully absorbed in Thy fulness? When shall I lose, in the love of Thee, all perception of myself; and have no sense of any being but Thine?

THOMAS À KEMPIS.

Living above the World.

"UPHOLD me, O God, with Thy free Spirit! strengthen me with might in the inner man!" that, being emptied of all selfish solicitude, I may no longer be the slave of restless and tormenting desires; but with holy indifference may consider all earthly good, of whatever kind, as continually passing away, and my own life as passing with it: for there is nothing permanent under the sun.

But what wisdom, O Lord! can consider this truly, but that which was present with Thee when Thou madest the world, and knew what was acceptable in Thy sight? O send me this wisdom "from the throne of Thy glory," that I may learn to know and seek Thee alone, and thus seeking find Thee. May I love Thee, and delight in Thee, above all beings; may I understand all that Thou hast made as it is in itself, and regard its various forms only according to that order in which Thy infinite mind hath disposed them!

Grant that I may carefully shun flattery, and patiently bear contradiction; that being neither disturbed by the rude breath of impotent rage, nor captivated by the softness of delusive praise, I may securely pass on in the path of life, which, by Thy grace, I have begun to tread.

O Eternal Light, infinitely surpassing all that Thou illuminatest, let Thy brightest beams descend upon my heart, and penetrate its inmost recesses! O purify, exhilarate, enlighten, and enliven my spirit, that with all its powers it may adhere to Thee in raptures of triumphant joy, for there is no hope nor refuge for me but in Thee, O Lord, my God!

THOMAS À KEMPIS. (A. D. 1388–1471.)

The Sufficiency of God.

O THE grace of God! O the purity of God! The goodness of God!

Is it possible, my Beloved, that men can love Thee, without experiencing consolation and happiness in their love?

To me every event is God; and whether it be joyful or afflictive, I receive it with equal gratitude, knowing that He will send me only what I need.

To me every object is God. I do not go into distinctions, and say, *this* is mine, or *that* is mine. But I say, God is mine; everything belongs to God; and I have an inward conviction, which is better understood than expressed, that in the possession of God I have all that God has.

O my Beloved! is it possible that Thou hast thus called me to Thyself with so great goodness? Is it possible that Thou hast delivered me from my doubt and anguish; and in a moment of time hast imparted a knowledge greater than language can express?

I have faith in Thee, O my God, that Thou wilt not leave me, that Thou wilt not permit me to go astray; but wilt keep me in all inward thought, as well as in all outward word and action.

CATHERINE ADORNA. (1447-1510.)

When she was urged to take Monastic Vows.

O MY Beloved! who shall hinder me from loving Thee? Can my situation in life shut up the avenues of my heart and prevent my loving? O, no. I could not cease to love, and to love Thee with all my heart, even if I were situated amid the tumult and strife of armies. How, then, can the relation of a wife, and the cares of a family, or any of the ordinary duties of life, be an obstacle to a life of holy love? Pure love is a grace which has strength enough to live and flourish in every situation. I need no other proof, no other evidence of it, than what I have felt in my own soul, the gift of Him whom my soul loves.

CATHERINE ADORNA.

Sufficiency of God.

I, BEING in the Bastile, said to Thee, —

O my God! if Thou art pleased to render me a spectacle to men and angels, Thy holy will be done! All I ask is, that Thou wilt be with and save those who love Thee; — so that neither life nor death, neither principalities nor powers, may ever separate them from the love of God which is in Jesus Christ. As for me, what matters it what men think of me, or what they make me suffer, since they cannot separate me from that Saviour whose name is engraven in the very bottom of my heart. If I can only be accepted of him, I am willing that all men should despise and hate me. Their strokes will polish what may be defective in me, so that I may be presented in peace to him, for whom I die daily. Without his favor I am wretched. O Saviour! I present myself before Thee an offering, a sacrifice. Purify me in Thy blood, that I may be accepted of Thee.

MADAME GUYON. (Autobiography.)

Peace in Affliction.

HAVE I not infinitely more than "an hundred-fold in this life," in so entire possession as Thou, my God, hast taken of me; in that unshaken firmness which Thou givest me in my sufferings; in that perfect tranquillity in the midst of a furious tempest, which assaults me on every side; in that unspeakable joy, enlargedness, and liberty which I enjoy, at the very time of an imprisonment, rigorous and severe? I have no desire that my imprisonment should end before the right time. I love my chains. Everything is equal to me, as I have no will of my own, but purely the love and will of Him who possesses me. My senses indeed have not any relish for such things; but my heart is separated from them, and borne over them; and my perseverance is not of myself, but of Him who is my life; so that I can say with the Apostle, "It is no more I that live, but Jesus Christ that liveth in me." And if His life is in me, so my life is in Him. It is He in whom I live and move and have my being.

MADAME GUYON. (A. D. 1648-1717.)

The Intimate Presence of God.

O GOD, it is not to know Thee, to regard Thee only as an all-powerful being, who gives laws to all nature, and who has created everything which we see; it is only to know a part of Thy being, it is not to know that which is most wonderful and most affecting to Thy rational offspring. That which transports and melts my soul is to know that Thou art the God of my heart. Thou doest there Thy good pleasure.

Thou art ever with me. When I do wrong, reproaching me with the evil which I commit, inspiring me with regret for the good which I have forsaken, and with outstretched arms offering me pardon. The good works which I do, they are Thy gifts, and they cease to be good works as soon as I regard them as mine, and lose sight of Thy bounty which gives them their true value.

I call to my mind all the wonders of nature that I may form some image of Thy glory. I ask for knowledge of Thee from Thy creatures, and I forget to seek for Thee in the depths of my own soul, where Thou ever art. We need not descend into the centre of the earth, nor go beyond the seas; we need not ascend to heaven to find Thee; Thou art nearer to us than we are to ourselves.

O God, so glorious and yet so intimately with us, so high above these heavens and yet stooping to the lowliness of Thy creatures, so immense and yet dwelling in the bottom of my heart, so awful and yet so worthy of love! When will Thy children cease to be ignorant of Thee? O for a voice loud enough to reproach the world with its blindness, and to declare with power all that Thou art. When we bid men to seek Thee in their own hearts, it is as if we were to propose to them to seek for Thee in some undiscovered parts of the earth. What is there to a vain and sensual man more foreign, more remote, than the bottom of his own heart? Does he know what it is to enter into himself? Has he ever sought the way? Can he even imagine what is this inward sanctuary, these impenetrable depths of the soul, where Thou would be worshipped in spirit and in truth? For me, my Creator, closing my eyes upon outward things, which are only vanity and vexation of spirit, I would enjoy in the recesses of my heart an intimacy with Thee through Jesus Christ, Thy Son.

O God! man does not know Thee, he knows not who Thou art. "The light shines in the midst of the darkness, but the darkness comprehendeth it not." It is through Thee that we live, that we think, that we enjoy the pleasures of life, and we forget Him from whom we receive all these things.

O God, when shall we return love for love! When shall we turn toward Him who is ever seeking us, and whose arms are ever around us? It is while resting on Thy paternal bosom that we forget Thee. The sweetness of Thy gifts makes us forget the giver. The blessings we every moment receive from Thee, instead of touching our hearts, turn our thoughts away from Thee. Thou art the source of all true pleasures. Thy creatures are only the gross channels through which they flow to us, and the stream has made us forget the Fountain-Head. This infinite love follows us everywhere, and we are ever trying to escape from it; it is everywhere, and we do not perceive it. We call ourselves alone when we have only God with us. He does all for us, and we do not trust in him; we despair when we have no other resource than his providence, and count for nothing infinite love and infinite power.

FENELON. (A. D. 1651-1715.)

For more ardent Love of God.

CAN we know Thee, O my God, and not love Thee? Thee, who surpassest in greatness, and power, and goodness, and bounty, in magnificence, in all sorts of perfections, and what is more to me, in Thy love for me, all that a created being can comprehend? Thou permittest me, Thou commandest me, to love Thee. Shall the mad passions of the world be indulged with ardor, and we love Thee with a cold and measured love? O no, my God; let not the profane be stronger than the divine love.

Send Thy Spirit into my heart; it is open to Thee, all its recesses are known to Thee. Thou knowest how far it is capable of loving Thee. Weak and helpless being that I am, I can give only my love; increase it, Almighty God, and render it more worthy of Thee.

FENELON.

Satisfied.

LORD, I know not if Thou art satisfied with me. I acknowledge that there are many reasons why Thou shouldst not be so; but, to Thy glory, I must confess that I am satisfied with Thee, and perfectly satisfied. To Thee it does not matter whether I be so or not. But, after all, it is the highest tribute that I can pay to Thee. For to say that I am satisfied with Thee, is to say that Thou art my God, since nothing less than God could satisfy me.

BOSSUET. (A. D. 1627–1704.)

Looking for God.

"WALK before me, and be thou perfect." These are the words of God to faithful Abraham. Whoever walks in Thy presence, O Lord, is in the path to perfection. We never depart from this holy way but we lose sight of Thee, and cease to behold Thee in everything. Alas; where shall we go when we no longer see Thee, Thee who art our light, and the only goal to which our steps should tend? To have our eyes fixed on Thee in every step we take, is our only security that we shall never go astray. Faith! beaming with light amidst the darkness that surrounds us, I behold Thee with Thy look of holy love and trust, leading man to perfection. O God, I will fix my eyes on Thee; I will behold Thee in everything that is around me. The order of Thy providence shall arrest my attention. My heart shall still see Thee in the midst of the busy cares of life, in all its duties, all its concerns; for they shall all be fulfilled in obedience to Thy will. "I will lift my eyes unto the holy hills, whence cometh my strength."

In vain does our own foresight strive to escape the snares that surround us: danger comes from below, but deliverance only from on high. Temptations are without and within us; we should be lost, O Lord, without Thee. To Thee I raise my eyes, upon Thee I rest my heart; my own weakness frightens me. Thy all-powerful mercy will support my infirmity.

FENELON.

Joy in God.

AH, Jesus, what canst Thou refuse me, when Thou hast given me Thyself?—and where is the confidence that can be too tender? Why should I envy Thy beloved disciple who leaned on Thy breast at Thy last supper? for dost Thou not at present rest in my heart? O let me, then, be forever inviolably attached to Thee! Let the sweets of Thy presence so captivate my soul that, disgusted with sin, it may be fixed in the contemplation of Thee, and listen with docility to Thy holy inspirations.

CATHOLIC MANUAL.

Act of Love.

O MY sweet Lord! my Creator and my Redeemer! my God and my all! whence is this to me, that my Lord, and so great a Lord, whom heaven and earth cannot contain, should come into this poor cottage, this house of clay of my earthly habitation? O that I could give Thee a hearty welcome! O that I could entertain Thee as I ought.

Let my soul, O Lord, be sensible of the sweetness of Thy presence. Let me taste how sweet Thou art, O Lord! that, being allured by Thy love, I may never more hunt after worldly joys; for Thou art the joy of my heart, and my portion forever.

O, true light! which enlightenest every man that cometh into this world, enlighten my eyes that I may never sleep in death.

O my God and my all! may the sweet flame of Thy love consume my soul, that so I may die to the world, for the love of Thee, who hast vouchsafed to die upon the cross for the love of me.

O my Jesus! teach me to be poor in spirit, and separate my heart from the love of these transitory things, and fix it upon eternity. Teach me, by Thy divine example, and by Thy most efficacious grace, to be meek and humble of heart, and in my patience to possess my soul. Grant that I may ever keep my body and soul chaste and pure.

Above all things, teach me to love Thee; teach me to be ever recollected in Thee, and to walk always in Thy presence. Teach me to love my friends in Thee, and my enemies for Thee: grant me to persevere to the end in this love, and so to come one day to that happy place, where I may love and enjoy Thee forever.

CATHOLIC MANUAL.

For Union with God.

O MY God and Father, Thou knowest better than I how much I love Thee. Thou knowest it as I cannot, for nothing is more completely hidden from me than the depths of my own heart. I desire to love Thee, and fear lest I should not love Thee as I ought. I ask of Thee an abundant and pure love. Thou seest this desire, for Thou hast implanted it in me, regard then the want which Thou beholdest in Thy creature. O God, whose love to me is sufficient to inspire a boundless affection in return, look not upon the torrent of iniquity in which I was almost swallowed up, but rather on Thy mercy.

Lord, Thou art the God of nature; all things obey Thy word. Thou art the soul of all being, and even of those things that as yet are not. Thine are all things, and shall not my heart be Thine, that heart which Thou hast formed, and dost keep in life? It is Thine, and no longer mine.

But, O Lord, Thou art mine, for I love Thee. Thou art my all, my eternal Portion. I ask not earthly consolations, nor extraordinary gifts, nor any of those blessings which, though they come from Thee, yet are not Thyself; — for Thee, Thee only do I hunger and thirst. Do with me as Thou wilt, I care not since I love Thee.

FENELON.

An Act of Love.

O MY God! I love Thee above all things with my whole heart and soul, purely because Thou art infinitely perfect and deserving of all love. I love also my neighbor as myself for the love of Thee. I forgive all who have injured me, and ask pardon of all whom I have injured.

COME, O Holy Ghost! replenish the hearts of Thy faithful, and kindle in them the fire of Thy divine love.

CATHOLIC MANUAL.

A Prayer of Thomas Bradwardine, Archbishop of Canterbury.

THYSELF, my God, I love for Thyself, above all things. For Thyself I long. Thyself I desire as a final end. Thyself, for Thyself, not for aught else, I always and in all things hitherto seek. With my heart and whole strength, with groaning and weeping, with continual labor and grief. What, therefore, wilt Thou give me as my final end? If Thou dost not bestow on me Thyself, Thou bestowest on me nothing. If Thou dost not give me Thyself, Thou givest me nothing. If I find not Thyself, I find nothing. Thou dost not, then, reward me, but torture me. For even before that I sought Thee, I hoped to hold and possess Thee at last. And with this honeyed hope, I was sweetly consoled in all my labors. But now, if Thou deniest me Thyself, and that forever, and not for a season, whatever else Thou shalt give me, shall I not always languish with love, mourn with languishing, grieve with mourning, weep with grieving, because I shall ever remain void and empty? Shall I not mourn inconsolably? complain unceasingly? grieve interminably? This is not Thy wont, God of goodness, of clemency, and love; it is in no wise fitting, in no point seemly. Grant, therefore, O my gracious God, that in the present life I may ever love Thyself, for Thyself, above all things; and in the future world may find Thee, and hold Thee forever.

QUOTED BY BISHOP ANDREWES.

Prayer of a Deaf and Dumb Boy.

WHEN my long-attached friend comes to me, I have pleasure to converse with him, and I rejoice to pass my eyes over his countenance; but soon I am weary of passing my time carelessly and unimproved, and I desire to leave him (but not in rudeness), because I wish to be engaged in my business. But Thou, O my Father, knowest I always delight to commune with Thee in my lone and silent heart; I am never full of Thee; I am never weary of Thee; I am always desiring Thee. I hunger with strong hope and affection for Thee, and I thirst for Thy grace and spirit.

When I go to visit my friends, I must put on my best garments, and I must think of my manner to please them. I am tired to stay long, because my mind is not free, and they sometimes talk gossip with me. But, O my Father, Thou visitest me in my work, and I can lift up my desires to Thee, and my heart is cheered and at rest with Thy presence, and I am always alone with Thee, and Thou dost not steal my time with foolishness. I always ask in my heart, Where can I find Thee?

THE DIAL. (1842.)

Drawing near to God.

O GOD! the Centre of all pure spirits, the Everlasting Goodness, we come to Thee. Thou art the happiness of heaven; and Thy presence, felt by the soul that communes with Thee, is the highest good. Ignorant of Thee, we know nothing aright; wandering from Thee, we lose all light and peace; forgetting Thee, we turn our minds from the noblest object of thought; and without love to Thee, we are separated from infinite loveliness, and from the only substantial and sufficient source of joy. Thou hast an inexhaustible fulness of life; and Thine unceasing communications take nothing from Thy power to bless. Thou art infinitely better than all Thy gifts, and through all we desire to rise to Thee.

We thank Thee for the proofs Thou givest of Thy essential, pure, and perfect benignity, so that through all clouds and darkness we can see a gracious Father. In this world of shadows, this fleeting tide of things, this life of dreams, we rejoice that there is a Reality, sure, unchanging, in which we may find rest; that there is a Power which can cleanse us from all sin, raise us to all virtue and happiness, and give us endless growth.

How great is our privilege, that we have such an object for our hope and trust, — that our souls may contemplate infinite loveliness, greatness, goodness, — that we may at all times commune with the Best of Beings!

For Thy inviolable faithfulness, Thy impartial justice, Thy unerring wisdom, Thy unfathomable counsels, Thy unwearied care, Thy tender mercy, Thy resistless power, we adore Thee. For the splendor spread over all Thy works, and still more for the higher beauty of the soul, of which the brightness of creation is but the emblem and faint shadow, we thank Thee. O, let thy love affect our hearts, let us feel its reality, constancy, tenderness! To Thee we owe all. Thine is the health of our bodies, the light of our minds, the warmth of affection, the guiding voice of conscience. Whatever knowledge or virtuous impressions we have derived from the society of friends, the conversation of the wise and good, the care of instructors, the researches of past ages, we desire to trace gratefully to Thee. We rejoice that we depend on Thee, the Father of Spirits, whose requisitions are so reasonable, whose government is so mild, whose influences are so ennobling. How unspeakably great is Thy goodness! And all our other blessings are as nothing, when compared with the sublime, pure, infinite glory, to which we are called by the Gospel of Thy Son.

May Christ be precious to us; teach us his worth, his glory, so that we may love him and rejoice in him with joy unspeakable. May a sense of the greatness of the evils from which he came to deliver, and of the blessings which he can bestow, excite our sensibility, gratitude, desire, and lead our minds to dwell on him.

Let sin be our greatest burden; may all life's ills seem light in comparison with it; may we groan for deliverance from it, and be more earnest in resisting it than in resisting all other evils; and may we welcome Christ as our Saviour from it.

WILLIAM ELLERY CHANNING. (1814.)

That we put our Trust wholly in God.

O LORD God, Thou art our refuge and our hope: on Thee alone we rest; for we find all to be weak and insufficient but Thee. Many friends cannot profit, nor strong helpers assist, nor prudent counsellors advise, nor the books of the learned afford comfort, nor any precious substance deliver, nor any place give shelter, unless Thou thyself doth assist, strengthen, console, instruct, and guard us.

To Thee, therefore, do we lift up our eyes; in Thee, our God, the Father of Mercies, do we put our trust. Bless and sanctify our souls, that they may become the holy habitation, and the seat of Thine eternal glory; and let nothing be found in us displeasing in Thy sight. Protect and keep us amidst all dangers; and, accompanying us by Thy grace, direct us along the way of peace to Thine everlasting home. *Amen.*

MARTINEAU'S SERVICE BOOK.

Continual Dependence upon God.

O GOD, who art, and wast, and art to come, before whose face the generations rise and pass away; age after age the living seek Thee, and find that of Thy faithfulness there is no end. Our fathers in their pilgrimage walked by Thy guidance, and rested on Thy compassion: still to their children be Thou the cloud by day, the fire by night. Where but in Thee have we a covert from storm or shadow from the heat of life? In our manifold temptations, Thou alone knowest and art ever nigh: in sorrow, Thy pity revives the fainting soul: in our prosperity and ease, it is Thy spirit only that can wean us from our pride and keep us low.

O Thou sole Source of peace and righteousness; take now the veil from every heart: and join us in one communion with Thy prophets and saints who have trusted in Thee, and were not ashamed. Not of our worthiness, but of Thy tender mercy, hear our prayer. *Amen.*

J. Martineau.

Communion with God.

MERCIFUL and Eternal God, Love inexhaustible, Father of the universe, my Father! If I have but Thee, all that life may bring is but a shadowy phantasm. If I have but Thee, I shall pass without fear through light and through darkness, and shall find my way, and shall not falter, though want and death may threaten. If I have but Thee, I am sufficiently rich, though all fail me that others call riches; I am sufficiently exalted though all the world look down upon me; I am strong enough, though thousands conspire against me; I am safe, though disasters may befall me, and all my earthly possessions be lost. If I have but Thee, death itself cannot rob me of my joy, should it even tear from my bleeding heart all the beloved souls to whom I am attached. Ah! death is Thy angel messenger, he brings them to Thee, and in the bosom of Thy love I shall find them again. If I have but Thee, I possess all things. *Amen.*

ZSCHOKKE.

PART IV.

PRAISE.

Praise.

O LORD, my Lord,
for my being, life, reason,
for nurture, protection, guidance,
for education, civil rights, religion,
for Thy gifts of grace, nature, fortune,
for redemption, regeneration, catechising,
for my call, recall, yea, many calls besides;
for Thy forbearance, long-suffering,
long, long-suffering
to me-ward,
many seasons, many years up to this time;
for all good things received, successes granted me,
good things done;
for the use of things present,
for Thy promise, and my hope
of the enjoyment of good things to come;
for my parents honest and good,
teachers kind,
benefactors never to be forgotten,

religious intimates congenial,
hearers thoughtful,
friends sincere,
domestics faithful,
for all who have advantaged me
by writings, homilies, converse,
prayers, patterns, rebukes, injuries;
for all these and all others
which I know, which I know not,
open, hidden,
remembered, forgotten,
done when I wished, when I wished not,
I confess to Thee and will confess,
I bless Thee and will bless,
I give thanks to Thee, and will give thanks,
all the days of my life.
Who am I, or what is my father's house,
that Thou shouldest look upon
the like of me?
What reward shall I give unto the Lord
for all the benefits which He hath done unto me?
What thanks can I recompense unto God
for all He hath spared and borne with me until now?
Holy, Holy, Holy,
worthy art Thou,
O Lord and our God, the Holy One,
to receive the glory, and the honor, and the power,
for Thou hast made all things,
and for Thy pleasure they are,
and were created.

BISHOP ANDREWES'S DEVOTIONS.

The Leper.

AND one of them, when he saw that he was healed, turned back, and with a loud voice glorified God,

And fell down on his face at his feet, giving him thanks: and he was a Samaritan.

And Jesus answering said, Were there not ten cleansed? but where are the nine?

There are not found that returned to give glory to God, save this stranger.

GOSPEL OF LUKE, xvii. 15, 16, 17.

An Act of Adoration, being the Song that the Angels sing in Heaven.

HOLY, holy, holy, Lord God Almighty, who was, and is, and is to come:* heaven and earth, angels and men, the air and the sea, give glory, and honor, and thanks to Him that sitteth on the throne, who liveth for ever and ever.† All the blessed spirits and souls of the righteous cast their crowns before the throne, and worship Him that liveth for ever and ever.‡

Thou art worthy, O Lord, to receive glory, and honor, and power, for Thou hast created all things, and for Thy pleasure they are and were created. Great and marvellous are Thy works, O Lord God Almighty: just and true are Thy ways, Thou king of saints.§ Thy wisdom is infinite, Thy mercies

* Rev. xi. 17. † Rev. v. 10, 13. ‡ Rev. iv. 10. § Rev. xv. 3.

are glorious, and I am not worthy, O Lord, to appear in Thy presence, before whom the angels hide their faces.

O holy and eternal Jesus, Lamb of God, who wert slain from the beginning of the world, Thou hast redeemed us to God by Thy blood out of every nation, and hast made us unto our God kings and priests, and we shall reign with Thee forever.

Blessing, honor, glory, and power be unto Him that sitteth on the throne, and to the Lamb, for ever and ever. *Amen.*

JEREMY TAYLOR.

Gratitude.

O LORD, when I reflect on the many favors Thou hast conferred on me, I am overwhelmed with confusion, and feel my heart penetrated with such a deep sense of gratitude, as cannot be expressed. I find myself, as it were, encompassed on all sides, and pressed by Thy goodness. It is Thou thyself, O Lord, who lovest me in all those creatures from whom I receive any benefit or advantage. My parents, from whom I received my existence, or my friends, who have given me such proofs of their tenderness, are but the instruments of Thy providence, and the channels of mercies in my behalf. Thou art not only the God of the universe, but Thou art also, in a particular manner, my God! — so interested art Thou in all that relates to me, that Thy attention seems as if it were entirely fixed on me alone. Thou hast given me all Thou hast made, all that I am, and all that Thou art Thyself: cannot I, therefore, with as much reason as David, call Thee "The God of my salvation and my mercy; my refuge and my support; my treasure and my inheritance!" O Spirit of Wisdom! enlighten my understanding, fortify my will, purify my heart, regulate all its motions, and grant me an attentive docility to all Thy holy inspirations. O pardon my continual infidelities, and the blindness with which I have so often refused to correspond with the most tender and moving inspirations of Thy grace. I purpose for the future, with Thy assistance, to cease to be rebellious, and to follow the motions of Thy grace with so much docility, that I may be enabled to taste those fruits, and enjoy those beatitudes, which are produced in our souls by the infusion of the sacred gifts. *Amen.*

CATHOLIC MANUAL.

Thanksgiving.

O LORD God, Fountain of comfort and help, of life and peace, of plenty and pardon, who fillest heaven with Thy glory and earth with Thy goodness; we give Thee the most humble and earnest returns of a glad and thankful heart for the blessings of nature and the blessings of grace, for the support of every minute and the gifts of every day. What are we, O Lord, and what is our father's house, that the great God of men and angels should multiply upon us the proofs of his loving-kindness? Praised be the Lord daily, even the Lord that helpeth us and poureth his blessings upon us. Blessed be the name of his Majesty for-ever, and let all the earth be filled with his glory. *Amen.*

MARTINEAU'S SERVICE BOOK.

For Gratitude.

WHAT gratitude is justly due from me a sinner, who have been brought from darkness into light, and I trust from the pursuit of earthly things to the prime love of things above! O God, purify my heart still more by Thy grace. Quicken my dead soul, and purify me by Thy spirit, that I may be changed from glory to glory, and be made even here in some degree to resemble my Heavenly Father.

May the God of hope fill me with all joy and peace in believing. O Lord, do Thou break, soften, quicken, warm, my cold heart; and teach me to feel an overflowing love and gratitude, or rather a deep and grateful sense of obligation, not as a transient effusion, but as the settled temper and disposition, the practical habit of my soul: that so I may here begin the song of praise, to be sung with more purified and warmed affections in heaven.

Lord, I cast myself before Thee. O spurn me not from Thee, unworthy though I am, of all Thy wonderful goodness. O grant me more and more of humility, and love, and faith, and hope, and longing for a complete renewal into Thine image. Lord, help me and hear me. I come to Thee as my only Saviour. O be Thou my help, my strength, my peace, and joy, and consolation; my Alpha and Omega; my all in all. *Amen.*

WILLIAM WILBERFORCR. (1807.)

Gratitude.

OUR Father who art in heaven, and on earth, and near unto every heart, we flee unto Thee, seeking to feel Thy presence, and conscious of Thee, to know Thee as Thou art, and to worship Thee with all our mind and conscience and heart and soul. We seek to commune with Thy spirit for a moment, that we may freshen our hearts, tired with the world's journey and sore travail, and bow our faces down and drink again at the living waters of Thy life. O Thou Infinite One, we reverence Thee, who art the permanent in things that change, the foundation of what lasts, the loveliness of things beautiful, and the wisdom and the justice and the love which make and hold and bless all this world of matter and of men. O Thou, who art without variableness or shadow of turning, we thank Thee that Thou needest not our poor prayers to teach Thee of our need, nor askest Thou our supplication's argument to quicken Thy mercy or to stir Thy love. Thou anticipatest before we call, and doest more and better for us than we can ever ask or think.

O Father, who adornest the summer and cheerest the winter with Thy presence, we thank Thee that we know that Thou art our father and our mother, that Thou foldest in Thine arms all the worlds which Thou hast made, and warmest with Thy mother's breath each mote that peoples the sun's beams, and blessest every wandering, erring child of man.

O Lord, how marvellous is Thy loving-kindness and Thy tender mercy, which Thou spreadest out over matter and beast and man. In loving-kindness hast Thou made them all, and in tender mercy Thou watchest over the wanderings of the world, blessing those that sorrow, and recalling such as go astray. O, whither can we flee from Thy presence? If we take the wings of the morning, and dwell in the uttermost parts of the sea, even there shall Thy hand lead us, and Thy right hand shall hold us up. Yea, Lord, our transgression hideth us not from Thee; but Thine eye seeth in sin as in righteousness, and when our hearts cry out against us, Thou, who art greater than our heart, still takest us up, bearest us on Thy wings, and blessest us with Thine infinite love.

Father, we remember before Thee our several wants and conditions of life, and we thank Thee for the happiness that crowns our days, for the success that attends our efforts here on earth, the brightness that we gather in our homes, and the hearts whose beating is the music round our fireside, and their countenance the blessing on our daily bread. We thank Thee for these things wherein our hearts rejoice.

But we remember also in our prayer the world's sternness and severity, the sorrows that stain our face with weeping, and make our hearts sometimes run over with our sadness, and our deep distress. Father, if we cannot thank Thee for the things that we suffer, we still will thank Thee that we know Thine eye pities us in our sorrows, and no sadness stains our face but Thou knewest it before we were born, and gatherest the tears which we shed, and changest them into glorious pearls, to shine in our crown of glory as morning stars that herald the coming of the heavenly kingdom here below.

We pray Thee that we may find comfort in every sorrow, and when the world turns its cold hard eye upon us, when the mortal fades from our grasp, and the shadow of death falls on the empty seat of child or wife or friend, O Lord, by the shining of Thy candle in our heart, may we see our way through darkness unto light, and journey from strength to strength, our hearts still stayed on Thee.

Help us to grow stronger and nobler by this world's varying good and ill, and while we enlarge the quantity of our being by continual life, may we improve its kind and quality not less, and become fairer, and tenderer, and heavenlier too, as we leave behind us the various events of our mortal life. So,

Father, may we grow in goodness and in grace, and here on earth attain the perfect measure of a complete man. And so in our heart, and our daily life, may Thy kingdom come, and Thy will be done on earth as it is done in heaven.

THEODORE PARKER.

Gratitude and Supplication.

O THOU Infinite One, who dwellest not only in temples made with hands, but art a perpetual presence, living and moving and having Thy being in every star that flowers above and every flower that flames beneath, we flee unto Thee, who art always with us, and pray that we may commune with Thy spirit face to face for a moment, feeling Thy presence with us, and pouring out our gratitude unto Thee; and amid all the noises of earth, may the still small voice of Thy spirit come into our soul, wakening our noblest faculties to new life, and causing the wings of the spirit to grow out on our mortal flesh. O Thou Infinite One, we lift our thoughts unto Thee, our dependent souls constraining us unto Thee, that we may rest us under the shadow of Thy wings, and be warmed by Thy love, and sheltered and blessed by the motherly tender mercy wherewith Thou regardest all of Thy children. We adore and worship Thee, calling Thee by every name of power, of wisdom, of beauty, and of love; but we know that none of these can fully describe Thee to ourselves, for Thou transcendest our utmost thought of Thee, even as the heavens transcend a single drop of dew which glitters in their many-colored light.

We remember before Thee the manifold works of Thy hand, and Thy providence which hedges us in on every side. We thank Thee for the genial warmth which is spread abroad along the sky, we bless Thee for the green grass growing for the cattle, and the new harvest of promise just springing from the sod, foretelling bread for men in months to come. Father, we thank Thee for the flowers, those later prophets of Spring, which on all the New England hills now utter their fragrant foretelling of the harvest which one day shall hang from the boughs, and glitter and drop and enrich the ground.

O Lord, we thank Thee for the nation within whose borders the lines of our lot have been cast. We thank Thee for our fathers, men of mighty faith, who came here and planted themselves in the wilderness, few in numbers and strangers in it, and yet not weak of heart, and lifting up valiant hands before Thee. We thank Thee for what truth they brought, what truth they learned, and all the noble heritage which is fallen to our hands.

We bless Thee for every good institution in the midst of us, for schools and churches, for the unbounded opportunity here in these Northern States to develop the freedom of our limbs and enjoy the liberty of our souls, wherewith Thou makest all men free.

We remember before Thee our daily lives, and we thank Thee for the bread we eat, the garments we put on, and the houses which more loosely clothe us, sheltering from the summer's heat or the winter's cold.

We bless Thee for the dear ones who garment us about, sheltering us more tenderly and nearly. We bless Thee for those who love us, and whom with answering love we love back again; those under the sight of our eye, or lifting up their prayer with us, and those far severed from the touch of our hand or the hearing of our voice. We thank Thee for these blessed relationships which set the solitary in families, making twain one, and thence manifold, beautifying the world with all the tender ties which join lover and beloved, husband and wife, parent and child, and with kindred blood and kindred soul joining many children, grown or growing, into one great family of love.

Father, we thank Thee for the great ideas of our nature, and the revelation and inspiration which Thou makest therein; for the grand knowledge of Thyself, our Father and our Mother, full of infinite perfection, doing good to each greatest and each smallest thing, and making all things work together for the good of each. O Lord, we thank Thee for the knowledge which comes from the inspiration of Thy spirit working in the human soul, and human souls obedient thereunto working with Thee.

We remember our own daily lives before Thee,

and we mourn that, gifted with a nature so large and surrounded with opportunities so admirable, we have yet often stained our bodies with our soul's transgression, and that unclean and unholy sentiments have lodged within us, yea, nestled there and been cherished and brooded over by our consciousness. We lament that we have had within us feelings which we would not that others should bear towards us, and have done unrighteous deeds. We take shame to ourselves for these things, and we pray Thee that we may gather suffering thence and sorrow of heart, till we learn to cast these evils behind us, and live nobler and more natural lives, inward of piety, and outward of goodness towards all.

We remember our daily duties before Thee, the hard toil which Thou givest us in our manifold and various avocations, and we pray Thee that there may be in us such a confidence in our nature, such earnest obedience to Thee, we reverencing all Thy qualities and keeping Thy commands, that we shall serve Thee every day, making all our life one great act of holiness unto Thee. May our continuous industry be so squared by the golden rule that it shall nicely fit with the interests of all with whom we have to do, and so by our handicraft all mankind shall be blessed. We remember the temptations that are before us, when passion from within is allied with opportunity from without, and that we have so often therein gone astray; and we pray

Thee that the spirit of religion may be so strong within us that it shall enable us to overcome evil and prove ourselves stronger from every trial.

We remember the sorrows and the disappointments we must bear, and we pray that this same spirit of religion may lift us up when we are bowed down, and strengthen us when we are weak, and give joy of heart to our inner man when the mortal flesh weeps and our eyes run down with tears.

In our sorrow and sadness we look up to Thee, and when mortal friends fail us, and the urn that held our treasured joys is broken into fragments, and the wine of life is scattered at our feet, O Lord, we rejoice to know that Thou understandest our lot, and wilt make every sorrow of our life turn out for our endless welfare, and our continual growth, so that Thou wilt take us home to Thyself with no stain of weeping on our face. O Lord, when ourselves have been false, when our own hearts cry out against us, and we stain our daily sacrifice with remorseful tears, we rejoice to know that Thou art greater than our heart, and wilt bring home every wandering child of Thine, with no stain of sin on our immortal soul. Father, we thank Thee that amid the joys of the flesh, amid the delights of our daily work, and all the sweet and silent blessedness of mortal friendship and love upon the earth, Thou givest us the joy of knowing Thee, the still and calm delight of lying low in thy hand, and feeling the breath of Thy spirit upon us. Yea, Lord, we thank Thee that Thou holdest each one of us, yea, all of Thy children, and the universe itself, as a mother folds her baby to her bosom, and blessest us all with Thine infinite loving-kindness and Thy tender mercy.

May we, then, be conscious of immortal life, and, lifting up holy hearts, enjoy that kingdom of heaven which is not meat and drink, and here on earth, by the various steps of joy and sorrow, may we mount up to that high dwelling-place where we taste those joys which the heart hath not conceived of, but which Thy spirit and our own spirit create for every earnest and noble and aspiring soul!

O Lord, we remember before Thee our country, and while we thank Thee for the noble fathers and mothers who here planted this national vine, and bless Thee for the truth those men brought, and the justice which secures for us the liberty of our flesh and the freedom of our soul, — we remember also the wickedness in high places, in our Northern lands and in many a Southern State, which is throned over the necks of the people. We remember the millions of our brother-men whose chained hands cannot this day be lifted up to Thee, whose minds are dark with the ignorance we have forced upon them, and whose souls are in bondage because we have fettered their feet and manacled their hands. O Lord, we pray Thee that the whole nation may suffer till the Church and State be ashamed of their wickedness, and the whole people rise in their majesty and cast out this iniquity from the midst of us, and righteousness covers the land as the waters cover the sea. And we pray Thee that in our humble way we may be useful in these great and good works, that our daily lives may be a gospel unto men, and the brave words that we speak and the noble sentiments that we cherish may be a prophecy of better things to come, which shall ring in the ears of the nation till they tingle, and its heart also be touched. So may Thy kingdom come, and Thy will be done on earth, as it is in heaven.

THEODORE PARKER.

Prayer in Spring.

O THOU Infinite Power, whom men call by varying names, but whose grandeur and whose love no name expresses and no words can tell; O thou Creative Cause of all, Conserving Providence to each, we flee unto Thee, and would seek for a moment to be conscious of the sunlight of Thy presence, that we may lift up our souls unto Thee, and fill ourselves with exceeding comfort and surpassing strength. We know that Thou wilt draw near unto us when we also draw near unto Thee. Father, we thank Thee that while heaven and the heaven of heavens cannot contain Thine all-transcendent being, yet Thou livest and movest and workest in all things that are, causing, guiding, and blessing all and each.

We bless Thee for the material world, wherewith Thou environest us beneath and about and overhead. We thank Thee for the night, where Thy moon walks in brightness, pouring out her beauty all around, with a star or two beside her; and we bless Thee for the sun, who curiously prepares the chambers of the East with his beauty, and then pours out the golden day upon the waiting and expectant ground. We thank Thee for the new life which comes tingling in the boughs of every great or little tree, which is green in the new-ascended grass, and transfigures itself in the flowers to greater brightness than Solomon ever put on. We thank Thee for the seed which the farmer has cradled in the ground, or which thence lifts up its happy face of multitudinous prophecy, telling us of harvests that are to come. We thank Thee also for the garment of prophecy with which Thou girdest the forests and adornest every tree all round our Northern lands. We bless Thee for the fresh life which teems in the waters that are about us, and in the little brooks which run among the hills, which warbles in the branches of the trees, and hums with new-born insects throughout the peopled land. O Lord, we thank Thee for a day so sweet and fair as this, when the trees lift up their hands in a psalm of gratitude to Thee, and every little flower that opens its cup and every wandering bird seem filled by Thy spirit, and grateful to Thee. We thank Thee for all Thine handwritings of revelation on the walls of the world, on the heavens above us and the ground beneath, and all the testimonies recorded there of Thy presence, Thy power, Thy justice, and Thy love.

We thank Thee not less for that perpetual spring-time with which Thou visitest the human soul. We bless Thee for the sun of righteousness which never sets, nor allows any night there, but, with healing in his beams, shakes down perennial day on eyes that open, and on hearts that, longing, lift them up to Thee. We thank Thee for the great truths which shine to us, the lesser light like the moon in the darkness of the night, and those great lights which pour out a continuous and never-ending day about us where'er we turn our weary mortal feet. We thank Thee for the generous emotions which spring up anew in every generation of mankind, for the justice that faints not nor is weary, for the truth which never fails, for that philanthropy which goes out and brings the wanderer home, which lifts up the fallen and heals the sick, is eyes to the blind and feet to the lame; yea, we thank Thee for that piety which inspired Thy sons in many a distant age, in every peopled land, and we bless Thee that it springs anew in our heart, drawing us unto Thee, and giving us a multitudinous prophecy of glories that are yet to come, while it sheds peace along the pathway where we turn our weary mortal feet.

O Thou who art Infinite Perfection, we thank Thee for Thyself; and we know that out of Thy power, Thy wisdom, Thy justice, and Thy love have flowed forth this world of matter, and this world of man, and that kingdom of heaven whereinto we all hope to enter at the last. We thank Thee for Thy loving-kindness and Thy tender mercy, which are over all Thy works, and where we cannot see, save through a glass darkly, we will still trust Thee, with infinite longing which casteth out every fear.

Father in heaven, so gifted as we are, surrounded so, and so destined for immortal welfare, we pray Thee that we may live great and noble lives on the earth, unfolding our nature day by day, using our bodies for their purpose, and the soul for its higher use, growing wiser and better as we change time into life, and daily work into exalted character. So may we live that every day we learn some new truth, practise some new virtue, and become dearer and more beautiful in Thine own sight. So may Thy kingdom come, and Thy will be done on earth as it is in heaven.

THEODORE PARKER.

Thanksgiving for All Saints.

OUR Father who art in heaven, and on earth, we thank Thee that while Thou drawest near unto us, we may draw near unto Thee, and in Thee live and move and have our being. May the words of our mouths and the meditations of our hearts be acceptable in Thy sight, O Lord, our Strength and our Redeemer.

We thank Thee that Thou hast nowhere left Thyself without a witness, but everywhere makest revelations of Thyself, where day unto day uttereth speech of Thee, and night unto night showeth knowledge; yea, where there is no other voice nor language, Thou, Lord, speakest, in Thine infinite wisdom and Thy boundless love. We thank Thee for the presence of Thy Holy Spirit everywhere, that Thou persuasively knockest at every closed heart, and into open souls comest like the sweetness of morning, spreading there the delight of truth and piety, and loving-kindness and tender mercy too.

We thank Thee for the noble institutions which have come down to us; for the church with its many words of truth and its recollections of ancient piety; for the state, with its wise laws; for the community, which puts its hospitable walls around us from the day of our birth, until we are cradled again in our coffin, and the sides of the pit are sweet to our crumbling flesh.

We remember before Thee the ages that are past and gone, and thank Thee for the great men whom Thou causedst to spring up in those days, great flowers of humanity, whose seeds have been scattered broadcast along the world, making the solitary place into a garden, and the wilderness to blossom like a rose. We bless Thee for the great men who founded the state, and for the inventors of useful things, large-minded men, who thought out true ideas, and skilful-handed folk who made their lofty thought an exceeding useful thing. We thank Thee for those strong men of science in whose hands the ark of truth has been borne ever onward from age to age, for poets and philosophers whose deep vision beheld the truth when other men perceived it not, and for those gifted women whose presentient soul ran before the mighty prophet's thoughtful eye, forefeeling light when yet the very East was dark with night. Yea, we thank Thee for the goodly fellowship of all these prophets of glory, the glorious company of such apostles, and the noble army of martyrs, who were faithful even unto death. We bless Thee for the ways of the world which were made smooth by the toil of these great souls, and that we can walk serene on paths once slippery with their blood and now monumented with their memorial bones.

Chiefliest of all do we bless Thee for that noble son of Thine, born of a peasant mother and a peasant sire, who in days of great darkness went before men, his life a pillar of fire leading them into marvellous light and peace and beauty. We thank Thee for his words, so lustrous with truth, for his life, fragrant all through with piety and benevolence; yea, Lord, we bless Thee for the death which sinful hands nailed into his lacerated flesh, where through the wounds the spirit escaped triumphant unto Thee, and could not be holden of mortal death. We thank Thee for the triumphs which attend that name of Jesus, for the dear blessedness which his life has bestowed upon us, soothing the pathway of toil, softening the pillow of distress, and brightening the way whereon truth comes down from Thee, and life to Thee goes ever ascending up. Father, we thank Thee for the blessings which this great noble soul has widely scattered throughout the world, and most of all for this, that his spark of fire has revealed to us Thine own divinity enlivening this mortal human clod, and prophesying such noble future of achievement here on earth and in Thine own kingdom of heaven with Thee.

Father, we thank Thee also for the unmentioned martyrs, for the glorious company of prophets whom history makes no written record of, but whose words and whose lives are garnered up in the great life of humanity.

O Lord, we thank Thee for our fathers who brought us up, who have gone before us and blessed us with manifold kindness and tenderness; and we bless Thee also for the mothers who bore and carefully tended us, and watched over our little heads, and trained our infantile feet to walk in the ways of pleasantness and in the paths of peace.

We thank Thee for the noble nature which Thou hast given to woman, for the various faculties wherein she differs from man, for her transcendent mind which anticipates his slower thought. We bless Thee for her generous instincts of morality, of loving-kindness and tender mercy, and that deep religious power of intuition whereby she communes with Thy spirit face to face, and knows Thee and loves Thee with an exceeding depth of noble heart. We thank Thee for the great and lustrous women of other times and our own age, who spoke as they were moved by Thy spirit, or who, with lives more eloquent than speech, ran before the world's great prophets and redeemers, smoothing the pathway which rougher feet were yet to tread, and shedding the balsam of their benediction on the air which mankind was to breathe. We bless Thee for the noble and generous women in our own day, engaged in the various callings and lots of human life. We thank Thee for those who relieve the sick, who recall the wandering from the way of wickedness, who smooth the pillow of suffering, who teach and instruct those that are ignorant, who lift up such as are fallen down, and overtake the aged or the juvenile wanderers who are outcasts from the world. Father, we bless Thee for all these blessings, which Thou givest to the world in this portion of humanity.

And for ourselves to whom Thou hast given so many talents, and the opportunity so glorious for their use, we pray Thee that we may distinguish between the doctrines of men and Thine eternal commandments, and that no reverence to the old may blind our eyes to evils that have come down from other days, and no fondness for new things ever lead us to grasp the hidden evil when we take the specious good; but may we separate between the right and the wrong, and choose those things that are wise to direct, and profitable for our daily use. O Lord, when we compare our own poor lives with the ideal germ which warms in our innermost soul, longing to be itself a strong and flame-like flower, we are ashamed that our lives are no better, and we pray Thee that in time present and in all time to come we may summon up the vigor of our spirit, and strive to live lives of such greatness and nobleness that we shall bless our children and all who come after us, giving them better institutions than ourselves have received, and bequeathing to them a more glorious character than was transmitted to us.

May we cultivate every noble faculty of our nature, giving to every limb of the body its proper place and enjoyment, and over all the humbler faculties may we enthrone the great commanding powers, which shall rule and regulate our life into order and strength and beauty, and fill our souls with the manifold delight of those who know Thee and serve Thee and love Thee with all their understanding and all their heart.

In the stern duties which are before us, Father in heaven, may Thy light burn clear in our tabernacle, and when Thou callest us may our lamps be trimmed and burning, our loins girt about, our feet ready sandalled for the road, and our souls prepared for Thee. Thus may Thy kingdom come, and Thy will be done on earth as it is in heaven.

THEODORE PARKER. (1856.)

PART V.

SELF-RENUNCIATION.

CONTEMN riches, and thou shalt be rich; contemn glory, and thou shalt be glorious; contemn injuries, and thou shalt be a conqueror; contemn rest, and thou shalt gain rest; contemn earth, and thou shalt find heaven.

St. Chrysostom.

IN having nothing, I have all things, because I have Christ. Having, therefore, all things in Him, I seek no other reward; for He is the universal reward.

Ibid.

WOULDST thou that thy flesh obey thy spirit? then let thy spirit obey thy God. Thou must be governed that thou mayest govern.

St. Augustine.

He that loseth his life shall find it.

O MY God, how true it is, that we may have of Thy gifts, and yet may be very full of ourselves! How very narrow is the way, how straight is the gate, which leads to the true life in God! How little must one become, by being stripped of all the various attachments which the world places about him, so that he shall have no desire and no will of his own, before he is small enough to go through this narrow place! But when, by death to ourselves, we have passed through it, what enlargements do we find! Our will, by being lost and dead to itself, is raised and magnified into the Divine will. David saith, "*He brought me forth into a large place.*" And what is this large place, what can it be, but God himself, that Infinite Being in whom all other beings and all other streams of life terminate. God is a large place indeed. And it was through humiliation, through abasement, through nothingness, David was brought into it.

MADAME GUYON. (1648–1717.)

Self-Renunciation.

HOW poor is the wisdom of men, and how uncertain their forecast! Govern all by Thy wisdom, O Lord, so that my soul may always be serving Thee, as Thou dost will and not as I may choose. Punish me not by granting that which I wish or ask, if it offend Thy love, which would always live in me. Let me die to myself, that so I may serve Thee: let me live to Thee, Thou who in Thyself art the true life. Reign Thou, and let me be the captive, for my soul covets no other freedom. Amen.

St. Theresa. (1515-1583. Translated by L. G. Ware.)

Harmony with God's Will.

THAT wherein God himself is happy, the holy angels are happy, in whose defect the devils are unhappy; that dare I call happiness. Whatsoever conduceth unto this, may with an easy metaphor deserve that name; whatsoever else the world terms happiness, is to me a story out of Pliny, an apparition, or neat delusion, wherein there is no more of happiness than the name. Bless me in this life but with peace of my conscience, command of my affections, the love of Thyself and my dearest friends, and I shall be happy enough to pity Cæsar. These are, O Lord, the humble desires of my most reasonable ambition, and all I dare call happiness on earth; wherein I set no rule or limit to Thy hand or providence: dispose of me according to the wisdom of Thy pleasure: Thy will be done, though in my own undoing.

Sir Thomas Browne. (Religio Medici. 1605-1682.)

Entire Devotion.

THE one prayer of his whole life, was that he might have an "objective, disinterested love of

Christ," and that he might have "that possession of God which arises from love for others."

"Bring into captivity every thought to the obedience of Christ. Take what I cannot give: my heart, body, thoughts, time, abilities, money, health, strength, nights, days, youth, age, and spend them in Thy service, O my crucified Master, Redeemer, God. O, let not these be mere words! Whom have I in heaven but Thee? and there is none upon earth that I desire in comparison of Thee. My heart is athirst for God, for the living God. When shall I come and appear before God?

F. W. ROBERTSON. (Memoir.)

Living for God.

O GOD, our everlasting hope, who holdest us in life, and orderest our lot; we ask not for any prosperity that would tempt us to forget Thee. As disciples of one who had not where to lay his head, may we freely welcome the toils and sufferings of our humanity, and seek only strength to glorify the cross Thou layest on us. Every work of our hand may we do as unto Thee; in every trouble, trace some lights of Thine; and let no blessing fall on dry and thankless hearts. Redeeming the time, may we fill every waking hour with faithful duty and well-ordered affections, as the sacrifice which Thou hast provided. Strip us, O Lord, of every proud thought; fill us with patient tenderness for others, seeing that we also are in the same case before

Thee; and make us ready to help, and quick to forgive. And then, fix every grace, compose every fear, by a steady trust in Thine eternal realities, behind the changes of time and the delusions of men. Thou art our Rock: we rest on Thee. *Amen.*

MARTINEAU'S SERVICE BOOK.

For Submission.

BE present with me, Lord Jesus! in all places, and at all times. May I find consolation in being willing to bear the want of all human comfort. And if Thy consolation also be withdrawn, let Thy will and righteous probation of me be to me as the highest comfort; for "Thou wilt not always chide, neither wilt Thou keep Thine anger forever!"

THOMAS À KEMPIS. (1388-1471.)

The Victory over the World.

O MY God, I would be guided by Thy counsel every step of my walk through life, and strengthened by Thee for every part of my warfare. I pray Thee to deliver me from all evil influences of this present world, while I am going through it to a better. O my God, give me a stranger's temper, and a pilgrim's frame. Let me live a sojourner here below, that the good things I meet with on my journey may not tempt me to make this my rest; and the evil things I meet with may not lead me to fret and murmur as if God was not my Father, and His heaven my home. O Holy Spirit, show me daily the glory of my Saviour's victory over the world, that I may share with him in it; and enable me to go forth conquering and to conquer, in His strength, and to His praise. Help me to look upon the world and to treat it as He did; that, feeling the emptiness of its offered happiness, I may with a single heart cleave to my God, and may be saved from the spirit of the world. Let me sit quite loose and free from the things about me; and let eternal things be always present to my faith, in their reality and blessedness; that I may grow more and more alive to them, and more dead to everything else. Preserve my heart, O my gracious God, that I may be in communion with Thee when I am in my worldly business. Enable me to cast all my cares and burdens upon Thee, believing that Thou carest for me. O, daily crucify the world to me, and me to it, that when its offers stand in competition with Thy love, I may have grace to reject them. In this holy war carry me on, glorifying Him who hath called me to be a soldier. Grant me this for Jesus' sake. *Amen.*

William Romaine, D.D.

For the Martyr-Spirit.

O GOD, Thou hast set us in the train of many martyrs and holy men; and given us, as author and finisher of our faith, one who offered himself up a living and dying sacrifice. We are not our own, but Thine. Freely may we crucify our shrinking will, surrender ourselves to the uttermost claims of Thy spirit, and seek no peace but in harmony with Thee

MARTINEAU'S SERVICE BOOK.

Self-Renunciation.

IF a man may attain thereunto, to be unto God as his hand is unto man, let him be therewith content, and not seek further. . . . .

That we may thus deny ourselves, and forsake and renounce all things for God's sake, and give up our own wills, and die unto ourselves, and live unto God alone and to his will, may He help us who gave up his will to his Heavenly Father, — Jesus Christ our Lord, to whom be blessing for ever and ever. *Amen.*

THEOLOGIA GERMANICA. (About A. D 1350.
Translated by Susanna Winkworth.)

PART VI.

FOR SPIRITUAL QUICKENING.

Divine Enticement.

O EXCELLENT hiding, which is become my perfection! My God, Thou hidest Thy treasure, to kindle my desire; Thou hidest Thy pearl, to inflame the seeker; Thou delayest to give, that Thou mayest teach me to importune; seemest not to hear, to make me persevere.

St. Anselm. (1034-1099.)

Healthful Disquiets.

BE always displeased at what thou art, if thou desirest to attain to what thou art not: for where thou hast pleased thyself, there thou abidest. But if thou sayest, I have enough, thou perishest: always add, always walk, always proceed; neither stand still, nor go back, nor deviate: he that standeth still proceedeth not; he goeth back that continueth not; he deviateth that revolteth; he goeth better that creepeth in his way than he that runneth out of his way.

St. Augustine. (354-403.)

Unrest.

MY heart is a vain heart, a vagabond and instable heart; while it is led by its own judgment, and wanting divine counsel, cannot subsist in itself; and whilst it divers ways seekest not, findeth none, but remaineth miserable through labor, and void of peace: it agreeth not with itself, it dissenteth from itself, it altereth resolutions, changeth the judgment, frameth new thoughts, pulleth down the old, and buildeth them up again: it willeth and willeth not; and never remaineth in the same state.

St. Bernard. (1091 - 1153.)

For Light and Guidance.

ETERNAL God, Thou uncreate and primal Light, Maker of all created things, Fountain of pity, Thou Sea of Bounty, fathomless deep of Loving-Kindness: lift Thou up the light of Thy countenance upon us! Lord, shine in our hearts, true Sun of Righteousness, and fill our souls with Thy beauty.

Teach us always to keep in mind Thy judgments, and to discourse of them, and own Thee continually as our Lord and Friend. Govern by Thy will the works of our hands; and lead us in the right way, that we may do what is well-pleasing and acceptable to Thee, that through us unworthy Thy holy name may be glorified.

To Thee alone be praise and honor and worship eternally. *Amen.*

St. Basil. (A. D. 329 - 379.)

For Heavenly Refreshment.

COME, Holy Spirit, and bring from heaven a ray of Thy light! Come, Thou father of the poor, Thou giver of gifts, Thou light of the world, the blessed Comforter, the dear guest of the soul, and its sweetest refreshment; Thou, our repose in labor, our coolness in heat, our comfort in affliction! O, most blessed Spirit, fill full the hearts of Thy faithful people! Without Thy influence there is nothing in man which is not weakness and guilt. O, cleanse that which is sordid; bedew that which is dried up; heal that which is wounded; bend that which is stubborn; cherish in Thy bosom that which is cold; guide that which is wandering; and grant unto Thy servants, putting their trust in Thee, the merit of Thy righteousness; grant them final salvation; grant them everlasting joy! O Lord, hear our prayer, and let our cry come unto Thee.

ST. BERNARD. (1091–1153.)

For Cleansing.

O GOD, the Father of our Lord God and Saviour Jesus Christ, Lord, whose name is great, whose nature is blissful, whose goodness is inexhaustible, Thou God and Master of all things, who art blessed forever: who sittest on the Cherubim, and art glorified by the Seraphim; before whom stand thousands of thousands and ten thousand times ten thousand, the hosts of holy angels and archangels; sanctify, O Lord, our souls and bodies and spirits, and touch our apprehensions and search out our consciences, and cast out of us every evil thought, every base desire, all envy, and pride, and hypocrisy, all falsehood, all deceit, all worldly anxiety, all covetousness, vainglory, and sloth, all malice, all wrath, all anger, all remembrance of injuries, all blasphemy, and every motion of the flesh and spirit that is contrary to Thy holy will. And grant us, O Lord, the Lover of men, with freedom, without condemnation, with a pure heart and a contrite soul, without confusion of face and with sanctified lips, boldly to call upon Thee, our holy God and Father who art in heaven.

LITURGY OF ST. JAMES.

The Spiritual Illumination.

HEAR us, O never-failing Light, Lord our God, our only Light, the Fountain of light, the Light of Thine Angels, Thrones, Dominions, Principalities, Powers, and of all intelligent beings; who hast created the light of Thy saints. May our souls be lamps of Thine, kindled and illuminated by Thee. May they shine and burn with the truth, and never go out in darkness and ashes. May we be Thy house, shining from Thee, shining in Thee; may we shine and fail not; may we ever worship Thee; in Thee may we be kindled, and not be extinguished. Being filled with the splendor of Thy Son our Lord Jesus Christ, may we shine forth inwardly; may the gloom of sins be cleared away, and the light of perpetual faith abide within us.

MOZARABIC SACRAMENTARY. (Earlier than 711.)

For Growth in Grace.

O GOD, Thou art Life, Wisdom, Truth, Bounty, and Blessedness, the Eternal, the only true Good! My God and my Lord, Thou art my hope and my heart's joy! I confess, and with thanksgiving do I exalt it, that Thou hast made me in Thy express image, therewith to direct all my thoughts to Thee and to love Thee! Lord, make me to know Thee aright, that I may more and more love, and enjoy, and possess Thee.

And since in the life here below, I cannot fully attain this blessedness, let it at least grow in me day by day, until it all be fulfilled at last in the life to come! Here be the knowledge of Thee increased, and there let it be perfected! Here let my love to Thee grow, and there may it ripen; that my joy being here great in hope, may there in fruition be made perfect!

O Lord, Thou dost counsel us through Thy son, yea, Thou dost charge us to ask, and hast promised to grant that our joy may be fulfilled. I pray Thee through Thy bidding, in him who is our Counsel and our Light, give what Thou hast promised, that my joy may be full! O God of Truth, I beseech Thee, let me so attain that my joy may be full.

Meanwhile let my mind be set to this, and of

this my tongue speak! This let my heart love, and of this my mouth discourse! For this let my soul hunger, and my heart thirst, and my whole being long, until I enter Thy eternal Joy. Amen.

St. Anslem. (A. D. 1044–1099. Translated by L. G. Ware.)

For Guidance in Prayer.

LORD, if Thou art not present, where shall I seek Thee absent? If everywhere, why do I not see Thee present? Thou dwellest in light inaccessible; and where is that inaccessible light? or how shall I have access to light inaccessible? I beseech Thee, Lord, teach me to seek Thee, and show Thyself to the seeker; because I can neither seek Thee, unless Thou teach me, nor find Thee, unless Thou show Thyself to me: let me seek Thee in desiring Thee, and desire Thee in seeking Thee: let me find Thee in loving Thee, and love Thee in finding Thee.

St. Anselm.

For Love of Jesus.

AH! sweet Jesus, pierce the marrow of my soul with the healthful shafts of Thy love, that it may truly burn, and melt, and languish, with the only desire of Thee; that it may desire to be dissolved, and to be with Thee; let it hunger alone for the bread of life: let it thirst after Thee, the spring and fountain of eternal light, the stream of true pleasure; let it always desire Thee, seek Thee, and find Thee, and sweetly rest in Thee.

St. Bonaventura. (1221–1274. Translated by Quarles.)

For Light.

O LORD, who art the light, the way, the truth, the life; in whom there is no darkness, error, vanity, nor death: the light, without which there is darkness: the way, without which there is wandering; the truth, without which there is error; the life, without which there is death: say, Lord, "Let there be light," and I shall see light, and eschew darkness; I shall see the way, and avoid wandering; I shall see the truth, and shun error; I shall see life, and escape death: illuminate, O illuminate my blind soul, which sitteth in darkness and the shadow of death; and direct my feet in the way of peace.

St. Augustine. (A. D. 354-403.)

Teach us how to Pray.

O LORD! I know not what I should ask of Thee. Thou only knowest what I want; and Thou lovest me, if I am Thy friend, better than I can love myself. O Lord! give to me, Thy child, what is proper, whatsoever it may be. I dare not ask either crosses or comforts. I only present myself before Thee. I open my heart to Thee. Behold my wants, which I myself am ignorant of; but do Thou behold, and do according to Thy mercy. Smite, or heal! Depress me, or raise me up. I adore all Thy purposes without knowing them. I am silent, I offer myself in sacrifice. I abandon myself to Thee. I have no more any desire but to accomplish Thy will. Lord, teach me how to pray! Dwell Thou thyself in me by Thy Holy Spirit.

FENELON. (1651-1715.)

The Soul's Need.

GREAT God! what then is man, thus to wrestle during his whole life, against himself, to wish to be happy without Thee, in spite of Thee, in declaring himself against Thee? To feel his wretchedness and yet to love it, to know his true happiness and yet to fly from it? What is man, O my God, and who shall fathom his ways and the eternal contradiction of his errors? Delivered up to his own understanding, he is continually deceived, and nothing appears to his eyes but under fictitious colors; he but imperfectly knows Thee; he hardly knows himself; he comprehends nothing in all that surrounds him; he takes darkness for light; he wanders from error to error; he quits not his errors when he returns to himself. The lights alone of Thy faith can direct his judgments, open the eyes of his soul, become the reason of his heart, teach him to know himself, lay open the folds of self-love, expose all the artifices of the passions, and exalt him to the spiritual man, who conceives and judges of all.

O my God! I know only too well that the world and its pleasures make none happy! Come, then, and resume Thine influence over a heart which in vain endeavors to fly from Thee; and which its own disgusts recall to Thee in spite of itself; come to be its Redeemer, its Peace, its Light, and pay more regard to its wretchedness than to its crimes. *Amen.*

MASSILLON. (1663-1742.)

For Direct Guidance.

"SPEAK, Lord, for Thy servant heareth. I am Thy servant; give me understanding, that I may know Thy testimonies." Incline my heart to the words of Thy mouth: "Let Thy speech distil as the dew!"

The children of Israel once said to Moses, "Speak thou with us, and we will hear: let not God speak with us, lest we die." I pray not in this manner: no, Lord, I pray not so; but, with the Prophet Samuel, humbly and ardently entreat, "Speak, Lord, for Thy servant heareth." Let not Moses speak to me, nor any of the prophets; but speak Thou, O Lord God, the inspirer and enlightener of all the prophets: for Thou alone, without their intervention, canst perfectly instruct me; but, without Thee, they can profit nothing.

Thy ministers can pronounce the words, but cannot impart the Spirit; they may entertain the fancy with the charms of eloquence; but if Thou art silent, they do not inflame the heart. They administer the letter, but Thou openest the sense; they utter the mystery, but Thou revealest its meaning; they publish Thy laws, but Thou conferrest the power of obedience; they point out the way to life, but Thou bestowest strength to walk in it; "they water, but Thou givest the increase"; their voice soundeth in the ear, but it is Thou that givest understanding to the heart. Therefore, do Thou, O Lord my God, Eternal Truth! speak to my soul: lest, being outwardly warned, but not inwardly quickened, I die, and be found unfruitful: lest the word heard and not obeyed, known and not loved, professed and not kept, turn to my condemnation. "Speak," therefore, "Lord, for Thy servant heareth": "Thou" only "hast the words of eternal life!" O speak, to the comfort of my soul, to the renovation of my nature, and to the eternal praise and glory of Thy own holy name!

THOMAS À KEMPIS. (1388–1471.)

For Spiritual Light.

O HEAVENLY Father, the author and fountain of all truth, the bottomless sea of all understanding, send down, we beseech Thee, Thy Holy Spirit into our hearts, and lighten our understandings with the beams of Thy heavenly grace. We ask this, O merciful Father, not in respect of our deserts, but for Thy dear Son, our Saviour, Jesus Christ's sake. *Amen.*

RIDLEY. (Martyred in 1555.)

For Spiritual Enlargement.

O THAT Christ would break down the old narrow vessels of these narrow and ebb souls, and make fair, deep, wide, and broad souls, to hold a sea and a full tide, flowing over all its banks, of Christ's love!

RUTHERFORD.

A Prayer at the Diet of Worms.

ALMIGHTY, eternal God! what a strange thing is this world! How doth it open wide the mouths of the people! How small and poor is the confidence of men toward God! How is the flesh so tender and weak, and the Devil so mighty and so busy through his apostles and the wise of this world! How soon do they withdraw the hand, and whirl away and run the common path and the broad way to hell, where the godless belong. They look only upon that which is splendid and powerful, great and mighty, and which hath consideration. If I turn my eyes thither also, it is all over with me; the bell is cast and the judgment is pronounced. Ah God! Ah God! O Thou my God! Thou my God, stand Thou by me against the reason and wisdom of all the world. Do Thou so! Thou must do it. Thou alone. Behold, it is not my cause but Thine. For my own person I have nothing to do here before these great lords of the world. Gladly would I too have good quiet days and be unperplexed. But Thine is the cause, my Lord; it is just and eternal. Stand Thou by me, Thou true, eternal God! I confide in no man. It is to no purpose and in vain. Everything halteth that is fleshly, or that savoreth of flesh. O God! O God! Hearest Thou not, my God? Art Thou dead? No! Thou canst not die. Thou only hidest Thyself. Hast Thou chosen me for this end? I ask Thee. But I know for a surety that Thou hast chosen me. Ha! then may God direct it. For never did I think, in all my life, to be opposed to such great lords; neither have I intended it. Ha! God, then stand by me in the name of Jesus Christ, who shall be my shelter and my shield, yea! my firm tower, through the might and strengthening of Thy Holy Spirit. Lord! where stayest Thou? Thou my God! where art Thou? Come, come! I am ready, even to lay down my life for this cause, patient as a little lamb. For just is the cause and Thine. So will I not separate myself from Thee forever. Be it determined in Thy name. The world shall not be able to face me against my conscience, though it were full of devils. And though my body, originally the work and creature of Thy hands, go to destruction in this cause, — yea, though it be shattered in pieces, — Thy word and Thy Spirit they are good to me still! It concerneth only the body. The soul is Thine and belongeth to Thee, and shall also remain with Thee forever. *Amen.* God help me! *Amen.*

MARTIN LUTHER. (A. D. 1521.
Hedge's "Prose Writers of Germany.")

Prayer to the Virgin.

ACCEPT, O blessed Virgin! my protestations of fidelity; look favorably on the confidence I have in thee; obtain for me, of thy dear Son, a lively faith, a firm hope, a tender, generous, and constant love. Obtain for me a purity that nothing can soil; a humility that nothing can elate; a patient submission to the will of God, that nothing can ever disturb. In fine, O glorious Virgin! obtain for me so faithful an imitation of thy virtue in my life, that I may experience the power of thy protection at my death. *Amen.*

CATHOLIC MANUAL.

Prayer to St. Theresa.

LOOK down upon me from heaven, blessed Saint Theresa, as I kneel before your image, looking upon the lover of Jesus, and fondly desiring that I may be like her! I pray you, let the sacred semblance be mine, — let me be like you in something! Transfer to me your heavenward eyes to seek God, your heart to love Him, your lips to pray to Him. Give me your fortitude in adversity, your sweetness in suffering, your constancy in the midst of temptation. Let my soul aspire only to heavenly joys, let me live only in the love divine; let all my affections be rooted in this love; let it consecrate them in me, and let it fill with its sweetness the brother whom I love as you loved yours!

EUGÉNIE DE GUÉRIN. (1835.)

A Prayer to St. Joseph.

O FAITHFUL servant, whom God had charged with the care of His family; thou whom He had established the guardian and protector of the life of Jesus, the consoler and support of his mother, and his own faithful Associate in the great affair of our redemption; thou who hadst the happiness to live with Jesus and Mary, and to expire in their arms: chaste Spouse of the Mother of God! thou model of pure, humble, and interior souls! be touched with the confidence we have in thee; and graciously accept these testimonies of our devotion. We return God thanks for the favors He hath bestowed on thee; and we beg, through thy intercession, that we may imitate thy virtues. Pray for us, then, O glorious Saint; and by that love thou always hadst for Jesus and for Mary, and which Jesus and Mary had also for thee, obtain always for us the incomparable advantage of living faithful to Jesus, and of dying in his love. *Amen.*

KEY OF HEAVEN.

Union with God.

O MY God! what is my life, what is my happiness, but a continual receiving? Thou art the bread of life; Thou must keep alive the living principle in my soul. In Thee "dwelleth all the fulness of the Godhead bodily." Thy people are complete in Thee; Thou art their Head, they are Thy body, and by joints and bands have nourishment ministered to them, and are knit together and increased with the increase of God.

This, O this is what my soul pants after; close and more intimate union and communion. I would be transformed into Thine image, I would be Thy temple, I would have Thee live in me, walk in me, and make me one with Thee. I would be delivered from self-will, self-wisdom, self-seeking; I would be delivered from that philosophy and vain deceit which spoil souls, and lead them off from their Head; then, and not till then, shall I cease to wander. Shall I "run and not be weary, walk and not faint." Then shall I "run in the way of Thy commandments," and no longer turn aside to crooked ways. Then shall I eat and drink, work and recreate, all to Thy glory. Lord, send Thy spirit into my heart, that He may continually take of the things of Christ and show them unto me; that I may grow and be no longer a babe, but arrive at the "fulness of stature in Christ Jesus," and more steadily and more freely, and more zealously, and O, more humbly, live to God, and glorify Him in the world. *Amen.*

MRS. ISABELLA GRAHAM.

For Regeneration.

ALMIGHTY Creator, Father of Jesus Christ my Lord! Thou didst breathe into me the breath of my natural life. Inspire me now, I beseech Thee, with the life that is spiritual and immortal. Thou didst frame this body, so fearfully and so wonderfully made. Hallow it by an indwelling soul devoted to Thy will. Let its frailty, its disorders, its perishableness, make me only the more diligent and faithful in consecrating all its powers to Thy service. The faculties of my mind were planted and attempered by Thy wondrous skill. Subdue them to Thy perfect authority and let them rejoice to bow at Thy righteous control. The affections and sympathies of my heart were all wakened by Thine unsleeping love. May they rise first of all to Thee, and find their noblest exercise in the adoration of Thy wisdom and mercy, so that all my mortal friendships shall be made stronger and purer by being mingled with the higher love which binds my heart to heaven.

But O, Thou searcher of hearts, Thou knowest I am stained within and without by the defilements of sin. I am not clean; I am not just; I am not good. The bright heavens over my head are impure in Thy sight; how much more this offending breast! The world has too much power over me. I am too much the victim of its delusions, and the slave of its passions. Grant me deliverance by Thy

Holy Spirit. I am too apt to conform to its wicked customs, to be overborne by its proud fashions, and to be led astray by its base examples. O, break this vile bondage, and bring me into the liberty of the sons of God. I am too self-seeking in my business, too harsh in my speech, too uncharitable in my judgments, too impatient in my temper, too fond of ease and indulgence, too devoted to the way that seems pleasant in my own eyes. Scatter these deceptions and snares. Show me my peril and guilt. Rouse me to repentance, and then, merciful Father, pardon me, and restore me unto Thyself.

But Thou seest, my God, that the root of all my outward transgressions is an unsubmissive and unreconciled heart. Bend my stubborn will, therefore, and break down every feeling that rebels at Thy law. The sin is in the depths of my heart. I feel that my disease is in the inmost dispositions and hidden state of my soul. Reach after it there, I pray Thee, and purge it thence. No superficial sorrow or fitful effort can drive it away. Nothing can save me but a renewal of my inmost being, through the inworking of Thy grace. Give me that hearty and thorough repentance which is unto life, and needeth not to be repented of. Pour into the springs of thought and feeling within me a quickening and converting energy. Hold up before me, in Thy word and providence, that law of awful purity which is a terror to the conscience, and which is the condemnation of my life. Alarm my indifference. Urge my sluggishness. Hasten my steps in the return from the far country to my Father's house. Reveal to me the promise and the peace that dwell forever in that blessed home, and so lead me, from under the stern and fearful discipline of a law which maketh nothing perfect, into the liberty of grace; from the obedience of a servant to the free and filial trust of a child; from the dread of penalties and the seeking of rewards, to a better hope and the love that casteth out all fear. Make me a true disciple of the cross.

Lord God Almighty, with Thee all things are possible. I implore this infinite good, this glorious salvation by Thy son. Work it out within me, I beseech Thee, in Thine own way, and by such instruments as Thou wilt; by pain or joy, by suffering or comfort, by sickness or health, by peace or by grief. Only so chasten me that I may be wholly Thine. So renew me that I shall say and feel, in all things, "Thy will be done." And so refashion my sinning soul, that I shall be a new creature in Christ Jesus, and by the power of His redemption. And Thine shall be all the glory, through Him who is the mediator of the new covenant. *Amen.*

ALTAR AT HOME.

That we may be good Soldiers of Christ.

O LORD Almighty, who art merciful and gracious, long suffering and of great goodness, we approach Thee as the God of mercy, imploring

Thee to hear these our prayers, and to pardon the multitude of our sins, for the sake of Jesus Christ. Day after day we add to the number of our transgressions; every night we have the sins of the preceding day to repent of; and every morning we have reason to fear lest we should again yield to temptation, and return to our former iniquities. We pray, therefore, for Thy persevering and protecting grace. O Lord, put Thy spirit into all our hearts; that we, being made pure and holy in our secret thoughts, may not fail to perform all that is good and acceptable in Thy sight.

Dispose each of us on this day habitually to employ our several faculties in Thy service. While we pursue the various duties of our calling, may we have a single eye to Thy glory; and may we undertake no employment on which we cannot hope for Thy blessing. And give us such a portion of Thy grace, O Lord, we beseech Thee, that we may desire to do not only that which is in some degree beneficial, but that which is most excellent and most extensively useful. May no spirit of self-indulgence, no love of ease, no dread of opposition, no fear of shame, prevent our laying out our lives heartily in Thy service. Make us willing in all respects to deny ourselves, that we may live unto Thee. Teach us to enter into the spirit of those Christians and Apostles of old, who counted not their lives dear unto themselves, so that they might finish their course with joy: and who rejoiced that they were counted worthy to suffer shame for the name of Christ; who, living in unity and godly love, were seen striving together for the faith of the Gospel, in nothing terrified by their adversaries.

Grant unto every member of this family Thy peace, and all Thy heavenly consolations; and make us to be of one heart and one mind, praising Thee for Thy mercies, praying to Thee for Thy grace, and uniting in the confession of our daily sins before Thee.

Establish us in Thy faith, and fear, and love; and enlighten us, that we may understand Thy whole will concerning us. Where we mistake, have pity on our errors; and if we have wandered from the right way, do Thou in mercy bring us back. Lead us, O Lord, into the paths of righteousness and peace. And if we have in any measure attained to the knowledge of Thy truth, may we bring our faith into active exercise. May we watch our hearts, and bridle our tongues, and govern our tempers. May we be ready to forgive, even as we hope to be forgiven. May we be steadfast and immovable, always abounding in the work of the Lord, knowing that our labor shall not be in vain in the Lord.

We now commit ourselves to Thee for this day; help us to live according to these our prayers; and thus may we be prepared for Thy heavenly kingdom: we ask it for our Saviour's sake. *Amen.*

Henry Thornton.

For Quickening.

O GOD, may our souls be warm with life. Save us from an inanimate and sluggish state. Teach us Thy purity; how great Thy abhorrence of evil, how irreconcilable Thy hatred of it; and may we all partake of the same abhorrence of sin.

Increase our sensibility to evil; may we shun every appearance of it, and repel the first temptation; and, in a world where example is so corrupt, we beseech Thee to arm us with a holy fortitude.

Inspire us with a generous love of virtue, of rectitude, of holiness. May we prefer it even to life. Animate us to adhere to good in every danger. May nothing on earth move us or shake our steadfastness. Increase our sensibility to good; may we see more and more its loveliness and beauty.

Animate us to cheerfulness. May we have a joyful sense of our blessings, learn to look on the bright circumstances of our lot, and maintain a perpetual contentedness under Thy allotments.

Fortify our minds against disappointment and calamity. Preserve us from despondency, from yielding to dejection. Teach us that no evil is intolerable but a guilty conscience; and that nothing can hurt us, if with true loyalty of affection we keep Thy commandments and take refuge in Thee.

May every day add brightness and energy to our conceptions of Thy lovely and glorious character. Give us a deeper sense of Thy presence, and instruct us to nourish our devoutness by every scene of nature and every event of Providence.

Assist us to consecrate our whole being and existence to Thee, our understandings to the knowledge of Thy character, our hearts to the veneration and love of Thy perfections, our wills to the choice of Thy commands, our active energies to the accomplishment of Thy purposes, our lives to Thy glory, and every power to the imitation of Thy goodness. Be Thou the centre, life, and sovereign of our souls!

WILLIAM ELLERY CHANNING. (1814.)

For Earnestness.

O GOD, let us not linger at the threshold of Christianity; conduct us into its inmost depths of life.

Help us to break through the obstacles, the doubts, despondency, lethargy, weakness, which hinder us. Open in us an unquenchable aspiration for truth and virtue. Give us a spirit of rational, filial, strong, unreserved, triumphant, glad obedience. Give us perfect confidence in Thee, whose laws are the dictates of fatherly wisdom and love, and who dost delight in the purity and glory of Thy children.

Dispose us to see Thy goodness everywhere, not only when descending upon us, but when diffused abroad, so that we may discern the love which pervades the universe and quickens all spirits.

Make us sensible of our inward wants, indigence,

destitution, weakness. Lay open to us our corrupt motives. Expose to us our hidden vices in all their depravity. Teach us to look steadily into ourselves, till we shall see, with something of Thine own abhorrence, every evil affection. Lead us away from false resources to a sure dependence on Thy perfect will, and may this reign supreme within us.

Help us to look through the disguises of self-love, to judge ourselves truly, to anticipate the revelations of the last day; and let not this knowledge of our deficiencies and deformities fill us with dejection, but rather endear us to Thy mercy, and lead us to Thy grace, while rousing us to vigilance and to firm and faithful conflict with every irregular desire.

William Ellery Channing. (1822.)

PART VII.

FOR A BENEVOLENT SPIRIT.

Charity.

WHAT fire is this that so warmeth my heart? What light is this that so enlighteneth my soul! O fire that always burneth, and never goeth out, kindle me! O light which ever shineth, and art never darkened, illuminate me! O that I had my heat from thee, most holy fire! how sweetly dost thou burn! How secretly dost thou shine! how desiredly dost thou inflame me!

St. Augustine.

IT maketh God man, and man God; things temporal, eternal; mortal, immortal; it maketh an enemy, a friend; a servant, a son; vile things, glorious; cold hearts, fiery; and hard things, liquid.

St. Bonaventura. (1221-1274.)

Sum of the Commandments.

JESUS said, the first of the commandments is, Hear, O Israel: the Lord our God is one Lord; and thou shalt love the Lord thy God with all thy heart, and with all thy soul, with all thy mind, and with all thy strength. This is the first commandment.

People. Write these words in our hearts, O Lord, we beseech Thee.

Minister. And the second is like, namely, this: Thou shalt love Thy neighbor as thyself.

People. Write these words in our hearts, O Lord, we beseech Thee.

Minister. There is none other commandment greater than these. On these two commandments hang all the law and the prophets.

People. Glory to God in the highest: on earth peace and good-will toward men. *Amen.*

MARTINEAU'S SERVICE BOOK.

For a Benevolent Spirit.

O FATHER, dispose us to a sincere sympathy with all men, not only to see extraordinary excellence with joy, but to take pleasure in the humblest improvements of our fellow-creatures, in the beginning of everlasting life within them. Incline us to respect the feelings of others, so that we may never wound, nor tempt, nor depress a human being.

May we understand the sublime heights of benevolence to which we are called by the Gospel, and aim at perfection in all social relations. Assist us to express with purer and unaffected simplicity the beauty of virtue, so that we may attract all around us to the heavenly life. Inspire us with an active, diffusive beneficence, and may we have the witnesses of our good-will in the improved virtues and happiness of our friends, associates, and all within the sphere of our influence. Affect our hearts with the loveliness, beauty, and joy of that mild, condescending, affectionate spirit which our Master breathed, and may we imbibe it till our lives overflow with usefulness and bounty.

Assist us in enlarging our benevolence, in diffusing our affections, so that we may embrace in kind regards all beings capable of happiness; and give us wisdom to design, and vigor to execute noble and extensive schemes of public and private good. May we learn to lose ourselves in disinterested services, from generous ardor, and to delight in imitating Thee, and in promoting the great ends of Thy providence, and the blessedness of creation.

We pray for the *fulness of Thy Spirit.* We beseech Thee to animate with new life our languid affections. Give us the fervor of devotion, the glow of philanthropy. Awaken us to a holy zeal, a joy in Thy service, a promptness to do and to suffer whatsoever Thou dost appoint.

May the labors of life become acts of religion and offerings to Thee, by the conscientiousness, purity of motive, and devotedness to Thy will of perfect good, from which they are performed.

May our sense of Thy presence be ever more clear, our conceptions of Thy character more bright, our gratitude more tender, our love of exalted virtue more generous, our good-will more overflowing. May a Divine life be ever growing within us!

WILLIAM ELLERY CHANNING. (1822.)

For Gentlemen.

ALBEIT whatsoever is born of flesh is flesh, and all that we receive of our natural parents is earth, dust and ashes and corruption, so that no child of Adam hath any cause to boast himself of his birth and blood, seeing we have all one flesh and one blood, begotten in sin, conceived in uncleanness, and born by nature the children of wrath; yet forasmuch as some by their wisdom, godliness, virtue, valiantness, strength, eloquence, learning, and policy be advanced above the common sort of people unto dignities and temporal promotions, as men worthy to have superiority in a Christian commonwealth, and by this means have obtained among the people a more noble and worthy name; we most earnestly beseech Thee from whom alone cometh the true nobility to so many as are born of Thee and made Thy sons through faith, whether they be rich or poor, noble or unnoble, to give a good spirit to our superiors, that as they be called gentlemen in name, so they may show themselves in all their doings, gentle, courteous, loving, pitiful, and liberal unto their inferiors; living among them as natural fathers among their children, not polling, pilling, and oppressing them, but favoring, helping, and cherishing them: not destroyers, but fathers of the commonalty; not enemies to the poor, but aiders, helpers, and comforters of them: that when Thou shalt call them from this vale of wretchedness, they afore showing gentleness to the common people, may receive gentleness again at Thy merciful hand, even everlasting life, through Jesus Christ our Lord. *Amen.*

LITURGIES OF KING EDWARD VI. (16th Century.)

For the Grace of Humility.

O HOLY and most gracious Master and Saviour Jesus, who by Thy example and by Thy precept, by the practice of a whole life and frequent discourses, didst command us to be meek and humble, in imitation of Thy incomparable sweetness and great humility, be pleased to give me the grace, as Thou hast given me the commandment: enable me to do whatsoever Thou commandest, and command whatsoever Thou pleasest.

O mortify in me all proud thoughts and vain opinions of myself; let me return to Thee the acknowledgment and the fruits of all those good things Thou hast given me, that, by confessing I am wholly in debt to Thee for them, I may not boast myself for what I have received, and for what

I am highly accountable; and for what is my own teach me to be ashamed and humbled, it being nothing but sin and misery, weakness and uncleanness.

Let me go before my brethren in nothing but striving to do them honor and Thee glory, never to seek my own praise, never to delight in it when it is offered; that, despising myself, I may be accepted by Thee in the honors with which Thou shalt crown Thy humble and despised servants, for Jesus' sake, in the kingdom of eternal glory. *Amen.*

JEREMY TAYLOR. (1613-1667.)

For Humility.

WHAT have we, O Heavenly Father, that we have not received? Every good gift, and every perfect gift, is from above, and cometh down from Thee, which art the Father of lights. Seeing, then, all that we have is Thine, whether it pertain to the body or the soul, how can we be proud, and boast ourselves of that which is none of our own; seeing also that as to give, so also to take away again, Thou art able and wilt, whensoever Thy gifts be abused, and Thou not acknowledged to be the giver of them? Take, therefore, away from me all pride and haughtiness of mind, graft in me true humility, that I may acknowledge Thee the giver of all good things, be thankful unto Thee for them, and use them to Thy glory and the profit of my neighbor. Grant also that all my glory and rejoicing may be in no earthly creatures, but in Thee alone, which dost mercy, equity, and righteousness upon earth. To Thee alone be all glory. *Amen.*

LITURGIES OF KING EDWARD VI.

For Landlords.

THE earth is Thine, O Lord, and all that is contained therein; notwithstanding Thou hast given the possession thereof unto the children of men. We heartily pray Thee to send Thy Holy Spirit into the hearts of them that possess the grounds, pastures, and dwelling-places of the earth, that they, remembering themselves to be Thy tenants, may not rack and stretch out the rents of their houses and lands: nor yet take unreasonable fines and incomes, after the manner of covetous worldlings, but so let them out to others, that the inhabitants thereof may both be able to pay the rents, and also honestly to live, to nourish their families, and to relieve the poor: give them grace also to consider that they are but strangers and pilgrims in this world, having here no dwelling-place, but seeking one to come; that they, remembering the short continuance of their life, may be content with that which is sufficient, and not join house to house, nor couple land to land, to the impoverishment of others, but so behave themselves in letting out their tenements, lands, and pastures, that after this life they may be received into everlasting dwelling-places, through Jesus Christ our Lord. *Amen.*

LITURGIES OF KING EDWARD VI.

For a Benevolent Spirit.

O GOD, we gather and bend before Thee again in this good home where we dwell in peace and in plenty. The power to make this home is from Thee; the power to sustain it is from Thee. Thou hast made us to differ from the homeless by Thy pure mercy; by Thy will our life is strong; by Thy will we fade away into bare need, and cry to Thee for bread. Father, hast Thou not made us to differ that we may give unto others as Thou hast given unto us? Deepen, we beseech Thee, our sense of Thy great bounty; help us to see why we are so blessed. May we know that these good things are given for great and generous uses. The poor we have always with us; the stranger comes to our door; friends dwell near us whose life will be more cheerful if they may freely enter with us into this cheerful place. O grant that Thy spirit may touch us, so that we may gladly give of our bread to them that hunger, and our shelter to the Son of man who has not where to lay his head. May we know that in all guises Thine angels come to us, and grow radiant only after they are gone. And may we make the presence of our home felt all about us, in this place where we dwell; may no sect or party name ever close our hearts and our home to the good, of ANY name or nation. So may these fruits of good living in all pureness make this dwelling to all what Thou hast made it to us, as the house of God and the very gate of heaven. Then, being faithful in our few things, may we know that Thou hast said "well done," and enter into Thy joy, through Jesus Christ. *Amen.*

ALTAR AT HOME.

For Vital Piety. A Morning Prayer.

GIVER of all good, and Fountain of all joy, what rich feasts for our senses and our souls does Thy fatherly love offer anew with each returning morning. How hast Thou filled the earth with bounty and adorned it with beauty for our benefit. We see Thy mercy freshly revealed in the light and privilege of this new day. Again we hear Thy gracious invitations to come up higher and enjoy the felicity of heavenly things.

Thanks we give Thee for the returning light and our daily bread; for home and health and friends; for the instructions of Thy truth and the opportunities of Thy service; for repeated warnings against sin, and the ample rewards that crown our fidelity; for the sweet and kindly ties that bind us one to another, and the pure affections that spring up in our hearts, fountains of bliss unspeakable; for all that renders this world a pleasant home, and fits us for the life to come.

Teach us, O Father, to imitate Thine own boundless beneficence. Freely as we have received, so freely may we give. We would not selfishly appropriate Thy favor, but would know the deeper bliss of ministering to others' needs. Quicken within us the fountains of generosity; warm our sympathies towards the sufferer of every class and clime; let no unbrotherly prejudice ever close our homes or hearts against any child of Thine. May our faith in Christ be no empty profession, but lead us to honor Him in the persons of the sick, the imprisoned, the unfortunate, — His brethren and ours. Following in the footsteps of His self-denial and brotherly service, may we become the almoners of Thy bounty and saviors of souls.

When Truth knocks at the door of our hearts, may no indifference or prejudice forbid its entrance, but as an angel visitant may it find hospitable welcome. Gladly would we hail every message from heaven, however severe the toil or costly the sacrifice to which it calls us. To Thy messengers, whether of joy or grief, of life or death, we would lend attentive ear. And to the heavenly visions Thou showest us may we never prove disobedient.

Father, forgive us as we forgive those who wrong us. Keep us this day without sin, and may its passing hours render us more worthy of Thy love. Let Thy kind providence extend to those near and dear to us, and to all for whom we should pray. And may the time speedily come when Thy glory shall fill the world as the waters fill the sea. *Amen.*

ALTAR AT HOME.

Against Anger.

BE ye angry, and sin not: let not the sun go down upon your wrath.

Give me, O Lord, a mild, a peaceable, a meek, and an humble spirit, that, remembering my own infirmities, I may bear with those of others; that, considering my character, I may rebuke with all long-suffering and gravity; that I may think lowly of myself, and not be angry when others also think lowly of me; that I may be patient towards all men, gentle and easy to be entreated; that God, for Christ's sake, may be so towards me. *Amen.*

BISHOP WILSON. (1722.)

That we may Forgive one another.

EVEN as Christ forgave you, so also do ye.*

If ye forgive men their trespasses, your Heavenly Father will also forgive you; but if ye forgive not men their trespasses, neither will your Father forgive your trespasses.†

Judge not, and ye shall not be judged; condemn not, and ye shall not be condemned; forgive, and ye shall be forgiven; give, and it shall be given unto you. For with the same measure that ye mete withal, it shall be measured to you again.‡

O that we may be kindly affectionate towards one another, tender-hearted, forgiving one another, even as God, for Christ's sake, hath forgiven us.§

* Col. iii. 13. † S. Matt. vi. 14, 15. ‡ Luke vi. 37, 38. § Eph. iv. 32.

May we ever remember Thy goodness, Thy mercy, Thy patience towards us, and the multitude of our offences against Thee, that we may, from our hearts, forgive all that have offended us.

Grant, O God, that I make all my prayers in the spirit of love and charity.

O that that mercy and pardon, which we hope for from Thee, may lead us to forgive all that have injured or offended us.

Give us grace to imitate Thy goodness, that we may forgive, and give, and love, as becomes the disciples of Jesus Christ.

Give us all, O God, such forgiving tempers, that we may close with the merciful condition of pardon.

Even the power to perform this must be from Thy grace.

Thou, O God, art all mercy towards us; O make us all so to one another, for Thy sake and for our own.

We beseech Thee for all that are our enemies, not for judgment and vengeance, but for mercy, for the remission of their sins, and for their eternal happiness.

BISHOP WILSON.

TO forgive our enemies, yet hope that God will punish them, is not to forgive enough. To forgive them ourselves, and not to pray God to forgive them, is a partial piece of charity.

SIR THOMAS BROWNE. (Christian Morals.)

For Enemies.

IF thine enemy hunger, feed him; if he thirst, give him drink.

O Jesu! whose charity all the malice of Thy bitterest enemies could not overcome, shed abroad in my heart that most excellent gift of charity, the very bond of peace, and of all virtues.

"Rejoice not over thy greatest enemy being dead; but remember that we die all." — Ecc. viii. 7.

Our enemies are our benefactors, procuring for us a new right to heaven. I pray God convert all those who hate us without cause.

I beseech Thee for my enemies, not for vengeance, but for mercy; that Thou wouldst change their hearts by Thy grace, or restrain their malice by Thy power.

BISHOP WILSON.

As we Forgive.

O THOU Searcher of hearts, by whom alone actions and words and thoughts are justly weighed; keep far from us all disposition to judge and censure our brethren. Standing in constant need of Thy forgiveness, may we not deprive ourselves of the appeal to Thy mercy by uncharitably judging our fellow-men; but, in our conduct to each other, let mercy still rejoice against judgment, as we pray that it may do when we stand before Thy awful tribunal. *Amen.*

MARTINEAU'S SERVICE BOOK.

Prayer at the Offertory.

BLESSED be Thou, O Lord God, for ever and ever: Thine, O Lord, is the greatness, and the glory, and the victory, and the majesty; for all that is in the heavens and the earth is Thine. Thine is the kingdom, O Lord, and Thou art exalted as head above all: both riches and honor come of Thee, and of Thy own do we give unto Thee. *Amen.*

SCOTCH LITURGY. (1636.)

PART VIII.

CONFESSION.

Self-Examination.

GO up, my soul, into the tribunal of thy conscience: there set thy guilty self before thyself: hide not thyself behind thyself, lest God bring thee forth before thyself.

St. Augustine.

A Distinction.

GOD hath promised pardon to him that repenteth, but he hath not promised repentance to him that sinneth.

St. Anselm.

Sin of Despair.

IT is no such heinous matter to fall afflicted, as, being down, to lie dejected. It is no danger for a soldier to receive a wound in battle, but, after the wound received, through despair of recovery, to refuse a remedy; for we often see wounded champions wear the palm at last; and, after fight, crowned with victory.

St. Chrysostom.

Evil a Help.

IF there be no enemy, no fight; if no fight, no victory; if no victory, no crown.

Savonarola.

Self-Examination.

A GOOD man would rather know his infirmity than the foundations of the earth or the heights of the heavens.

St. Augustine.

BUT that knowledge of our own infirmity is not attained but by diligent inquisition: without which the mind is for the most part blind, and sees nothing of that which pertains to it.

We see that God himself concluded each day of the old Creation in no other manner than by an examination of the works of each.

And He beheld that all were good.

BEWARE that thou show thyself the judge, and not the patron of thy sins; and say in the tribunal of thy mind, say with grief and indignation, who will set scourges over my thoughts, and the discipline of wisdom over my heart?

Bishop Andrewes.

Self-Study.

IN vain he lifteth up the eye of his heart to behold his God, who is not first rightly advised to behold himself: First, thou must see the visible things of thyself, before thou canst be prepared to know the invisible things of God; for if thou canst not apprehend the things within thee, thou canst not comprehend the things above thee; the best looking-glass, wherein to see thy God, is perfectly to see thyself.

Hugo.

Introduction to Confession.

THOU who hast created me
by Thy goodness,
let not Thy work come to naught
through my iniquity.
What is Thine in me acknowledge;
what is mine, take away.
Look on me, the wretched,
O boundless Loving-Kindness:
on me, the wicked,
O Compassion that extendest to all!
Infirm I come to the Almighty,
wounded I hasten to the Physician:
reserve for me the gentleness
of Thy compassion,
Who hast so long held suspended the sword
of Thy vengeance.

Blot out the number of my crimes,
renew the multitude of Thy compassions.
However unclean, Thou canst cleanse me;
however blind, enlighten me;
however weak, restore me;
yea, though dead, raise me.
Of what kind soever I am, be it good or bad,
I am ever Thine.
If Thou cast me out, who shall take me in?
If Thou disregard me, who shall look on me?
More canst Thou remit, than I commit;
more canst Thou spare, than I offend.
Let not noxious pleasures overcome me;
at the least, let not any perverse habit overwhelm me.
(Preserve me)
from depraved and lawless desires;
from vain, hurtful, impure imaginations;
from the illusions of evil spirits;
from pollutions of soul and of body.

Bishop Andrewes.

Self-Examination.

HAVE I penitence, grief, shame,
pain, honor, weariness for my sin?
(Do I pray,) if not seven times, as David,
yet at least thrice, as Daniel?
If not, as Solomon, at length,
yet shortly, as the Publican?
If not, like Christ, the whole night,
at least for one hour?

If not on the ground, and in ashes,
at least not in my bed?
If not in sackcloth,
at least not in purple and fine linen?
If not altogether freed from all,
at least from immoderate desires?
(Do I give,) if not, as Zaccheus, fourfold,
at least, as the law commands, with the fifth
part added? (Lev. v. 16.)
If not as the rich,
yet as the widow?
If not the half,
yet the thirtieth part?
If not above my power,
yet up to my power?

BISHOP ANDREWES'S DEVOTIONS.

Penitence.

LORD! Thou hast said there is joy in heaven over one sinner that repenteth, more than over ninety-nine just: O, give me now grace to be a true penitent indeed, that thereby heaven may rejoice at my conversion.

I know Thou willest not the death of a sinner, but rather that he may repent and live. Let me no longer remain dead in my sins! O let me now at least begin to live to Thee.

Create a clean heart in me, O God! and renew a right spirit within me. Grant that I may now serve Thee in good earnest! O, let this be the change of the right hand of the Most High.

Too late have I known Thee, O eternal truth! too late have I loved Thee, O eternal beauty! too long have I gone astray from Thee! From this moment, O my Sovereign Good! I desire to be forever Thine. O, let nothing in life or death ever separate me from Thee any more!

O Divine love! how little art Thou known in this wicked world; how little art Thou loved! Come now to me, and take full possession of my whole heart and soul, for time and eternity.

I am resolved, by Thy grace, never more to return to my sins. Rather let me die, than offend Thee wilfully any more. I am resolved to avoid all evil company, and dangerous occasions; and to take proper measures for a thorough amendment of my life for the future. All this I resolve; but Thou knowest my frailty, O my God! and if Thou assist me not with Thy grace, all my resolutions will prove ineffectual, and I shall be forever miserable. O look to me, O Lord! that I may never betray Thee any more.

THE CHRISTIAN'S GUIDE. (A Catholic Manual.)

Confession.

I AM perfectly sensible, O my God, that I have in many ways offended Thy Divine Majesty, and provoked Thy wrath in my sins; and that if I obtain not pardon, I shall be cast out of Thy sight forever; I desire therefore at present to call myself to an account, and look into all the sins whereby I have displeased Thee: but, O my God, how miserably shall I deceive myself, if Thou assist me not in this work by Thy heavenly light. Grant me, therefore, at present Thy grace, whereby I may discover all my imperfections, — see all my failings, — and duly call to mind all my sins, — for I know that nothing is hidden from Thy sight. But I confess myself in the dark as to my own failings: my passions blind me, self-love flatters me, presumption deludes me; and though I have many sins which stare me in the face, and cannot be hidden, yet how many too are there quite concealed from me! But discover even these to me, O Lord; enlighten my darkness, cure my blindness, and remove every veil that hides my sins from me, that I may be no longer a secret to myself, nor a stranger to my own failings; nor ever flatter myself with the thoughts of having repented, and at the same time nourish folly and vice within my breast. Come, Holy Ghost, and by a beam of Thy divine light illumine my understanding, that I may have a perfect view of all my sins and iniquities, and that, sincerely repenting of them, I may know Thee, and be again received into Thy favor.

KEY OF HEAVEN.

Confession.

I CONFESS, O my God, not only in Thy presence, who seest the secrets of hearts, but also in the presence of all the blessed in heaven, and faithful on earth, that I have often and grievously offended Thee, in thought, word, and deed; through my fault, through my fault, through my most grievous fault. Yes, Lord, I have sinned; I acknowledge it to my shame, and with the most bitter regret, that I have ungratefully abused all Thy gifts; and therefore I humbly beseech Thee, O blessed Virgin Mary, and all ye saints and angels, to intercede for me. Vouchsafe, O Lord, to listen to them; grant to the ardor of their prayers what Thou mayest justly refuse to the coldness of mine; and to their services, that pardon to which my offences can have no claim.

MANUAL OF PIETY.

Desire for Repentance.

O ALMIGHTY and most merciful God! who hast made me out of nothing, and redeemed me by the precious blood of Thy Son, — who hast with so much patience borne with me to this day, notwithstanding all my sins and ingratitude; ever calling after me to return to Thee from the ways of vanity and iniquity, in which I have been quite wearied out in the pursuit of empty toys and mere shadows; seeking in vain to satisfy my thirst with muddy waters, and my hunger with husks, like swine: behold, O most gracious Lord! I now sincerely desire to leave all these my evil ways, to forsake this region of death, where I have so long lost myself, and to return to Thee, the fountain of life. I desire, like the prodigal son, to enter seriously into myself, and, with the like resolutions, to rise without delay, and to go home to my Father, though I am infinitely unworthy to be called his child, in hopes of meeting with the like reception from his most tender mercy. My Lord and my all! I am confounded at the multitude of offences against so good a God; I dare not lift up my eyes to heaven, after so many treasons against Thee. Alas! what shall I now do, O Lord,—what shall I say,—but, with the humble publican, strike my breast, and cry unto Thee, O God! be merciful to me a sinner.

Father! I have sinned against heaven and in Thy sight, and am not worthy to be called Thy child. O, receive me as one of the least of Thy servants, and never suffer me to stray from Thee any more.

THE CHRISTIAN'S GUIDE.

Promise of Amendment.

THAT the world may know that I love the Father; and as the Father gave me a commandment, so I do: arise, let us go.

JOHN XIII.

BEHOLD, O my God, the moment is now come wherein I am to sacrifice those inclinations to Thee which Thou hast so often demanded, and which I was so miserably slothful as to have refused Thee. I now see the danger to which my sluggish languor has exposed me, and am determined to avoid it. I will labor incessantly against my vicious habits; I am determined to quit the immediate occasion of sin. I pledge myself to Thee, and am satisfied to be treated as Thine enemy, if those promises be not most sincere and determined. I will no longer resist Thy inspirations, nor allow myself those pleasures which Thy law forbids, nor expose myself to the danger of offending Thee. There shall be no more remissness in my duty, nor languor in my devotion. I do not make these promises through a spirit of presumption, — I am convinced of my own insufficiency, and know that, if abandoned by Thee I must necessarily fall back into all my former disasters; but being now united to Thee, I flatter myself that, in spite of my frailty, I shall constantly persevere in Thy grace. Why should I not find the same strength in this divine sacrament, which Thy glorious martyrs have derived from it? It was here they imbibed that generous spirit of suffering which could brave the power of tyrants, and smile on the horrors of death. And art Thou now less faithful, less liberal, or less able to fortify me against the attacks of the enemies of my salvation? No. Come, then, it is full time I should begin the work of my salvation. Thy will has been sufficiently declared to me; I will hesitate no longer to put it into execution, how great soever the conflict may be against myself and the world. In fine, let me feel, O Lord, an experimental conviction of such a reformation of life as may edify those whom my past conduct has scandalized, by convincing them that I do now really love Thee. Confirm, O God, what Thou hast wrought in us. *Amen.*

MANUAL OF CATHOLIC PIETY. (Compiled in 1840.)

Penitence.

LORD, I am not worthy that Thou shouldest come under my roof, but, relying on Thy loving-kindness, I draw near to Thine altar; — a sick man, to the Physician of life; a blind man, to the Light of eternal brightness; poor, to the Lord of heaven and earth; naked, to the King of glory; a sheep, to its Shepherd; a creature, to its Creator; desolate, to the loving Comforter; miserable, to the Merciful; a criminal, to the Giver of pardon; ungodly, to the Justifier; hardened, to the Infuser of grace; beseeching Thine exuberant and infinite mercy, that it may please Thee to heal my weakness, to wash my foulness, to enlighten my blindness, to enrich my poverty, to clothe my nakedness, to bring me back from my wanderings; to console my desolation, to reconcile my guiltiness, to give pardon to the sinner, forgiveness to the miserable, life to the criminal, justification to the dead; so that I may be enabled to receive Thee, the Bread of angels, the King of kings, and Lord of lords, with such chastity of body and purity of mind, such contrition of heart and plenteous sorrow, such spiritual gladness and heavenly joy, such fear and trembling, such reverence and honor, such faith and humility, such purpose and love, such devotion and thanksgiving, as are due and meet; so that it may profit me unto life eternal and remission of all my sins.

St. Thomas Aquinas. (1224–1274. With additions. Bright.)

Trust and Penitence.

RECEIVE my confession, O my only hope of Salvation, Jesus Christ, my Lord and God. For in . . . . I am lost, and altogether in thought, word, and deed, and in all evils, I am overwhelmed. Thou who justifiest the ungodly and quickenest the dead, Lord my God, justify me and revive me. Save me, O Lord, King of eternal glory, who canst save. Grant me to will and to do, and to accomplish, what is pleasing to Thee, and profitable to myself; give me aid in distress, consolation in persecution, and strength in all temptation; vouchsafe me pardon for past evils, amendment for present evils, and be pleased to send me protection against evils to come. Thine it is to give the sinner a stricken heart and a fountain of tears. It is mine, if Thou shalt vouchsafe it, to weep for my sins; it is Thine to efface them speedily, as a cloud. I beseech Thee, O Lord, to forget my sins, and to remember Thy mercies. O Christ, spare me, pity me, not according to my deserts, but according to Thy mercy. Do not despise me a sinner. Do not cast me away, but receive me according to Thy word, that I may live, and not be disappointed of my hope. Give me a fountain of tears, O Fountain of life. My hope of salvation is in no works of mine; but my soul hangs simply on the boundlessness of Thy love, and confides in the multitude of Thy mercy.

ANCIENT MISSAL. (First published by Matthias Illyricus, in 1557. Translated by Bright.)

For Forgiveness.

O MY God, hear the prayers and cries of a sinner who calls earnestly for mercy. O just and dear God, my sins are innumerable; they are upon my soul in multitudes; they are a burden too heavy for me to bear; they already bring sorrow and sickness, shame and displeasure, guilt and a decaying spirit, a sense of Thy present displeasure and fear of worse, of infinitely worse. But it is to Thee so essential, so delightful, so usual, so desired by Thee to show mercy, that, although my sin be very great, and my fear proportionable, yet Thy mercy is infinitely greater than all the world, and my hope and my comfort rise up in proportions towards it, that I trust the devils shall never be able to reprove it, nor my own weakness discompose it. Lord, Thou hast sent Thy son to die for the pardon of my sins; Thou hast given me Thy Holy Spirit as a seal of adoption; Thou hast, for all my sins, still continued to invite me to conditions of life by Thy ministers the prophets; and

Thou hast, with variety of holy acts, softened my spirit and possessed my fancy, and instructed my understanding, and bended and inclined my will, and directed or overruled my passions, in order to repentance and pardon; and why should not Thy servant beg passionately, and humbly hope for the effects of all these Thy strange and miraculous acts of loving-kindness? Lord, I deserve it not, but I hope Thou wilt pardon all my sins: and I beg it of Thee for Jesus Christ's sake, whom Thou hast made the great endearment of Thy promises, and the foundation of our hopes, and the mighty instrument whereby we can obtain of Thee whatsoever we need and can receive.

JEREMY TAYLOR.

For Steadfastness.

I WILL "confess my transgressions unto the Lord," and acknowledge my infirmity. How small are the afflictions by which I am often cast down, and plunged in sorrow! I resolve to act with fortitude, but by the slightest evil am confounded and distressed. From the most inconsiderable events the most grievous temptations rise against me; and while I think myself established in security and peace, the smallest blast, if it be sudden, hath power to bear me down.

Behold, therefore, O Lord, my abject state, and pity the infirmity which Thou knowest infinitely better than myself! Have mercy upon me that I sink not; that the deep may not swallow me up forever! So apt am I to fall, and so weak and irresolute in the resistance of my passions, that I am continually driven back in the path of life, and covered with confusion in Thy sight. Though sin does not obtain the full consent of my will, yet the assaults of it are so frequent, and so violent, that I am often weary of living in perpetual conflict. My corruption and weakness are experimentally known; for the evil thoughts that rush upon me take easy possession of my heart, but are with difficulty driven out again.

O that Thou, the mighty God of Israel, the zealous lover of faithful souls, wouldst look down with compassion on the labors and sorrows of Thy servant, and perfect and fulfil his desire of reunion with Thee. Strengthen me with heavenly fortitude, lest the old man, this miserable flesh, which is not yet brought under subjection to the Spirit, should prevail and triumph over me: against him I am bound to struggle as long as I breathe.

THOMAS À KEMPIS.

Confession.

HOW does this little check of sickness impress on me the duty of working while it is day; the night cometh when no man can work! Let me not take my estimate of myself from others who do not know me, but from my own self-knowledge and conscience. O what cause have I for contrition! What misspent time, what wasted talents, what means of grace (no one so many and so great), with how little profit; what self-indulgent habits; what softness, instead of the hardness of a good soldier of Christ! It may be shown in any improper want of self-denial. O Lord, may my faith and love be more active, bringing forth more the fruits of the Spirit.

I cast myself at the foot of the cross, bewailing my exceeding sinfulness and unprofitableness deeply, most deeply aggravated by the infinity of my mercies. I plead Thy precious promises, and earnestly pray to Thee to shed abroad in my heart more love, more humility, more faith, more hope, more peace and joy; in short, to fill me with all the fulness of God, and make me more meet to be a partaker of the inheritance of the saints in light. Then shall I also be better in all the relations of life in which I am now so defective, and my light will shine before men, and I shall adorn the doctrine of my Saviour in all things.

O let me deal honestly with myself. Let me give up, however entertaining, even however instructive, whatever it seems the intimation of God that I should relinquish. O Lord, cause me to be so full of love, and zeal, and grateful loyalty, and child-like affection for my Saviour, that I may love them that love Thee; and may I thus become more in my tempers and frames of mind an inhabitant of heaven.

William Wilberforce. (1812 and 1827.)

Confession.

O LORD God Almighty, who understandest the secrets of every heart, — who art also a God of infinite perfection and purity, and claimest not only the outward service of Thy creatures, but requirest truth in the inward parts, — we sinners, who in thought, word, and deed have offended against Thee, desire most humbly to confess our sins, and to implore Thy merciful forgiveness.

O Lord, we acknowledge that forgetfulness of Thee, and that rebellion of heart against Thee, which have been the cause of so many disorders in our lives. We have not honored Thee as God: but have set up our own will as our law; choosing to follow our own vain imaginations. We have neglected Thy written word; we have not duly attended to the instructions of Thy ministers; we have been careless under the means of grace.

Thou hast called us by many dispensations of Thy providence: Thou hast shown us the vanity of all our earthly hopes; and hast taught us lessons of wisdom, both by the mercies and by the afflictions, and by all the various trials and disappointments with which Thou hast visited us. But we have too often repined at Thy dispensations, instead of profiting by them; and have complained of our condition in life instead of turning our thoughts to a happier and better world.

Or if Thou hast multiplied our comforts, how

prone have we been to place our chief happiness in these, and not in Thee, who art the Giver! How many and various have been our sins, both secret and open, from our youth until this time! How many have been the sinful thoughts which we have indulged; of which Thou and Thou only hast been the witness! How many rash and angry words, also, have we continually spoken! How often have we injured our neighbors; judging harshly of others, while we hope to be judged mercifully by Thee; — not willing to forgive, though we ourselves hope to be forgiven!

We would confess, O Lord, the ungodliness of our hearts and lives, and the frequent impatience of our spirits. Thou hast appointed our lot in life, and hast ordered all things concerning us; but how little have we adorned the stations in which Thou hast placed us! how unfaithfully have we employed the talents intrusted to us; and how soon have we been weary in well doing!

O Lord, in the time to come defend us, we most humbly beseech Thee, from these evils. Save us from the sins which most easily beset us. Let us command our tempers and restrain our tongues. Let us add to faith, virtue; and to virtue, knowledge; and to knowledge, temperance; and to temperance, patience; and to patience, brotherly kindness; and to brotherly kindness, charity! Let us be rich in good works, to the praise and glory of Thy name. And while we are thus receiving Thy truths into an honest heart, and are endeavoring, by Thy grace assisting us, to walk according to the precepts of Thy written word; may Thy providence direct our steps in life, and watch over us, for good. Defend us, we beseech Thee, to the end of our lives; and let Thy good Spirit abide within us, that we may not faint in our Christian course, nor become weary of well doing.

We pray for Thy blessing on all our friends and relations. May they walk by the light of the same blessed Gospel. May both they and we possess in this world the knowledge of Thy truth, and in the world to come life everlasting.

We offer up these and all our supplications in the name of Jesus Christ, our only Mediator and Redeemer. *Amen.*

HENRY THORNTON.

Confession.

FATHER and Friend, Thou who art all holy and pure, burdened with a sense of sin and a weight of transgression, weighed down by a heavy heart, all-conscious of its evil, we come to Thee. We come, though we are sinners, — yes, we come because we are sinners. There is no better reason, Thou hast taught us in Christ, for coming to Thee, than we have in our sin. If we were pure and righteous, we should not need Thy pardoning love; but because we are sinful, we need it; and because Thou knowest that we need it, Thou art sending it. O Thou, who art in Christ reconciling sinners to

Thyself, reconcile us to Thyself. Change this death into life; let the burden drop from us; lift us out of this mire and deep water, in which we can neither stand nor go, — lift us, and put our feet upon the rock which shall never be moved. Let Thy forgiveness teach us to love; because Thou forgivest much, may we love much in return. Looking behind us, we see our lives imperfect, our souls stained, our best works poor, our plainest duties unfulfilled. How much time have we wasted, how many opportunities have we lost. In thought and affection, in word and deed, against each other and against Thee, how much have we done wrong, and omitted to do of right. Looking around us, we see so much that we ought to do, and are doing so little, so many who need, and we so poor and negligent to give. Looking within us, how little we find of faith, love, and peace. Dark, stormy, and wild are our thoughts and feelings, too often, — how seldom filled with the sense of Thy mercies and love. Looking before us, what can we hope? We can hope nothing away from Thee, or without Thee. In Thee alone, God of our life, is our hope. In Thee alone, through Thy Son our Saviour. In Thee alone, through the power of redemption and pardon in him. In Thee, in Thee, Infinite Love, abyss of mercy, ever-flowing Fountain, inexhaustible in grace, — in Thee we will trust, hope, and have rest. Help us to trust and be forgiven, to trust and be saved, to trust now and forever. *Amen.*

ALTAR AT HOME.

A Confession of Sin.

ALMIGHTY and most merciful Father; we have erred and strayed from Thy ways like lost sheep. We have followed too much the devices and desires of our own hearts. We have offended against Thy holy laws. We have left undone those things which we ought to have done; and we have done those things which we ought not to have done. But Thou, O Lord, have mercy upon us, miserable offenders. Spare Thou those, O God, who confess their faults. Restore Thou those who are penitent; according to Thy promises declared unto mankind, in Christ Jesus our Lord. And grant, O most merciful Father, for His sake, that we may hereafter live a godly, righteous, and sober life, to the glory of Thy holy name. *Amen.*

EPISCOPAL SERVICE BOOK.

For Forgiveness.

ALMIGHTY God, Father of our Lord Jesus Christ, Maker of all things, Judge of all men, we acknowledge and bewail our manifold sins and wickedness, which we from time to time most grievously have committed, by thought, word, and deed, against Thy divine Majesty; provoking most justly Thy wrath and indignation against us. We do earnestly repent, and are heartily sorry for these our misdoings; the remembrance of them is grievous unto us; the burden of them is intolerable. Have mercy upon us, have mercy upon us, most merciful Father; for Thy Son, our Lord Jesus Christ's sake, forgive us all that is past; and grant that we may ever hereafter serve and please Thee in newness of life, to the honor and glory of Thy name, through Jesus Christ our Lord. *Amen.*

SERVICE BOOK. (Church of England.)

Confession.

O GOD, ever-blessed and holy; none but the Angels and Thy Redeemed can serve Thee with a perfect joy. On us, as we look up to the light of Thy countenance, the shadows of shameful remembrance fall; and to all Thy mercies we must still answer with a cry for more. Called in our measure to be perfect as Thou art perfect, we have been most unlike to Thee, and are not worthy to be deemed Thy children. Thirsting with momentary desires, we have forsaken the living springs of heavenly wisdom, of which he that drinketh shall never thirst again. We have been slow to the calls of affection, heedless of the duties, hard under the sorrows, which are Thy gracious discipline: yet are oppressed with cares Thou layest not on us, with ease Thou dost not permit, and wants Thou wilt never bless. O Lord, regard our complaint; it is only against our faithless hearts. We have nothing to plead, and renounce our pride before Thee. Only leave us not to ourselves. Visit us with the wrestlings of Thy Spirit, and lay on us the cross, if we may but grow into the holiness of Christ. *Amen.*

MARTINEAU'S SERVICE BOOK.

Confession.

HOLY Lord God; how can we lift up our face, and make mention of Thy loving-kindness? for Thy praise is only our abasement, and the greatness of Thy mercy is the measure of our guilt. Yet turn us not back from Thy presence. Look upon us according to our deep need, not our poor deservings. Lift off the burden of our many sins, and revive the contrite that fly to Thee. When Thou art nigh, we are weary of our selfish desires, our faithless cares, our unresisted temptations: wasted moments, and bitter words, and vain ambitions rise up in judgment against us: we lay at Thy feet with shame the vows we have not kept, and the sorrows we have not sanctified. No secret thing is hid from Thee. Thou knowest the spirit we are of. Chasten us with Thy rebuke, seek us with Thy pity, recall us by Thy grace, ere we are quite estranged from Thee. Let the saving word, once heard on earth, be renewed from heaven, "Your sins are forgiven; go in peace." *Amen.*

J. MARTINEAU.

PART IX.

IN TROUBLE.

The Heart's Hunger.

THE heart is a small thing, but desireth great matters. It is not sufficient for a Kite's dinner; yet the whole world is not sufficient for it.

HUGO.

Trouble Everywhere.

SECURITY is nowhere; neither in heaven nor in paradise, much less in the world. In heaven the angels fell from the divine presence; in paradise, Adam fell from his place of pleasure; in the world, Judas fell from the school of our Saviour.

ST. BERNARD.

Inconsistency.

BEHOLD, the world is withered in itself, yet flourisheth in our hearts, everywhere death, everywhere grief, everywhere desolation. On every side we are smitten: on every side filled with bitterness; and yet, with the blind mind of carnal desire, we love her bitterness. It flieth, and we follow it; it falleth, yet we stick to it; and because we cannot enjoy it falling, we fall with it, and enjoy it fallen.

ST. GREGORY.

POLICARP being sentenced to die for his religion, and being brought to the fire, prayed, —

Thou God and Father of our Lord Jesus Christ, by whom I have received the knowledge of Thee! O God of the angels and powers, and of every living creature, and of all sorts of just men which live in Thy presence, I thank Thee that Thou hast graciously vouchsafed this day and this hour to allot me a portion among the number of martyrs, among the people of Christ, unto the resurrection of everlasting life; among whom I shall be received in Thy sight, this day, as a fruitful and acceptable sacrifice, wherefore for all this, I praise Thee, I bless Thee, I glorify Thee through the everlasting High Priest, Jesus Christ, Thy well-beloved Son; to whom, with Thee and the Holy Ghost, be all glory, world without end. *Amen.*

In Trouble.

BLESSED be Thy name, O Lord, forever, who hast permitted this tribulation to come upon me! I am not able to fly from it; but it is necessary for me to fly to Thee, that Thou mayst support me under it, and make it instrumental to my good. I am in deep distress, and my heart faints and sinks under the burden of its sorrows. Dearest Father, encompassed thus with danger, and oppressed with fear, what shall I say? O save me from this hour! But for this cause came I unto this hour, that, after being perfectly humbled, Thou mightest have the glory of my deliverance. Be pleased, O Lord to deliver me! Poor and helpless as I am, what can I do, and whither shall I go, without Thee? O fortify me under this new distress; be Thou my strength and my support; and whatever be its weight, whatever its continuance, I will not fear.

Lord, Thy will be done! This tribulation and anguish I accept as my due: O that I may bear it with patience till the dark storm be overpast, and light and peace succeed! Yet Thy omnipotent arm, O God, my mercy! as it hath often done before, can remove even this trial from me, or so graciously mitigate its severity that I shall not utterly sink under it. Though difficult it seems to me, how easy to Thee is this change of Thy right hand, O Most High!

THOMAS À KEMPIS. (1388-1471.)

Submission in Distress.

O FATHER, ever to be praised, now is the hour of Thy servant's trial! O merciful Father, ever to be loved, it is well that Thy servant should suffer something for Thy sake! O Father, infinitely wise, and ever to be adored, that hour is come, which Thou didst foreknow from all eternity, in which Thy servant shall be oppressed and enfeebled in his outward man, that his inward man may live to Thee forever! It is necessary I should be disgraced, humbled, and brought to nothing, in the sight of men; should be broken with sufferings, and worn down with infirmities; that I may be prepared to rise again in the splendor of the new and everlasting day, and be glorified with Thee in heaven!

It is Thy peculiar favor to him whom Thou hast condescended to choose for Thy friend, to let him suffer in this world, in testimony of his fidelity and love: and be the affliction ever so great, and however often, and by whatever hand it is administered, it comes from the counsels of Thy infinite wisdom, and is under the direction of Thy merciful providence; for without Thee nothing is done upon the face of the earth. Therefore, "it is good for me, O Lord, that I should be afflicted, that I may learn Thy statutes," and utterly cast from me all self-confidence and self-exaltation. It is good for me, that "shame should cover my face": that in seeking comfort, I may have recourse, not to men, but to Thee; that I may learn to adore in silence Thy unsearchable judgments.

I give Thee thanks, O Father of mercies! that Thou hast not spared the evil that is in me; but hast humbled my nature by severe chastisements, inflicting pains, and accumulating sorrows, both from within and from without; and of all in heaven and on earth, there is none that can bring me comfort but Thou, O Lord my God, the sovereign physician of diseased souls; "who woundest and healest, who bringest down to the grave, and raisest up again!" Thy chastisement is upon me, let Thy rod teach me wisdom!

Behold, dear Father, I am in Thy hands, and bow myself under the rod of Thy correction! O teach my untractable spirit a ready compliance with Thy righteous will! Thou knowest what is most expedient for my advancement in holiness, and how effectually tribulation contributeth to wear away the rust of corruption. Do with me, therefore, O Lord, according to Thy own will.

Grant, O Lord, that from this hour I may know only that which is worthy to be known; that I may love only that which is truly lovely; that I may praise only that which chiefly pleaseth Thee; and that I may esteem what Thou esteemest, and despise that which is contemptible in Thy sight! Suffer me no longer to judge by the imperfect perception of my own senses, or of the senses of men ignorant like myself; but enable me to judge both of visible and invisible things, by the Spirit of Truth; and, above all, to know and to obey Thy will.

THOMAS À KEMPIS. (1388–1471.)

For Submission.

O LORD, take from me that sorrow which the love of self may produce from my sufferings, and from my unsuccessful hopes and designs in this world, while regardless of Thy glory; but create in me a sorrow resembling Thine. Let me not henceforth desire health or life, except to spend them for Thee, with Thee, and in Thee. I pray not that Thou wouldst give me either health or sickness, life or death; but that Thou wouldst dispose of my health and my sickness, my life and my death, for Thy glory, for my own eternal welfare, for the use of the church, for the benefit of the saints, of whose number, by Thy grace, I hope to be. Thou alone knowest what is good for me; Thou art Lord of all; do, therefore, what seemeth Thee best. Give to me, or take from me; conform my will to Thine! and grant that with humble and perfect submission, and in holy confidence, I may be disposed to receive the orders of Thy eternal providence; and may equally adore every dispensation which will come to me from Thy hand, through Jesus Christ our Lord. *Amen.*

PASCAL. (1623-1662.)

Submission in Chastisement.

"MY Father, I have sinned against heaven and in Thy sight." I know my duty to Thee, but my heart fails to fulfil it. If Thou shouldst allow me to fix my own punishment, I should flatter and spare myself, and should be deceived in so doing. But Thy gracious hand executes that which I should not have the courage to inflict. It chastises me in love. Grant that I may bear with patience these salutary blows; for what less can a sinner do than to receive meekly the chastisement which he would not have the courage to choose? Yea, I thank Thee, O God, for all things; for afflictions as well as for benefits, for afflictions become benefits when Thou bestowest them. I would no longer murmur at the dispensations of Thy providence, but I would adore its wisdom. I recognize Thy will, O Lord, as fulfilled in the motions of the stars, in the order of the seasons, and in the events of life. Let that will be accomplished also in me: let it be my delight, let it sweeten every trial. May my own will be annihilated, that Thine may reign in me; for it is Thine, O Lord, to will, and mine to obey.

FENELON. (1651-1715.)

In Prison.

O LORD, Thou God and Father of my life, hear me, a poor and desolate woman who takes refuge with Thee only, in all troubles and miseries! Thou, O Lord, art the only defender and deliverer of those that put their trust in Thee; and therefore I, being defiled with sin, encumbered with affliction, and disquieted with troubles, wrapped in cares, overwhelmed with miseries, vexed with temptations, and grievously tormented with the long imprisonment of this vile mass of clay, my sinful body, do come unto Thee, O merciful Saviour, craving Thy mercy and help, without which so little hope of deliverance is left, that I may utterly despair.

Albeit it is expedient that, seeing our life is full of trials, we should be visited with some adversity, whereby we might be tried whether we are of Thy flock or not, and also know Thee and ourselves the better; yet Thou that saidst Thou wouldst not suffer us to be tempted above our power, be merciful unto me now, miserable wretch; I beseech Thee, and with Solomon do cry unto Thee! humbly desiring that I may neither be too much puffed up with prosperity, nor be too much pressed down with adversity; lest I, being full, should deny Thee my God; or being brought too low, should despair, and blaspheme Thee, my Lord and Saviour.

O merciful God, consider my misery, best known unto Thee; and be Thou now unto me a strong tower of defence, I humbly entreat Thee. Suffer me not to be tempted above my power; but either be Thou a deliverer unto me out of this great misery, or else give me grace patiently to bear Thy heavy hand and sharp correction. It was Thy right hand that delivered the people of Israel out of the hands of Pharaoh, who for the space of four hundred years did oppress them and keep them in bondage. Let it, therefore, likewise, seem good to Thy fatherly goodness to deliver me, sorrowful wretch (for whom Thy Son Christ shed his precious blood on the cross), out of this miserable captivity and bondage wherein I now am. How long wilt Thou be absent? forever? O Lord, hast Thou forgotten to be gracious, and hast Thou shut up Thy loving-kindness in displeasure? Wilt Thou be no more entreated? Is Thy mercy gone forever, and Thy promise come utterly to an end, forevermore? Why dost Thou make so long tarrying? Shall I despair of Thy mercy, O God? Far be that from me. I am Thy workmanship, created in Christ Jesus; give me grace, therefore, to await Thy leisure, and patiently to bear what Thou doest unto me; assuredly knowing that as Thou canst, so Thou wilt deliver me when it shall please Thee, nothing doubting or mistrusting Thy goodness towards me; for Thou knowest what is good for me better than I do. Therefore do with me in all things what Thou wilt, and visit me with affliction in what way Thou wilt; only in the mean time arm me, I beseech Thee, with Thy armor, that I may stand fast; my loins being girt about with truth, having on the breastplate of righteousness, and shod with the preparation of the Gospel of peace; above all things, taking to me the shield of faith, wherewith I may be able to quench all the fiery darts of the wicked; and taking the helmet of Salvation, and the sword of the Spirit, which is Thy most holy word; praying always, with all manner of prayer and supplication, that I may refer myself wholly to Thy will, abiding Thy pleasure, and comforting myself in those troubles which it shall please Thee to send me, seeing such troubles are profitable for me; and seeing I am assuredly persuaded that all Thou doest cannot be but well. Hear me, O merciful Father! for His sake whom Thou wouldst should be a sacrifice for my sins; to whom, with Thee and the Holy Ghost, be all honor and glory. *Amen.*

LADY JANE GREY. (1553.)

Submission.

WHAT is to happen to him, O my God, I cannot know; all I do know is, that nothing will happen that has not been arranged, foreseen, ordained by Thee from all eternity. This suffices me, my God, this suffices me! I adore Thy eternal and impenetrable designs; I submit to them with all my heart for love of Thee! I will everything; I accept everything, — I sacrifice everything to Thee; and I unite this sacrifice to that of Jesus Christ, my Saviour. I ask Thee in His name for perfect submission to all Thou willest and permittest to happen. May the most just, most exalted, and most gracious will of God be accomplished in all things.

Prayer of Madame Elizabeth in the Temple tower, very often repeated by me in the little room.

JOURNAL OF EUGÉNIE DE GUÉRIN.

The LITANIES OF GRIEF *that I made in a burst of Anguish.*

O CHRIST, who didst come to suffer, take pity on my sadness;

O Christ, who tookest our sorrows on Thyself;
O Christ, who wert neglected at Thy birth;
O Christ, who livedst in a foreign land;
O Christ, who hadst not where to lay Thy head;
O Christ, who wert misunderstood;
O Christ, who hast suffered temptations;
O Christ, who hast suffered contradictions;
O Christ, who hast seen Lazarus die;
O Christ, who in agony hast sweated blood in the Garden of Olives;
O Christ, who hast been sorrowful unto death;
O Christ, who hast received the kiss of Judas;
O Christ, who hast been abandoned by Thy disciples;
O Christ, who hast been denied by a friend;
O Christ, who hast been crowned with thorns;
O Christ, who hast been scourged;
O Christ, who hast borne Thy cross;
O Christ, who didst sink down on the way to Calvary;
O Christ, who didst see the women of Jerusalem weeping;
O Christ, who didst meet Thy mother;
O Christ, who sawest at the foot of the cross the disciple whom Thou lovedst.
O Christ, who hast looked on the unrepentant thief at Thy side;
O Christ, who hast suffered so much for sinners;
O Christ, who didst end Thy life by a mighty groan, have pity on my sadness.

EUGÉNIE DE GUÉRIN.

Suffering from Enemies.

ALL-SEEING Light, and Eternal Life of all things, to whom nothing is either so great that it may resist, or so small that it is contemned; look upon my misery with Thine eye of mercy, and let Thine infinite power vouchsafe to limit out some portion of deliverance unto me, as to Thee shall seem most convenient.

Let not injury, O Lord, triumph over me; and let my faults by Thy hand be corrected; and make not mine unjust enemy the minister of Thy justice.

But yet, my God! if in Thy wisdom this be the aptest chastisement for my inexcusable folly, if this low bondage be fittest for my overhigh desires, if the pride of my not-enough humble heart be thus to be broken, O Lord, I yield unto Thy will, and joyfully embrace what sorrow Thou wilt have me suffer.

Only thus much let me crave of Thee, (let my craving, O Lord, be accepted of Thee, since even that proceeds from Thee,) let me crave even by the noblest title, which in my greatest affliction I may give myself, that I am Thy creature, and by Thy goodness (which is Thyself), that Thou wilt suffer some beam of Thy majesty so to shine into my mind, that it may still depend confidently on Thee.

Let calamity be the exercise but not the overthrow of my virtue; let their power prevail, but prevail not to their destruction; let my greatness be their prey; let my pain be the sweetness of their revenge: let them (if so it seem good unto Thee) vex me with more and more punishment. But, O Lord! let never their wickedness have such a hand, but that I may carry a pure mind in a pure body.

PRAYER OF PAMELA. (Sir Philip Sidney's Arcadia.)

In Temptation.

O ALMIGHTY God, infinite and eternal, Thou fillest all things with Thy presence; Thou art everywhere by Thy essence and by Thy power; in heaven by glory, in holy places by Thy grace and favor, in the hearts of Thy servants by Thy Spirit, in the consciences of all men by Thy testimony and observation of us.

Teach me to walk always as in Thy presence, to fear Thy majesty, to reverence Thy wisdom and omniscience; that I may never dare to commit any indecency in the eye of my Lord and my Judge; but that I may with so much care and reverence demean myself that my Judge may not be my accuser but my advocate; that I, expressing my belief of Thy presence here by careful walking, may feel the effects of it in the participation of eternal glory, through Jesus Christ. *Amen.*

JEREMY TAYLOR.

In Time of Political Defeat.

O LORD, take not Thy holy spirit from me: take away the heart of stone, and give me a heart of flesh; that under Thy chastisements, I may lift up to Thee a humble, reverential, and even thankful eye, and desire that Thy correction may work its due effect, and keep me closer to Thee for strength, and light, and warmth, and all things.

O quicken me in Thy righteousness. Give me all holy affections in their just measure of vigor and force. Give me Thy spirit to help me to pray, and praise Thee acceptably, to worship in spirit and in truth.

Let me aim at universal holiness, but especially guard against self-indulgence, and love of human estimation. O how that vile passion will creep in! Even now it is at work fold within fold. Lord, Thou knowest me; I cast myself on Thy pardoning mercy and sanctifying grace.

O Lord, teach me to extract good from present evil, and turn temporary suffering into everlasting happiness. Lord, purify my heart, and make me meet for the blessed society above. Alas, how sadly do I still find myself beset by my constitutional corruptions! I trust the grief I felt on the defeat of my Bill (for the abolition of slavery) on Thursday last, proceeded from sympathy with the wretched victims, whose sufferings are before my mind's eye, yet I fear in part also less pure affections mixed and heightened the smart, — regret that I had not made a greater and better fight in the way of speaking; vexation at the shame of the defeat. O Lord, purify me. I do not, God be merciful to me, deserve the signal honor of being the instrument of putting an end to this atrocious and unparalleled wickedness. But, O Lord, let me earnestly pray Thee to pity these children of affliction, and to terminate their unequalled wrongs; and O, direct and guide me in this important conjuncture, that I may act so as may be most agreeable to Thy will. O may I never forsake Thee. Guide me, guard me, purify me, strengthen me. Keep me from falling, and at length present me faultless before the presence of Thy glory with exceeding joy. *Amen.*

W. WILBERFORCE. (1805.)

In Trouble.

CALL upon me in the time of trouble, so will I hear thee, and thou shalt praise me.

PSALM. i. 15.

O GOD, who seest all my weaknesses, and the troubles I labor under, have regard unto the prayers of Thy servant, who stands in need of Thy comfort, Thy direction, and Thy help.

Grant, O God, that I may suffer like a Christian, and not grieve like an unbeliever; that I may receive this trouble as a punishment due to my past offences, as an exercise of my faith, and patience, and humility, and as a trial of my obedience.

Thou alone knowest what is best for me; let me not dispute Thy wisdom or Thy goodness, for this is not the effect of chance, but according to Thy just appointment.

Direct my reason, subdue my passions, put a stop to my roving thoughts and fears, and let me have the comfort of Thy promise, and of Thy protection, both now and ever.

Grant that I may improve all my afflictions to the good of my soul, and Thy glory.

O Jesu, who hast known what troubles and sorrows are, have compassion upon me in my trouble; Thou who wast despised and rejected of men; whose life was sought for by Herod; who wast tempted by the Devil; who wast hated by the world which Thou camest to save, and set at naught by Thine own people; who wast called a deceiver and a dealer with the Devil; who wast driven from place to place, and had not where to lay Thy head; who wast betrayed by one disciple, and forsaken by all the rest; wast falsely accused, spitted on and scourged; set at naught by Herod and his men of war; given up by Pilate to the will of the Jews; hadst a murderer preferred before Thee; wast condemned to a most shameful death; crucified betwixt two thieves; reviled by those that passed by; hadst gall and vinegar given Thee to drink; and suffered a most bitter death, submitting with patience to the will of Thy Father.

O Jesu, who now sittest at the right hand of God, to succor all those who suffer for righteousness' sake, be Thou my advocate with God for grace;

that in all my sufferings, I may follow Thy example, and be supported under all the difficulties and discouragements with which God shall see fit to exercise the patience and fidelity of His poor servant. *Amen.*

BISHOP WILSON. (1722.)

For Resignation.

NEVERTHELESS not my will but Thine be done.

O God, who takest delight in helping the afflicted, help a soul too often distressed with an inward rebellion against Thy just appointments.

Who am I, that I should make exceptions against Thy will, O God, infinitely great, and wise, and good!

Lord, Thy will be done, and grant that I may ever be pleased it should be so.

I know not the things that are for my own good.

My most earnest desires, if granted, may prove my ruin.

The things I complain of, and fear, may be the effects of the greatest mercy.

The disappointments I meet with may be absolutely necessary for my eternal welfare.

I do therefore protest against the sin and madness of desiring to have my own will done, and not Thine, O God.

Grant, gracious Father, that I may never dispute the reasonableness of Thy will, but ever close with it, as the best that can happen.

Prepare me always for what Thy providence shall permit or bring forth.

Let me never murmur, be dejected, or impatient, under any of the troubles of this life; but ever find rest and comfort in this; *this is the will of my Father and of my God:* grant this for Jesus Christ's sake. *Amen.*

BISHOP WILSON. (1722. Sacra Privata.)

For Peace.

O PEACE, dear object of my heart! O God, who art my peace, who makest us at peace with ourselves, with all the world, who by this means pacifieth heaven and earth! When shall I, my God, when shall I, by the tranquillity of my conscience, by a sweet confidence in Thy power, by an entire acquiescence, or rather an attachment to, a delectation in Thy eternal will in all the events of this life, possess that peace which is in Thee, which comes from Thee, and which Thou thyself art.

QUOTED BY EUGÉNIE DE GUÉRIN.

Prayer of John Woolman.

O LORD my God, the amazing horrors of darkness were gathered around me and covered me all over, and I saw no way to go forth: I felt the depth and extent of the misery of my fellow-creatures separated from the divine harmony, and it was heavier than I could bear, and I was crushed down under it. I lifted up my hand, I stretched out my arm, but there was none to help me; I looked round about and was amazed; in the depths of misery, O Lord, I remembered that Thou art omnipotent, that I had called Thee Father, and I felt that I loved Thee, and I was made quiet in Thy will, and I waited for deliverance from Thee; Thou hadst pity upon me when no man could help me; I saw that meekness under suffering was showed to us in the most affecting example of Thy Son, and Thou taught me to follow Him, and I said, "Thy will, O Father, be done."

A Prayer of Job Scott in 1788.

O MY God! Thou hast given me to see the wonders of Thy ways, in degree, and the strength of Thine arm! Thou hast led me through the deeps! hast bowed my soul in the deepest prostration! stripped me and emptied me of all things, and then marvellously displayed both Thy wisdom, Thy goodness, and Thy power! In lifting me up again from the dust, Thou hast given me indeed "beauty for ashes, the oil of joy for mourning, and the garment of praise for the spirit of heaviness." Thou art my God, and through Thy aid I will serve Thee forever; be Thou with me; go before me, and I will follow Thee; for in Thy presence there is life; at Thy right hand a river of pleasure; therefore to whom could I wish to go, seeing I know, to my inexpressible consolation, that Thou hast the words of eternal life! Thou hast graciously redeemed my soul, and delivered me, as it were, from the den of lions; to Thee and to Thy service I therefore once more dedicate the remainder of my days; draw me and I will run after Thee, command me and I will obey; I fear to offend Thee, for Thou hast shown me Thy purity; I adore Thee, for Thou hast wrought wonders for my soul; I love Thee, for Thou art my life. Hold me fast, O Lord, forever; keep my heart clean by the word of Thy power, and never, O never, I pray Thee, suffer my foot to slide! continue to fill me with the joy of Thy salvation, since Thou hast so continually shown it unto me. Take not Thy holy spirit from me; guide me by the right hand of Thy power; continue to my soul the quickening efficacy of the live coal from Thine altar; then will I, at Thy bidding, teach transgressors Thy way, and sinners, through the operation of Thy baptizing spirit, shall be converted to Thee. Even so, O Lord, hasten Thou Thy great work in the earth, draw thousands by the cords of Thy love, and tens of thousands by a clear discovery of, and a living desire, after a full establishment in the beauty of holiness; till the nations come to serve Thee, and the kingdoms of the earth to bow before Thy throne; till righteousness cover the earth, as waters do the sea, and light and life reign triumphant over death and darkness, forever. *Amen.*

O LORD, my God, I humbly crave of Thee to enable me, rightly, to settle, or to have and know, through Thy help, rightly settled in my mind, every necessary rule, limit, and regulation of life, and that Thou wouldest steadily hold my hand and guide my feet in ways that will please Thee, until every such rule and limitation receive the sanction in my heart of a divine law that is not to be broken again forever; yea, until a confirmed and habitual observance of them shall have conformed my whole life thereunto, and therein to Thy divine will and heavenly image. *Amen.*

Prayer of George Fox the Younger,

Written in Prison. 1660.

SURELY it was Thou, O Lord, that gave bounds unto the sea, that the floods thereof could not overwhelm Thy chosen: Thou canst let forth the winds, and suffer a storm; and Thou canst make a calm when Thou pleasest. Have Thou the glory of all, Thou King of saints, Thou Saviour of Israel. Thou canst do whatever Thou pleasest, therefore will we trust in Thy name, neither will we fear what men can do unto us, because Thou wilt not forsake us; but Thou wilt plead our cause in the sight of our adversaries, and they shall know that Thou art God, who art able to save to the uttermost. O Lord, our righteousness, we will praise Thy name; for Thy mercies endure forever. Our eyes, O God, are unto Thee, for we have no other helper. Our faith, O Lord, standeth in Thee, who canst not forget Thy people. Thou hast revealed and brought up Jacob, who wrestleth with Thee, and prevaileth as a prince; therefore must the blessing come. O Lord, the birth, the birth crieth unto Thee, Thy own elect, which long hath been oppressed. Thou canst not deny Thyself, therefore have we faith, and hope, which maketh not ashamed.

O Lord, how unsearchable are Thy ways! Thou hast even amazed Thy people with the depth of Thy wisdom: Thou alone wilt have the glory of their deliverance; and therefore hast Thou suffered these things to come to pass. O Lord, Thou art righteous in all Thy judgments: only preserve Thy people which Thou hast gathered, and wilt gather unto Thyself, in the day of trial; that so they may sing of Thy power, and magnify Thy name in the land of the living.

Communion with God.

Prayer of C. C. Sturm.

O GOD, who art so worthy of all adoration! I will continually reflect with gratitude and veneration on the wonders of Thy power and wisdom, which fill the whole universe. I will raise myself from earth to heaven, by the chain of beings Thou hast formed, in order to know Thee, to feel and to enjoy Thy goodness. Everything around me, everything within myself, will serve to lead me to Thee as the source of all; everything will more and more contribute to inflame me with love and piety. These, O Heavenly Father, are the engagements I make before Heaven and earth, in presence of every creature Thou hast formed. This sun which shines upon me, this air which I breathe, this earth which bears me, and gives me food; all nature, so wisely framed for our wants and pleasures, shall one day rise as witnesses against me, if I neglect to contemplate and admire Thy works.

PART X.

OLD AGE AND SICKNESS.

Evening Prayer for an Aged Person.

THE day is gone,
and I give Thee thanks, O Lord.
Evening is at hand,
make it bright unto us.
As day has its evening,
so also has life;
the even of life is age,
age has overtaken me,
make it bright unto us.
Cast me not away in the time of age,
forsake me not when my strength faileth me.
Even to my old age be Thou He,
and even to hoar hairs carry me;
do Thou make, do Thou bear,
do Thou carry and deliver me.
Abide with me, Lord,
for it is toward evening,

and the day is far spent
of this fretful life.
Let Thy strength be made perfect
in my weakness.
Day is fled and gone,
life too is going,
this lifeless life.
Night cometh,
and cometh death,
the deathless death.
Near as is the end of day,
so too the end of life.
We then, also, remembering it,
beseech of Thee
for the close of our life,
that Thou wouldst direct it in peace,
Christian, acceptable,
sinless, shameless,
and, if it please Thee, painless,
Lord, O Lord,
gathering us together
under the feet of Thine Elect,
when Thou wilt, and as Thou wilt,
only without shame and sins.
Remember we the days of darkness,
for they shall be many,
lest we be cast into outer darkness.
Remember we to outstrip the night
doing some good thing.
Near is judgment;—

a good and acceptable answer
at the dreadful and fearful judgment-seat
of Jesus Christ
vouchsafe to us, O Lord.
By night I lift up my hands in the sanctuary,
and praise the Lord.
The Lord hath granted his loving-kindness
in the daytime;
and in the night season did I sing of Him,
and made my prayer unto the God of my life.
As long as I live will I magnify Thee on this manner,
and lift up my hands in Thy name.
Let my prayer be set forth in Thy sight
as the incense,
and let the lifting up of my hands
be an evening sacrifice.
Blessed art Thou, O Lord our God,
the God of our fathers,
who hast created the changes of days and nights,
who givest songs in the night,
who hast delivered us from the evil of this day,
who hast not cut off like a weaver my life,
nor from day even to night made an end of me.

LORD,
as we add day to day,
so sin to sin.
The just falleth seven times a day;
and I, an exceeding sinner,
seventy times seven;
a wonderful, a horrible thing, O Lord.

But I turn with groans
from my evil ways,
and I return into my heart,
and with all my heart I turn to Thee,
O God of penitents and Saviour of sinners;
and evening by evening I will return
in the innermost marrow of my soul;
and my soul out of the deep
crieth unto Thee.
I have sinned, O Lord, against Thee,
heavily against Thee;
alas, alas, woe is me! for my misery.
I repent, O me! I repent, spare me, O Lord.
I repent, O me, I repent,
help Thou my impenitence.
Be appeased, spare me, O Lord;
be appeased, have mercy on me;
I said, Lord, have mercy upon me,
heal my soul, for I have sinned against Thee.
Have mercy upon me, O Lord,
after Thy great goodness,
according to the multitude of Thy mercies
do away mine offences.
Remit the guilt,
heal the wound,
blot out the stains,
clear away the shame,
rescue from the tyranny,
and make me not a public example.
O bring Thou me out of my trouble,

cleanse Thou me from secret faults,
keep back Thy servant also from presumptuous sins.
My wanderings of mind
and idle talking
lay not to my charge.
Remove the dark and muddy flood
of foul and wicked thoughts.
O Lord,
I have destroyed myself;
whatever I have done amiss, pardon mercifully.
Deal not with us after our sins,
neither reward us after our iniquities.
Look mercifully upon our infirmities;
and for the glory of Thy All-Holy Name,
turn from us all those ills and miseries,
which by our sins, and by us through them,
are most righteously and worthily deserved.

TO my weariness, O Lord,
vouchsafe Thou rest,
to my exhaustion
renew Thou strength.
Lighten mine eyes that I sleep not in death.
Deliver me from the terror by night,
the pestilence that walketh in darkness.
Supply me with healthy sleep,
and to pass through this night without fear.
O Keeper of Israel,
who neither slumberest nor sleepest,

guard me this night from all evil,
guard my soul, O Lord.
Visit me with the visitation of Thine own,
reveal to me wisdom in the visions of the night.
If not, for I am not worthy, not worthy,
at least, O loving Lord,
let sleep be to me a breathing time
as from toil, so from sin.
Yea, O Lord,
nor let me in my dreams imagine
what may anger Thee,
what may defile me.
Let not my loins be filled with illusions,
yea, let my reins chasten me in the night season,
yet without grievous terror.
Preserve me from the black sleep of sin;
all earthly and evil thoughts
put to sleep within me.
Grant to me light sleep,
rid of all imaginations
fleshly and Satanical.
Lord, Thou knowest
how sleepless are mine unseen foes,
and how feeble my wretched flesh,
who madest me;
shelter me with the wing of Thy pity;
awaken me at the fitting time,
the time of prayer;
and give me to seek Thee early,
for Thy glory, and for Thy service.

INTO Thy hands, O Lord, I commend myself,
my spirit, soul, and body:
Thou didst make, and didst redeem them;
and together with me all my friends
and all that belongs to me.
Thou hast vouchsafed them to me, Lord,
in Thy goodness.
Guard my lying down and my rising up,
from henceforth and forever.
Let me remember Thee on my bed,
and search out my spirit;
let me wake up and be present with Thee;
let me lay down in peace, and take my rest:
for it is Thou, Lord, only
that makest me dwell in safety.

BISHOP ANDREWES'S DEVOTIONS.

Evening Prayer. For the Aged.

ALMIGHTY and Everlasting God, in whose favor is life, and in whose presence there are joys forever; whom angels and archangels continually adore; and whom all Thy saints in heaven delight to worship; we, who are not worthy to take Thy name upon our lips, desire nevertheless to join with all the heavenly host, in blessing and praising and magnifying Thy holy name.

We beseech Thee to inspire us with a spirit of Christian kindness to all around us. Thou hast been very bountiful and gracious to us. Thou hast multiplied our temporal comforts; and Thou pardonest our numberless transgressions. O, grant that we may follow the example of Thy beneficence; and that we may also be like Thee, ready to forgive. May we be watchful over ourselves, but tender towards the infirmities of others; full of meekness, and gentleness, and patience, and loving-kindness, and charity.

Enlighten us, O Lord, by Thy good Spirit, that we may exercise every holy temper, and understand every part of our Christian duty. Strengthen us in our seasons of trial and temptation; guide us through all the difficulties into which we may fall; and bless us in all the scenes of life through which we may pass. If affliction should come upon us, inspire us with humble resignation to Thy will: Thou, O Lord, dost not willingly grieve the children of men; O visit us not in Thine indignation, but turn the mournful events of Thy providence to our spiritual and endless good.

Prepare us, by all the events of life, for our great and final change; for we know not how soon it may come upon us. May every opportunity of holy meditation, and of public, social, and secret prayer, and all the other means of edification which we so abundantly possess, concur with the successive events of Thy wise and merciful providence, in so calling off our minds from this earthly scene, that we may be fitted for that everlasting state, on the borders of which we stand.

May Thy good Spirit sustain and strengthen us

in our last hours: when the shadows of the evening shall come upon us, when age and sickness shall arrive, and human help shall fail, be Thou, O Lord, the strength of our hearts and our portion forevermore; and let an abundant entrance be ministered unto us into the Everlasting Kingdom of our Lord and Saviour.

With these prayers for ourselves, we desire to join our intercessions for others also. We pray Thee to bestow Thy blessing on our dear friends and relations; on our country; and on all for whom it is our privilege to pray. Pity those who are afflicted, and who shall pass this night in wakefulness and pain. Succor the tempted. Give peace to the troubled in mind. Be Thou a Father to the fatherless, and a God of consolation to those who are desolate and oppressed. And give us all grace, that we may abound in charity one towards another; and do good unto all men, according to our Lord's example and commandment. Be favorable to the rising generation. Keep them from the follies and vanities of youth; and let them learn to walk in Thy fear, and in the way of Thy commandments.

And finally, we beseech Thee to take us all under Thy protection this night. Grant unto these our frail bodies that refreshment which is needful for them; and enable us to lie down, exercising a holy trust in Thee, and having fervent charity towards all men.

We offer up these our imperfect prayers in the name of our blessed Saviour, Jesus Christ. *Amen.*

HENRY THORNTON.

In Old Age. To Christ.

O THOU merciful and faithful High Priest, Jesus Christ, I bless Thee for Thy kind promises to the aged. Thou hast suited them in great mercy to all their infirmities, and Thou art always with them to help in time of need. O grant me continual supplies of Thy Spirit, that I may profit by my infirmities, may exercise and improve my faith in Thee; that they may keep me humble and I may pray more in faith, and keep me thankful that I may be more in praise. Thine arm is not shortened, nor can Thy compassions fail. Stand by me, then, and hold me up according to Thy word. Make me strong in Thy strength, that I may daily put more honor upon Thy love and Thy power. In the decline of life let me not doubt Thy faithfulness to support, and when Thou seest it best, to comfort me. Vouchsafe me the consolations of God; when my heart and my flesh fail me, then be Thou the strength of my heart, and my portion forever. When I am weakest in myself, then make me strongest in the Lord; and if it be Thy holy will that I should become quite helpless, an infant again, make me to lie quiet in Thy hand without murmuring or repining, but believing that Thou art all my salvation, and enjoying in Thee all my desire. Grant me this, Lord Jesus, and for Thy mercies' sake let me die in faith. *Amen and Amen.*

WILLIAM ROMAINE, D.D.

Acts of Patience, by way of Prayer and Ejaculation.

I WOULD seek unto God, and unto God would I commit my cause;

Which doeth great things and unsearchable; marvellous things without number;

To set up on high those that be low; that those which mourn may be exalted to safety.

So the poor hath hope, and iniquity stoppeth her mouth.

Behold, happy is the man whom God correcteth: therefore despise not thou the chastening of the Almighty;

For he maketh sore, and bindeth up: he woundeth, and his hands make whole.

He shall deliver thee in six troubles: yea, in seven there shall no evil touch thee.

JOB V. 8, 9, 11, 16-20.

WHEN I remember Thee upon my bed, and meditate on Thee in the night-watches.

Because Thou hast been my help, therefore in the shadow of Thy wings will I rejoice.

My soul followeth hard after Thee: Thy right hand upholdeth me.

PSALM LXIII. 6-8.

GOD restoreth my soul: he leadeth me in the paths of righteousness for his name's sake. Yea, though I walk through the valley of the shadow of death, I will fear no evil; for Thou art with me; Thy rod and Thy staff they comfort me.

PSALM XXIII. 3, 4.

FOR he hath looked down from the height of his sanctuary; from heaven did the Lord behold the earth;

To hear the groaning of the prisoner; to loose those that are appointed to death.

PSALM CII. 19, 20.

I CRIED unto God with my voice, even unto God with my voice; and he gave ear unto me.

In the day of my trouble I sought the Lord: my sore ran in the night, and ceased not: my soul refused to be comforted.

I remembered God, and was troubled: I complained, and my spirit was overwhelmed. Selah.

Thou holdest mine eyes waking: I am so troubled that I cannot speak.

Will the Lord cast off forever? and will he be favorable no more?

Is his mercy clean gone forever? doth his promise fail forevermore?

Hath God forgotten to be gracious? hath he in anger shut up his tender mercies? Selah.

And I said, This is my infirmity; but I will remember the years of the right hand of the Most High.

PSALM LXXVII. 1-4, 7-10.

THERE hath no temptation taken you but such as is common to man: but God is faithful, who will not suffer you to be tempted above that ye are able; but will with the temptation also make a way to escape, that ye may be able to bear it.

1 CORINTHIANS X. 13.

IT is the Lord; let him do what seemeth him good.

1 SAMUEL III. 18.

THERE was given to me a thorn in the flesh, the messenger of Satan to buffet me, lest I should be exalted above measure.

For this thing I besought the Lord thrice that it might depart from me.

And he said unto me, My grace is sufficient for thee; for my strength is made perfect in weakness. Most gladly therefore will I rather glory in mine infirmities, that the power of Christ may rest upon me.

Therefore I take pleasure in infirmities, in reproaches, in necessities, in persecutions, in distresses, for Christ's sake: for when I am weak, then am I strong.

2 CORINTHIANS XII. 7-10.

O LORD, Thou hast pleaded the causes of my soul; Thou hast redeemed my life.

It is of the Lord's mercies that we are not consumed, because his compassions fail not. They are new every morning; great is Thy faithfulness. The Lord is my portion saith my soul; therefore will I hope in him.

The Lord is good to them that wait for him; to the soul that seeketh him. It is good that a man should both hope and quietly wait for the salvation of the Lord. For the Lord will not cast off forever. But though he cause grief, yet will he have compassion according to the multitude of his mercies. For he doth not afflict willingly, nor grieve the children of men.

LAMENTATIONS III. 58, 22–26, &c.

WHEREFORE doth a living man complain,—a man for the punishment of his sins?

JOB XIV. 13.

SHALL we receive good at the hand of God, and shall we not receive evil?

JOB II. 10. (Cento by Jeremy Taylor.)

Resignation in Sickness.

O ETERNAL God, Thou hast made me and sustained me; Thou hast blessed me in all the days of my life, and hast taken care of me in all variety of accidents; and nothing happens to me in vain, nothing without Thy providence; and I know Thou smitest Thy servants in mercy, and with designs of the greatest pity in the world: Lord, I humbly lie down under Thy rod; do with me as Thou pleasest; do Thou choose for me not only the whole state and condition of being, but every little and great accident of it. Keep me safe by Thy grace, and then use what instrument Thou pleasest of bringing me to Thee. Lord, I am not solicitous of the passage, so I may get to Thee. Only, O Lord, remember my infirmities, and let Thy servant rejoice in Thee always, and feel, and confess, and glory in Thy goodness. O be Thou as delightful to me in this my medicinal sickness as ever Thou wert in any of the dangers of my prosperity; let me not peevishly refuse Thy pardon at the rate of a severe discipline. I am Thy servant and Thy creature, Thy purchased possession, and Thy son; I am all Thine; and because Thou hast mercy in store for all that trust in Thee, I cover mine eyes, and in silence wait for the time of my redemption. *Amen.*

JEREMY TAYLOR. (1613-1667.)

Submission in Loss of Health.

"THE Lord gave, and the Lord hath taken away." This, O Lord, is what Thy servant Job said in the excess of his sufferings. It is Thy mercy that has put these precious words into the heart and lips of a sinner like me. Thou gavest me health, and I forgot Thee; Thou deprivest me of it and I return to Thee. Blessed be God, who has taken away His gifts, to bring me to Himself.

O Lord, deprive me of all else, but restore to me Thyself. All things are Thine; Thou art the Lord. Take from me riches, honor, health; everything that would separate me from Thee.

FÉNELON. (1651-1715.)

Promise of Amendment.

O MOST just and most merciful Lord God, who hast sent evil diseases, sorrow and fear, trouble and uneasiness, briers and thorns, into the world, and planted them in our houses, and round about our dwellings, to keep sin from our souls, or to drive it thence; I humbly beg of Thee that this my sickness may serve the ends of the Spirit, and be a messenger of spiritual life, an instrument of reducing me to more religious and sober courses. I say, O Lord, that I am unready and unprepared in my accounts, having thrown away great portions of my time in vanity, and set myself hugely back in the accounts of eternity, and I had need live my life over again, and live it better; but Thy counsels are in the great deep, and Thy footsteps in the water; and I know not what Thou wilt determine of me. If I die, I throw myself into the arms of the holy Jesus, whom I love above all things; and if I perish, I know I have deserved it; but Thou wilt not reject him that loves Thee. But if I recover, I will live, by Thy grace and help, to do the work of God, and passionately pursue my interest in heaven, and serve Thee in the labor of love with the charities of a holy zeal, and the diligence of a firm and humble obedience. Lord, I will dwell in Thy temple, and in Thy service; religion shall be my employment, and alms shall be my recreation, and patience shall be my rest, and to do Thy will shall be my meat and drink, and to live shall be Christ, and then to die shall be gain.

O spare me a little, that I may recover my strength before I go hence, and be no more seen. Thy will be done on earth as it is in heaven. *Amen.*

JEREMY TAYLOR.

For Persons who come to the Baths for Cure.

I HUMBLY beg of Thee, O merciful Father, that this affliction may strengthen my faith, which Thou sawest was growing weak; fix my hope which was staggering, quicken my devotion which was languishing, unite me to my first love which I was forsaking, rekindle my charity which was cooling, revive my zeal which was dying, confirm my obedience which was wavering, recover my patience which was fainting, mortify my pride which was presuming, and perfect my repentance which was daily decaying: for all these and the like infirmities, to which my soul is exposed, O make this affliction my cure.

O my Father, if it be Thy blessed will the waters should not be effectual to me, make them effectual to all other infirm persons besides; I will rejoice in Thy goodness for removing their affliction, I will acquiesce in Thy goodness for continuing mine.

THOMAS KEN. (1685. Bishop of Bath and Wells.)

For one who is Bed-ridden.

O LORD, who maketh all things work together for good to them that love Thee, make Thy servant thankful that Thou hast, it may be, by confinement and affliction, kept *him* from the company of those whose evil communication might have corrupted *him;* and hast taken *him* out of a world, by whose snares and temptations *he* might have been led to forsake Thee, and turn from the way of Thy commandments; and that Thou hast taken this way to secure *him* to Thyself and make *him* a partaker of Thy joy. O grant that *he* may not, by murmuring and repining hinder this Thy desire being fulfilled in *him;* through Jesus Christ our Lord. *Amen.*

VISITATIO INFIRMORUM.

For Patience.

THOU who art the God of patience and consolation, strengthen me in the inner man, that I may bear the yoke and burden of the Lord without any uneasy and useless murmurs and ineffective unwillingness. Lord, I am unable to stand under the cross, unable of myself; but Thou, O holy Jesus, who didst feel the burden of it, who didst sink under it, and wert pleased to admit a man to bear part of the load, when Thou underwentest all for him, be Thou pleased to ease this load by fortifying my spirit, that I may be strongest when I am weakest, and may be able to do and suffer everything Thou pleasest through Christ, who strengthens me. Lord, if Thou wilt support me, I will forever paise Thee; if Thou wilt suffer the load to press me yet more heavily, I will cry unto Thee, and complain unto my God; and at last I will lie down and die, and by the mercies and intercession of the holy Jesus, and the conduct of Thy blessed Spirit, and the ministry of angels, pass into those mansions where holy souls rest and weep no more. Lord, pity me; Lord, sanctify this my sickness; Lord, strengthen me; holy Jesus, save me and deliver me. Thou knowest how shamefully I have fallen with pleasure: in Thy mercy and very pity let me not fall with pain too. O let me never charge God foolishly, nor offend Thee by my impatience and uneasy spirit, nor weaken the hands and hearts of those that charitably minister to my needs: but let me pass through the valley of tears and the valley of the shadow of death with safety and peace, with a meek spirit and a sense of the Divine mercies, and though Thou breakest me in pieces, my hope is Thou wilt gather me up in the gatherings of eternity. Grant this, eternal God, gracious Father, in the name of our ever-blessed Saviour Jesus.

JEREMY TAYLOR. (1613-1667.)

For the Sick.

SOVEREIGN Lord our God, Almighty, we beseech Thee to save us all, Thou only Physician of souls and bodies. Sanctify us all, Thou that healest every disease; and heal also this Thy servant. Raise *him* up from the bed of pain by Thy tender mercy; visit *him* in mercy and compassion; drive away from *him* all sickness and infirmity; that, being raised up by Thy mighty hand, *he* may serve Thee with all thankfulness; and that we, being made partakers of Thine ineffable benignity, may praise and glorify Thee, who doest works great and wonderful, and worthy to be praised. For it is Thine to pity and to save; and to Thee we ascribe glory, Father, Son, and Holy Ghost, now and forever, and unto ages of ages.

GREEK OFFICE FOR THE SICK. (Bright.)

PART XI.

DEATH.

Ejaculations for the Sick and Dying.

O BLESSED Lord, who scourgest every son whom Thou receivest, let me not be weary of Thy correction.

Give me such a perfect submission to Thee, the Father of Spirits, that this chastisement may be for my profit, and that I may thereby be made a partaker of Thy holiness.

I confess, O Lord, that I have deserved much greater punishments than I now feel.

O make me cheerfully and thankfully to bear my present pains; chasten me as Thou seest fitting; do with me what Thou pleasest here, so I may not be condemned in the world hereafter.

O Christ, who first sufferedst many and grievous things, and then enteredst into Thy glory, make me to suffer with Thee, that I may also be glorified with Thee.

O Lord God most holy, O Lord most mighty, O

holy and most merciful Saviour, deliver me not, I beseech Thee, into the bitter pains of eternal death.

O cast not off the bowels of Thy tenderest compassions, but, even as a father that pitieth his own children, be Thou so merciful unto me, Thy sinful but repenting servant.

O blessed High Priest, who art able to save to the utmost them who come unto God by Thee, save me, I beseech Thee, who have no hopes but in Thy merits and intercession.

Suffer not, O my Redeemer, my soul, which Thou hast purchased with the invaluable price of Thy own blood, to perish; but say unto me, I am thy salvation.

O dear Jesus, who humbledst Thyself even to the death of the cross for me, let that precious death of Thine sweeten all the bitterness of mine.

I believe that Thou shalt come to be my Judge.

I pray Thee, therefore, help Thy servant, whom Thou hast redeemed with Thy most precious blood.

Make me to be numbered with Thy saints in glory everlasting.

O receive me into that place of rest, where all tears shall be wiped from my eyes; where there shall be no more death, nor sorrow, nor crying, nor pain.

O take me where I shall forever behold Thy face, and follow the Lamb whithersoever he goeth.

Into Thy hands I commend my spirit, for Thou hast redeemed me, O Lord, Thou God of truth.

O Lord, in Thee is my trust; O cast not out my soul.

O Lord, in Thee have I trusted; let me never be confounded.

HENRY THORNTON.

Prayer for the Dying.

O MY God! Thou hast created, redeemed, and sanctified me. Thou hast preserved me in many dangers, both of soul and body. Thou hast shown unwearied patience in bearing with my repeated sins, and often called me to repentance. For these and all other blessings bestowed upon me, a most ungrateful sinner, I offer Thee innumerable thanks.

And now, O God, I cheerfully receive the certain summons of my death. It is a greater happiness to fulfil Thy will than to enjoy ten thousand lives. O happy news of my departure! I shall soon hear the choirs of angels sing Thy immortal praises. Let slow death hasten on, that dying I may no more offend Thee, but live with Thee, and love Thee eternally.

I am truly and heartily sorry for all my sins, not through the fear of hell, or hope of reward; but for the love of Thee my God, and only God; and were I beginning as I am ending my life, I would not offend Thee for a thousand worlds. O my God, do not despise a contrite and humble heart.

THE KEY OF HEAVEN. (A Catholic Manual.)

On a Sick-Bed, after having received the Holy Communion.

GLORY and thanksgiving be to Thee, O Lord, who in Thy sweetness hast been pleased to visit and refresh my poor soul. Now let Thy servant depart in peace, according to Thy word.

Now Thou art come to me, I will not let Thee go; now I willingly bid farewell to the world; and with joy I go to Thee, my God.

Nothing more, O dear Jesus, nothing more shall separate me from Thee. Now I am united to Thee, in Thee I will live, in Thee I will die, and in Thee I hope to abide forever.

Now life seems uneasy to me; I desire to be dissolved, and to be with Christ; for Christ is my life, and to die will be my gain.

Now I will fear no evils, though I walk through the shadow of death, because Thou art with me. O Lord, as the hart pants after the fountains of water, so does my soul after Thee; my soul thirsts after the Fountain of Living Water: O when shall I come and appear before the face of my God!

Give me Thy blessing, O Jesus, and establish my soul in everlasting peace: such peace as only Thou canst give; such peace as it may not be in the power of my enemy to destroy.

O that I were happily united to Thee forever; that I were wholly swallowed up and buried in Thee: O that my soul were at rest in Thy happiness, and in the enjoyment of Thee, my God, forever.

What have I more to do with the world? And in heaven what have I to desire but Thee, my God?

Into Thy hands I commend my spirit; receive me, sweet Jesus! In Thee may I rest, and in Thy happiness rejoice without end. *Amen.*

KEY OF HEAVEN.

Prayer for the Dying.

O OUR God, we beseech Thee, by that love which sent Thy Son from heaven, to have compassion on the soul of this Thy servant; forgive him all his sins and failings, and supply his defects. Let him now experience the multitude of Thy tender mercies, and be sensible how good a God Thou art. Grant him, we beseech Thee, true patience and perfect resignation in his pains and anguish. Confirm his faith, strengthen his hope, and perfect his charity, that, departing hence, his soul may be received into Thy mercy.

O dear Redeemer! by that distress which Thou sufferedst on the cross, when Thou criedst out to Thy eternal Father, we pray Thee show mercy to this Thy servant in his extremity; hear the sighs and desires of his heart; and since he cannot speak for himself, speak Thou for him, we beseech Thee, who art the Eternal Word, and to whom the Father will refuse nothing.

Let those hands which were once nailed to the

cross now plead for him, and, obtaining his pardon, conduct him into Thy eternal rest. *Amen.*

DEPART, Christian soul! out of this world, in the name of God the Father Almighty who created thee; in the name of Jesus Christ, Son of the living God, who suffered for thee; in the name of the Holy Ghost that sanctified thee; in the name of the Angels, Archangels, Thrones and Dominations, Cherubim and Seraphim; in the name of the Patriarchs and Prophets, of the holy Apostles and Evangelists, of the holy martyrs and confessors, of the holy monks and hermits, of the holy virgins, and of all the saints of God; let thy place be this day in Peace, and thy abode in holy Sion: through Christ our Lord. *Amen.*

I RECOMMEND thee, dear brother, to Almighty God and leave thee to His mercy, whose creature thou art, that, having paid the common debt, by surrendering thy soul, thou mayest return to thy Maker, who formed thee out of the earth. Let, therefore, the noble company of Angels meet thy soul at its departure; let the court of the Apostles receive thee; let the triumphant army of glorious Martyrs conduct thee; let the crowds of joyful confessors encompass thee; let the choir of blessed virgins go before thee; let a happy rest be thy portion in the company of the Patriarchs; and let Jesus Christ appear to thee with a mild and cheerful countenance, and give thee place among those who are to be in his presence forever. May the wicked Enemy depart from thee. Let no evil spirit dare to stop thee in the way; let them tremble at thy approach in the company of Angels. Christ Jesus, Son of the living God, place thee in his garden of Paradise; and may He, the true Shepherd, own thee for one of his flock. May He absolve thee from all thy sins, and place thee at his right hand, in the inheritance of his elect. We pray it may be thy happy lot to behold thy Redeemer face to face, to be ever in his presence, and in the vision of that truth which is the joy of the blessed. And thus placed among those happy spirits, may'st thou be ever filled with heavenly sweetness. *Amen.*

COME to his assistance, all ye saints of God! meet him, all ye angels of God! receive his soul, and present it now before its Lord! May Jesus Christ receive thee, and the Angels conduct thee to thy place of rest; may they receive his soul, and present it now before its Lord.

Response. Eternal rest grant him, O Lord! and let perpetual light shine unto him. May they present him now before his Lord.

V. May he rest in peace.

R. Amen.

V. O Lord, hear our prayer.

R. And let our cry come unto Thee.

To Thee, Lord, we recommend the soul of Thy

servant, that, being dead to this world, he may live to Thee. And whatever sins he has committed through human frailty, we beseech Thee in Thy goodness mercifully to pardon, through Christ our Lord. *Amen.*

OFFICE OF ROMAN CATHOLIC CHURCH.

The Manner of commending the Sick into the Hands of God at the Hour of Death.

THE Priest, on entering the sick person's presence, shall say,

Peace be unto you.

Those present are to kneel, while the Priest, standing over the dying, shall say,

God the Father, who hath created thee; God the Son, who hath redeemed thee; God the Holy Ghost, who hath infused His grace into thee, assist thee in all thy trial, and lead thee the way to everlasting peace.

Answer. Amen.

God grant thy place may be Abraham's bosom. *Amen.*

God grant thou mayest behold thy blessed Saviour in the state of glory. *Amen.*

God grant thy death may be precious in His sight, in whom thou art to rest forever. *Amen.*

Then the Priest shall read these sections of comfort.

We brought nothing into this world, neither may we carry anything out of this world. The Lord giveth and the Lord taketh away. Even as the Lord pleaseth, so cometh everything to pass. Blessed be the name of the Lord.

We owe God a death: all our life have we been gathering manna to comfort us in our last agony: what hurt is it in going to Paradise? after a while we shall have greater joys than now we do feel pain: we shall go to one of those mansions which Christ is gone to prepare for us: our Head is in heaven already, to assure we shall, before it be long, follow after; we cannot have our happiness unless we go unto it.

Christ went not up to glory, but first He suffered; our way to life is to die with Christ.

Let not pains dismay us, for we are passing from death to life, from sorrow to joy; from a vale of misery to a Paradise of all comfort and consolation.

Let not our sins dismay us; Christ hath died for them, who is your advocate with the Father.

Wherefore, we are very unnatural to ourselves, if we should give testimony of discontentment, when our souls should be delivered into His hands who is the best Preserver of all. Again, where is our desire, with St. Paul, to depart, and to be with Christ? Where is our complaining, with the prophet David, that we are not yet come to appear in the presence of God? Where is the longing of St. Augustine, to see that head which was crowned, those hands which were pierced for our sins? Had we the love and faith which these good men had, we should rather wish for the hour of rest, than show any unwillingness to depart when God is about to call us hence.

Then, kneeling with those present, let the Priest say:

Preserve, O Lord, the soul of Thy servant, as Thou didst Noah in the flood. *Amen.*

Preserve, O Lord, the soul of Thy servant, as Thou didst Lot from the fire of Sodom. *Amen.*

Preserve, O Lord, the soul of Thy servant, as Thou didst Job in all his adversities. *Amen.*

Preserve, O Lord, the soul of Thy servant, as Thou didst the Israelites from the power of Pharaoh and the oppression of Egypt. *Amen.*

Preserve, O Lord, the soul of Thy servant from the malice of Satan, as Thou didst David from all his enemies. *Amen.*

Preserve, O Lord, the soul of Thy servant, as Thou didst Daniel from the mouth of the lions. *Amen.*

Preserve, O Lord, the soul of Thy servant, as Thou didst the three children from the fiery flames. *Amen.*

Preserve, O Lord, the soul of Thy servant, as Thou didst Elijah from the false Prophets that sought his overthrow. *Amen.*

Preserve, O Lord, the soul of Thy servant, and deliver *him*, as Thou didst the Apostles Paul and Silas out of prison at midnight. *Amen.*

From that rueful darkness,
Deliver *him*, O Lord.
From the pains of hell,
Deliver *him*, O Lord.
From everlasting malediction,
Deliver *him*, O Lord.

By Thy Nativity,
O Lord, deliver *him*.
By Thy Fasting and Prayer,
O Lord, deliver *him*.
By Thy Hunger and Thirst,
O Lord, deliver *him*.
By Thy Cross and Passion,
O Lord, deliver *him*.
By Thy Descension into Hell,
O Lord, deliver *him*.
By Thy Resurrection from the dead the third day,
O Lord, deliver *him*.
By Thine Ascension into Heaven,
O Lord, deliver *him*.
By Thy sitting at the right hand of the Father in glory,
O Lord, deliver *him*. *Amen.*

Our Father, &c.
But deliver us from evil. *Amen.*

The act of commendation to be said by the Priest, standing, over the dying.

O Almighty God, with whom do live the spirits of just men made perfect, after they are delivered from their earthly prisons; we humbly commend the soul of this Thy servant, our dear *brother*, into Thy hands, as into the hands of a Faithful Creator, and most merciful Saviour; most humbly beseeching Thee, that it may be precious in Thy sight. Wash it, we pray Thee, in the blood of that immaculate Lamb, that was slain to take away the sins of the world; that whatsoever defilements it may have contracted in the midst of this miserable and naughty world, through the lusts of the flesh, or the wiles of Satan, being purged and done away, it may be presented pure and without spot before Thee. And teach us who survive, in this and other like daily spectacles of mortality, to see how frail and uncertain our own condition is; and so to number our days, that we may seriously apply our hearts to that holy and heavenly wisdom, whilst we live here, which may in the end bring us to life everlasting; through the merits of Jesus Christ Thine only Son our Lord. *Amen.*

Into Thy merciful hands, O Heavenly Father, we commend the soul of Thy servant now departing from the body. Acknowledge, we meekly beseech Thee, a sheep of Thine own fold, a lamb of Thine own flock, a sinner of Thine own redeeming. Receive *him* into the arms of Thy mercy, into the blessed rest of everlasting peace, into the glorious estate of Thy chosen Saints in Heaven. O most merciful Jesu, that thing cannot perish which is committed to Thy charge; receive, we beseech Thee, *his* spirit in peace. *Amen.*

Jesus Christ absolve thee from all sins.

Answer. Amen.

Jesus Christ remit all the evil which thou hast committed by thy hearing, by thy seeing, by Thy touching, by thy tasting howsoever. *Amen.*

Jesus Christ, that redeemed thee with His agony and bloody Death, have mercy on thee, and strengthen thee in this agony of death. *Amen.*

Jesus Christ, that rose again the third day from death, raise thee, body and soul, in the resurrection of the just. *Amen.*

Jesus Christ, that ascended into heaven, thither bring thee whither He Himself has gone before to the Paradise of bliss. *Amen.*

The Lord bless thee and keep thee. The Lord make his face to shine upon thee, and be gracious unto thee. The Lord lift up his countenance upon thee, and give thee peace, both now and evermore. *Amen.*

Depart, O Christian Soul, in the name of God the Father who created thee; of God the Son, who redeemed thee; of God the Holy Ghost, who sanctified thee; One Living and Immortal God; to whom be glory for ever and ever. *Amen.*

And should the dying be still sensible, let the Priest distinctly, and with slow and solemn utterance, say:

Lord, now lettest Thou Thy servant depart in peace. Remember not, we beseech Thee, the sins and offences of *his* youth; but according to Thy mercy think Thou upon *him*, O Lord, for Thy goodness. Into Thy hands, O God, we commend *his* spirit; for Thou hast redeemed it, O Lord, Thou God of truth. Bring *his* soul out of prison, that it may praise Thee. O deliver *him* from the body of this death. Say unto *his* soul, I am Thy salvation. Say unto *him*, To-day shalt Thou be with me in Paradise. Let *him* now feel the salvation of Jesus, let *him* now feel the anointing of Christ, even the oil of gladness wherewith Thou art anointed. Guide Thou *him* through the valley of the shadow of death. Let *him* see the goodness of the Lord in the land of the living. O Lord, command *his* spirit to be received up to Thee in peace. O Lord, bid *him* come to Thee. Lord Jesus, receive *his* spirit, and open to *him* the gates of everlasting glory. Let Thy loving spirit lead *him* forth into the land of righteousness, into Thy holy will, into Thy heavenly kingdom. Send Thine Angel to meet *him* and carry *him* into Abraham's bosom. Place *him* in the habitation of light, and peace, and joy, and gladness. Receive *him* into the arms of Thy mercy, and give *him* an inheritance with Thy Saints in light, there to reign with Thy elect Angels, Thy blessed Saints departed, Thy holy prophets and glorious Apostles, in all joy, glory, felicity, and blessedness, for ever and ever. *Amen.*

Then the following.

Lord Jesu, Thy servant calleth upon Thee:
Come, Lord Jesu, come quickly.

I know that my Redeemer liveth, and that I shall
be raised again in the last day.
I desire to be dissolved and to be with Christ.
Thou art my Helper and Redeemer;
Make no long tarrying, O my God.
Go to Thy rest, O my soul;
From death to life,
From sorrow to joy,
From a vale of misery to a paradise of mercy.
Come, Lord Jesu, come quickly.
Lord Jesu, receive my spirit.

This is to be repeated till the soul be departed. And when this shall be, the Priest, if possible, subduing the lamentations of the near relations, shall say:

Almighty God, with whom do live the spirits of them that depart hence in the Lord, and with whom the souls of the faithful, after they are delivered from the burden of the flesh, are in joy and felicity; we give Thee hearty thanks for that it hath pleased Thee to deliver this our *brother* out of the miseries of this sinful world; beseeching Thee that it may please Thee, of Thy gracious goodness, shortly to accomplish the number of Thine elect, and to hasten Thy kingdom; that we, with all those that are departed in the true faith of Thy holy name, may have our perfect consummation in bliss, both in body and soul, in Thy eternal and everlasting glory; through Jesus Christ our Lord. *Amen.*

The grace of our Lord Jesus Christ, and the love of God, and the fellowship of the Holy Ghost, be with us all evermore. *Amen.*

VISITATIO INFIRMORUM.

An Office to be used with Parents on the Death of Young Children.

The Priest, when he cometh into the house, shall say:

PEACE be unto you.

The Lord gave and the Lord hath taken away;
Blessed be the name of the Lord. *Amen.*

Then addressing the parents, let him say:

Dearly beloved, hear what comfortable words our blessed Lord Jesus Christ saith to those that mourn for young children.

Suffer little children to come unto me, and forbid them not: for of such is the kingdom of God. — LUKE xviii. 16.

Take heed that ye despise not one of these little ones: for I say unto you, That in heaven their angels do always behold the face of my Father which is in heaven.— MATTHEW xviii. 10.

Verily I say unto you, Except ye be converted, and become as little children, ye shall not enter into the kingdom of heaven.— MATTHEW xviii. 3.

Hear also what the wise King saith.

Better it is to have no children, and to have virtue: for the memorial thereof is immortal: because it is known with God and with men. When it is present, men take example at it; and when it is gone, they desire it: it weareth a crown, and triumpheth forever, having gotten the victory, striving for undefiled rewards.— WISDOM iv. 1, 2.

Hear also what the son of Sirach saith.

Trust not thou in their life, neither respect their multitude; for one that is just is better than a thousand, and better it is to die without children, than to have them that are ungodly.—ECCLUS. xvi. 3.

Hear also the Word of God by the Prophet Jeremiah.

Refrain thy voice from weeping, and thine eyes from tears: for thy work shall be rewarded, saith the Lord; and there is hope in thine end, saith the Lord, that thy children shall come again to their own border.—JER. xxxi. 16, 17.

Then shall he say the Psalms following.

Domini est terra. Psalm XXIV.

The earth is the Lord's and all that therein is: the compass of the world, and they that dwell therein.

For He hath founded it upon the seas: and prepared it upon the floods.

Who shall ascend into the hill of the Lord: or who shall rise up in His holy place?

Even he that hath clean hands and a pure heart: and that hath not lift up his mind unto vanity, nor sworn to deceive his neighbor.

He shall receive the blessing from the Lord: and righteousness from the God of his salvation.

This is the generation of them that seek Him: even of them that seek thy face, O Jacob.

Glory be to the Father, &c.

As it was in the beginning, &c. *Amen.*

Laudate, pueri, Dominum. Psalm CXIII.

Praise the Lord, ye servants: O praise the Name of the Lord.

Blessed be the Name of the Lord: from this time forth for-evermore.

The Lord's name is praised: from the rising up of the sun unto the going down of the same.

The Lord is high above all heathen: and His glory above the heavens.

Who is like unto the Lord our God, that hath His dwelling so high and yet humbleth himself to behold the things that are in heaven and earth?

He taketh up the simple out of the dust: and lifteth the poor out of the mire; that He may set him with the princes: even with the princes of his people.

He maketh the barren woman to keep house: and to be a joyful mother of children.

Glory be to the Father, &c.

As it was in the beginning, &c. *Amen.*

Then shall he say, Hear the words of the Holy Scripture written in the twenty-second chapter of the Book of Genesis.

And it came to pass, after these things, that God did tempt Abraham, and said unto him, Abraham: and he said, Behold, here I am.

And He said, Take now thy son, thine only son Isaac, whom thou lovest, and get thee into the land of Moriah; and offer him there for a burnt-offering upon one of the mountains which I will tell thee of.

And Abraham rose up early in the morning, and saddled his ass, and took two of his young men with him, and Isaac his son, and clave the wood for the burnt-offering, and rose up, and went unto the place of which God had told him.

Then on the third day Abraham lifted up his eyes, and saw the place afar off.

And Abraham said unto his young men, Abide ye here with the ass, and I and the lad will go yonder and worship, and come again to you.

And Abraham took the wood of the burnt-offering, and laid it upon Isaac his son; and he took the fire in his hand and a knife: and they went both of them together.

And Isaac spake unto Abraham his father, and said, My father: and he said, Here am I, my son. And he said, Behold the fire and the wood; but where is the lamb for a burnt-offering?

And Abraham said, My son, God will provide himself a lamb for a burnt-offering: so they went both of them together.

And they came to the place which God had told him of; and Abraham built an altar there, and laid the wood in order; and bound Isaac his son, and laid him on the altar upon the wood.

And Abraham stretched forth his hand, and took the knife to slay his son.

And the angel of the Lord called unto him out of heaven, and said, Abraham, Abraham. And he said, Here am I.

And he said, Lay not thy hand upon the lad, neither do thou anything unto him: for now I know that thou fearest God, seeing thou hast not withheld thy son, thine only son, from me.

And Abraham lifted up his eyes, and looked, and, behold, behind him a ram caught in a thicket by his horns: and Abraham went and took the ram, and offered him up for a burnt-offering in the stead of his son.

And Abraham called the name of that place Jehovah-jireh; as it is said to this day, In the mount of the Lord it shall be seen.

And the angel of the Lord called unto Abraham out of heaven the second time,

And said, By myself have I sworn, saith the Lord; for because thou hast done this thing, and hast not withheld thy son, thine only son;

That in blessing I will bless thee, and in multiplying I will multiply thy seed as the stars of the heaven, and as the sand which is upon the sea-shore; and thy seed shall possess the gate of his enemies:

And in thy seed shall all the nations of the earth be blessed: because thou hast obeyed my voice.

You hear in this Scripture, dearly beloved, how God did prove Abraham, and make trial of his faith. For on former occasions Abraham had shown his faith in God's promises in no common degree: but now God proved his faith by putting it to the severest trial; namely, by requiring the life of his beloved and only son. And if the death of a dear child be to every parent a heavy affliction, consider, from the circumstances of the case, what the death of Isaac must have been to Abraham. He was the child of promise, granted to Abraham's faith. The previous trials Abraham had to endure were all sweetened by this, that a great blessing was to come upon the earth, and to extend to all nations, in and by his offspring. And the word of God which could not fail, had further assured him that this promise was to be accomplished in Isaac; For in Isaac, it was said, shall thy seed be called. The certainty of the fulfilment of this promise had sustained Abraham through all his previous trials; yet he, through and in whom it was to be fulfilled, was now to die in his childhood. Consider, too, the natural affection and love Abraham must have borne to this child, who was born to him in his old age, and when the hope of having children must have all but passed away from him. Consider, too, the requirement that God made of him, that he should take the life of this beloved and longed-for child with his own hand. Yet none of these things moved Abraham to repine or to attempt to withhold his child when God desired him to yield him up. Doubtless he felt all these things as we should feel them; but he knew that God required not such a sacrifice without good reason. Whatever his difficulties were, he knew that God would certainly accomplish His promise, even were the external means of its accomplishment removed. However great his love for his beloved child was, his love for God was greater. He felt that what God required must be very good, however the present accomplishment of it might grieve or distress him. Wherefore he conferred not with flesh and blood; he hesitated not, but took his son and went his way, resolved to submit to what God required of him, and to do speedily and readily what He commanded. But God's command had been to prove him, for He Himself knew what He would do. He not only restored to him his child, but He twice sent His Angel to assure him of His approval of his ready faith and willing obedience, and to promise him a blessing on account of them. And, dearly beloved, be sure that this blessing was not pronounced for Abraham alone, but that a blessing will also come on all those who, being put to a like trial with Abraham, like him withhold not their beloved children from God, but readily and cheerfully obey His voice. Wherefore, in His heavy affliction with which God has made trial of your faith, endeavor to imitate the ready submission and patient resignation of Abraham. Remember how much you have to confirm and strengthen your faith which Abraham had not. You have the full assurance of those things of which Abraham had but the promise. God has now provided Himself a Lamb for an offering, even his own Son, whom He gave up for the sins of the world. He has by His sacrament of Baptism, adopted this your child as His own, and has now summoned *him* to take possession of that inheritance, which in that holy Sacrament He vouchsafed to *him;* and has assured us, as you have heard, that of such as little children His heavenly kingdom is composed; and that the angels of such little ones do always behold the face of their Heavenly Father. Wherefore, dearly beloved, do not pine or grieve, but be strong in faith as Abraham was: be willing, as he was, to give up your dear child when God calls: be sure that you have placed *him* in the arms of *his* Heavenly Father; and that if you bear this your trial in faith and patience, He will restore *him* to you in that day when you come to stand before Him. For if you imitate Abraham's faith and Abraham's obedience, to you is this promise: By myself have I sworn, saith the Lord, for because thou hast done this thing, and hast not withheld thy son, thine only son, that in blessing I will bless thee, because thou hast obeyed my voice.

Then, all kneeling, the Priest shall say, Let us pray.

Lord, have mercy upon us.

Christ, *have mercy upon us.*

Lord, have mercy upon us.

Our Father, &c.

But deliver us from evil. *Amen.*

O Almighty and most merciful God, who, without anything to deserve it on their part, dost grant everlasting life to all little children who depart this life, after having been born again in Thy holy Baptism, as we believe Thee to have done with the soul of the child of these sorrowing parents; mercifully grant, we beseech Thee, that we may so serve Thee with pure and clean hearts here, that hereafter we may dwell eternally with glorified children; through the merits and mediation of Jesus Christ our Lord. *Amen.*

O Almighty and Everlasting God, the lover of holiness and purity, who hast been graciously pleased now to call the soul of a little child of this family into Thine heavenly Kingdom; so vouchsafe, O Lord, to deal mercifully with us who survive, that through the merits of Thy most sacred Passion, Thou mayest cause us ever to rejoice with all Thy Blessed Saints and Thine Elect, in the same Thy Kingdom, who livest and reignest with the Father in the unity of the Holy Spirit, One God, world without end. *Amen.*

O Lord Jesu Christ, who didst restore the widow's son to his weeping mother, and the daughter of the Ruler of the Synagogue to her lamenting parents, we beseech Thee to have compassion on the (*father* and *mother*) of this little child, whom Thou hast now called to *his* Heavenly Father's Kingdom. Make *them* know and feel, O Lord God, that *he* is committed to Thy merciful arms, and ever beholdeth Thy blissful presence. Let this assurance assuage *their* tears and mitigate *their* present sorrow. And grant, O Lord, that as *they* have experienced the blessing Thou gavest *them* in this child, and now feel the affliction Thou hast laid upon *them*, in taking *him* from *them;* so *they* may know assuredly that Thou wilt comfort *them* by restoring *him* to *them* in Thine everlasting kingdom; to which vouchsafe to conduct *them* by Thy merits, O Saviour, who with the Father and the Holy Ghost, livest and reignest, One God, world without end. *Amen.*

Then standing up, the Priest shall pronounce this blessing:

Our Lord Jesus Christ Himself, and God, even our Father, which hath loved us, and hath given us everlasting consolation and good hope through grace, comfort your hearts, and stablish you in every good word and work. *Amen.*

VISITATIO INFIRMORUM.

On the Death of a Parent.

MY God and my Lord, whose goodness is boundless and past searching out, bear my dear (*father's*) soul up to the dwelling-place of comfort and the abiding of Eternal Rest, where shineth the light of Thy countenance.

In that Land of the Living give (*him*) everlasting joy, and bring me again to see (*him*) in the heavenly Transfiguring, so that, united forever, we may taste the blessedness of the saints, and with each other, sing the praises of Thy glory everlastingly. *Amen.*

German Prayer Book. (Translated by Rev. L. G. Ware.)

THANKS be unto God for all his loving-kindness, and His gracious promise of an endless peace.

For one about to make a Will.

O LORD, who puttest into our heart good desires, and hast inclined Thy servant to set *his* house in order; grant that *he* may do it with wisdom and piety according to the precepts of our holy religion and the dictates of right reason, that so being freed from all earthly cares and anxieties *he* may be the better able before *he* go hence to set in order the inward house of *his* soul; through Jesus Christ our Lord. *Amen.*

O Lord, from whom cometh all good understanding and the right ordering of our desires; give Thy servant strength of mind and heart, in the time of *his* trouble, wisely and happily to settle *his* affairs. Grant that *his* memory may be perfect; *his* judgment sound; and *his* heart so rightly disposed, that *he* may do nothing amiss, or through partiality; but that justice and integrity may rule the whole conduct and disposition of *his* affairs. Grant that *he* may be just to all men, thoughtful of *his* relations, grateful to his friends, kind to *his* servants, and a benefactor to religion. Add moreover this, O Lord, to all Thy favors, that in making *his* last will, *he* may so faithfully discharge all engagements and fulfil all responsibilities, that no curse may cleave to *him*, or to anything *he* shall leave behind *him;* through Jesus Christ our Lord. *Amen.*

Grant, gracious Lord, that this Thy servant may part with those things with which Thou hast blessed *him* here, willingly and without grudging. Bless them to those into whose hands *he* commits them, that they may serve both to their temporal and eternal welfare. And grant to Thy servant, that when *his* earthly house of this tabernacle shall be dissolved, *he* may receive a better and an enduring substance in Thine everlasting Kingdom; where with the Son, and the Holy Ghost, Thou livest and reignest, One God, world without end. *Amen.*

VISITATIO INFIRMORUM.

In View of Death.

BLESSED, yea blessed are they who die in the Lord, for their works do follow them, and mine also will follow me!

O God of life, Judge of the dead! O merciful Saviour of sinners! My works also will follow me, the evil as the good! I look back with dismay at my past life. How often I may have erred I do not even know. Lord, Lord, wilt Thou remember my offences? When Thou enterest into judgment with me, how shall I stand before Thee? The good that was in me was but feebly sustained by my will, and, alas! it was often set at naught by frivolity, thoughtlessness, or passion, while vanity frequently detracted from the merit of my best deeds. How often have I been failing in love, how often in perseverance, how often in meekness and humility.

But Thou, O merciful God, art my comfort and my trust! Accept my will for half the deed, my endeavors for half success, my conflicts for half the victory. Forgive me my trespasses! Thou knowest how often I try to lift myself up, though I fall back each time in helpless impotence!

But perhaps life is but one long struggle against evil, and that he may find mercy before Thee who has had courage enough not to shrink from the combat, but carry it on to the best of his power.

And I will never weary in this struggle after

perfection. As Thy soldier I will die, full of faith, and full of hope in Thy mercy, O Father, who ever granteth more than we deserve. *Amen.*

ZSCHOKKE's Stunden der Andacht.

Trust, in View of Death.

O JESUS, in Thy holy revelation I will live, and in it I will die. Blessed is the power of Thy word; to it the power of death must yield. I live to Thee, and I shall not die. There is no death, there is no grave; it is but change and glorification. God is no God of death; he is our life. He created life, and my spirit is his work. My spirit is life, while it animates my body; and remains life, when the dust which for a time clothed it as a garment, and which was to it as an instrument, returns again to dust.

Heavenly and Eternal Father, Source of all being, Thou from whom I spring, unto whom I shall return, — Thine I shall ever be! Sweet is life, in truth, but death has nevertheless no terrors; no fear of it shall overwhelm me, shall turn me away from Thee and from the path of virtue. I hold as naught the days that I do not adorn with good deeds, I hold as naught a life which I cannot glorify by virtue.

And me also, me also, O God, Thou wilt call unto Thyself when my hour comes, when my earthly goal is reached. Blessed shall I then be if I can say unto myself, *I have fought a good fight;* as far as my powers allowed, I have completed a life of well-doing; *the crown of eternal life awaits me also!*

And when in the last hour I have to taste the bitterness of death, to drain the final cup of trial; when my stiffened hand can no longer bestow a blessing on my loved ones, from whose sorrowful eyes the tears of parting are falling on my pillow, my closed lips can no longer utter words of love, of love true unto death; when the stir of the world and all the sweet sounds of life cease to fall upon my ear, — then, then, O Lord, I commend my soul to Thee. Joyfully I turn away my dimmed eyes from those who are dear to my heart, for I know they are in Thy keeping. Thou abidest with them as Thou abidest with me, forevermore in the regions of eternal life.

No, I fear not death, *O Father of life!* For death is not eternal sleep; it is the transition to a new life, a moment of great and glorious transformation, an ascension towards Thee.

How could that be an evil, and Thou, the All-good! that cometh from Thy hand? Lord of the seraph and the worm, Ruler of life and death, I am in Thy hand; do unto me as Thou deemest fit; for what Thou dost is well done. When Thou didst call me from nothing into life, Thou didst will my happiness; when Thou callest me away from life, will my happiness be less Thy care? No, no, Thou art Love, and whosoever dwells in love, dwells in Thee, O Lord, and Thou in him. Thou, Lord, art my light and my salvation; why should I tremble? Thou art the Lord of my life; what should I dread?

ZSCHOKKE.

PART XII.

COLLECTS.

For Heavenly-Mindedness.

GRANT us, O Lord, not to mind earthly things, but to love things heavenly; and even now, while we are placed among things that are passing away, to cleave to those that shall abide; through Jesus Christ our Lord.

LEONINE SACRAMENTARY. (Fifth Century.)

For Deliverance from Temptation.

WE beseech Thee, O Lord, to renew Thy people inwardly and outwardly, that as Thou wouldst not have them to be hindered by bodily pleasures, Thou mayest make them vigorous with spiritual purpose; and refresh them in such sort by things transitory, that Thou mayest grant them rather to cleave to things Eternal; through Jesus Christ our Lord.

LEONINE SACRAMENTARY.

O LORD, our support and our refuge, deliver us from temptation, give us the defence of Thy salvation, hold us up with Thy right hand, teach us by Thy discipline, and make our way and our life undefiled.

MOZARABIC SACRAMENTARY. (Earlier than 711.)

Invocation.

LORD God, of might inconceivable, of glory incomprehensible, of mercy immeasurable, of benignity ineffable; do Thou, O Master, look down upon us in Thy tender love, and show forth, towards us and those who pray with us, Thy rich mercies and compassions.

LITURGY OF ST. CHRYSOSTOM. (Fourth Century.)

For Cleansing.

CLEANSE us, O Lord, from our secret faults, and mercifully absolve us from our presumptuous sins, that we may receive Thy holy things with a pure mind; through Jesus Christ our Lord.

SACRAMENTARY OF LEO THE GREAT. (Fifth Century.)

After Communion.

WE have received the body of Christ, and drunk His blood. We will fear no evil, for the Lord is with us. May Thy blood be always life to us, and salvation to our souls, O our God.

AMBROSIAN MISSAL. (Fourth Century.)

To Jesus.

JESU, our Master, do Thou meet us while we walk in the way, and long to reach the (Heavenly) Country, so that following Thy light, we may keep the way of righteousness, and never wander away into the horrible darkness of this world's night, while Thou, who art the Way, the Truth, and the Life, art shining within us.

MOZARABIC SACRAMENTARY. (Earlier than A. D 711.)

For Perseverance.

O GOD, who bestowest this upon us by Thy grace, that we should be made righteous instead of ungodly, blessed instead of miserable; be present to Thine own works, be present to Thine own gifts; that they in whom dwells a justifying faith may not lack a strong perseverance; through Jesus Christ our Lord.

ANCIENT GALLICAN MISSAL.

GIVE perfection to beginners, give intelligence to the little ones, give aid to those who are running their course. Give compunction to the negligent, give fervor of spirit to the lukewarm, give to the perfect a good consummation.

GALLICAN SACRAMENTARY.

For Spiritual Growth.

O GOD, who buildest for Thy Majesty an eternal habitation out of living and elect stones, assist Thy suppliant people, that as Thy Church gains in material extent, it may also be enlarged by spiritual increase: through Jesus Christ our Lord.

GREGORIAN SACRAMENTARY.

Benediction.

OUR Lord Jesus Christ be near thee to defend thee, within thee to refresh thee, around thee to preserve thee, before thee to guide thee, behind thee to justify thee, above thee to bless thee. Who liveth and reigneth, &c.

MS. RITUAL OF 10TH CENTURY.

Benediction.

THE Lord bless us and keep us; the Lord make his face to shine upon us, and be gracious unto us; the Lord lift up the light of his countenance upon us, and give us peace. *Amen.*

NUMBERS VI. 24-26.

NOW the Lord of Peace himself give us peace always by all means. The Lord be with us all. *Amen.*

2 THESSALONIANS III. 16.

THE grace of our Lord Jesus Christ, and the love of God, and the fellowship of the Holy Spirit, be with us all evermore. *Amen.*

2 CORINTHIANS XIII. 14.

THE grace of our Lord Jesus Christ be with you all. *Amen.*

PHILEMON IV. 23.

THE peace of God, which passeth all understanding, keep our hearts and minds through Christ Jesus. *Amen.*

PHILEMON IV. 7.

Benediction.

THE Almighty Lord, who is a most strong tower to all them that put their trust in Him, to whom all things in heaven, in earth, and under the earth, do bow and obey, be now and evermore thy defence; and make thee know and feel that there is none other name under Heaven given to man, in whom, and through whom, thou mayest receive health and salvation, but only the name of our Lord Jesus Christ. *Amen.*

VISITATIO INFIRMORUM.

For Harmony.

O GOD the Father, Origin of Divinity, Good beyond all that is good, Fair beyond all that is fair, in Whom is calmness, peace, and concord; do Thou make up the dissensions which divide us from each other, and bring us back into an unity of love, which may bear some likeness to Thy sublime Nature. And as Thou art above all things, make us one by the unanimity of a good mind, that through the embrace of charity and the bonds of affection we may be spiritually one, as well in ourselves as in each other, through that peace of Thine which maketh all things peaceful, and through the grace, mercy, and tenderness of Thine Only-begotten Son.

JACOBITE LITURGY OF ST. DIONYSIUS.

O GOD, who of Thy great love to this world didst reconcile earth to heaven through Thine Only-begotten Son; grant that we who, by the darkness of our sins, are turned aside from brotherly love, may by Thy light shed forth in our souls be filled with Thine own sweetness, and embrace our friends in Thee, and our enemies for Thy sake, in a bond of mutual affection.

MOZARABIC SACRAMENTARY.

For Peace.

O GOD, who art peace everlasting, whose chosen reward is the gift of peace, and who hast taught us that the peacemakers are Thy children, pour Thy sweet peace into our souls, that everything discordant may utterly vanish, and all that makes for peace be sweet to us forever.

MOZARABIC.

For Forgiveness.

WE beseech Thee, Almighty God, to receive with Fatherly tenderness Thy people fleeing from Thine anger to Thyself; that they who dread the scourge that comes from Thy Majesty may be enabled to rejoice in Thy forgiveness; through Jesus Christ our Lord.

GELASIAN SACRAMENTARY.

For a good use of Blessings.

ALMIGHTY and everlasting God, who healest us by chastening, and preservest us by pardoning; grant unto Thy suppliants, that we may both rejoice in the comfort of the tranquillity which we desired, and also use the gift of Thy peace for the effectual amendment of our lives; through Jesus Christ our Lord.

SACRAMENTARY OF LEO. (Fifth Century.)

Collects. For Illumination.

LET Thy mercy, O Lord, be upon us, and the brightness of Thy spirit illumine our inward souls; that He may kindle our cold hearts, and light up our dark minds, who abideth evermore with Thee in glory.

MOZARABIC SACRAMENTARY. (About 700 A. D.)

For a Saint's Day.

O GOD, the strength of all Thy saints, who hast granted them in Thine abundant bounty the grace to come to their present glory, vouchsafe, we beseech Thee, pardon to our sins, that we may be able worthily to celebrate their solemnities; through Jesus Christ our Lord.

LEONINE SACRAMENTARY. (Fifth Century.)

For Firm Faith.

ARISE, O Lord, who judgest the earth; and as Thou dwellest in and possessest the faith of all nations, suffer us not to abide in darkness; and grant that we may not lay the foundations of our faith on the sand where the whirlwind may overthrow them, but be established on the rock which is steadfast in Thee.

MOZARABIC.

Easter.

THE day of Resurrection has dawned upon us, the day of true light and life, wherein Christ, the Life of believers, arose from the dead. Let us give abundant thanks and praise to God, that while we solemnly celebrate the day of our Lord's Resurrection, He may be pleased to bestow on us quiet peace and special gladness; so that being protected from morning to night by His favoring mercy, we may rejoice in the gift of our Redeemer.

MOZARABIC SACRAMENTARY. (About 700 A. D.)

On a Fast-Day.

O GOD, who in Thy deep counsel and foresight for mankind hast appointed holy fasts, whereby the hearts of the weak might receive salutary healing, do Thou purify our souls and bodies, O Saviour of body and soul, O loving Bestower of eternal happiness! through Jesus Christ our Lord.

GELASIAN SACRAMENTARY.

Good Friday.

TO-DAY, O good Jesus, for us Thou didst not hide Thy face from shame and spitting. To-day, Jesus our Redeemer, for us Thou wast mocked, buffeted by unbelievers, and crowned with thorns. To-day, O good Shepherd, Thou didst lay down Thy life on the Cross for the sheep, and wast crucified with robbers, and hadst Thy sacred hands nailed through. To-day Thou wast laid in the guarded sepulchre, and the saints burst open their tombs. To-day, O good Jesus, put an end to our sins, that on the day of Thy Resurrection we may joyfully receive Thy holy Body, and be refreshed with Thy sacred Blood.

MOZARABIC SACRAMENTARY.

Ascension-Day.

SAVIOUR and Lord, who, ascending into heaven, wast pleased to show Thyself in glory to the eyes of beholders, while Thou didst promise to come as our Judge in like manner as Thou hadst ascended; make us to welcome this feast-day of Thine Ascension with pure and devout hearts; that we may in such wise ascend continually in Thee to a better life, that when Thou comest to the judgment we may see Thy face and not be confounded.

MOZARABIC SACRAMENTARY. (Earlier than 711.)

For Christian Graces.

GIVE me, O Lord, purity of lips, a clean and innocent heart, and rectitude of action. Give me humility, patience, abstinence, chastity, prudence, justice, fortitude, temperance. Give me the spirit of wisdom and understanding, the spirit of counsel and strength, the spirit of knowledge and godliness, and of Thy fear. Make me ever to seek Thy face with all my heart, all my soul, all my mind; grant me to have a contrite and humbled heart in Thy presence, — to prefer nothing to Thy love. Most high, eternal, and ineffable Wisdom, drive away from me the darkness of blindness and ignorance; most high and eternal Strength, deliver me; most high and eternal Fortitude, assist me; most high and incomprehensible Light, illuminate me; most high and infinite Mercy, have mercy on me.

GALLICAN SACRAMENTARY. (Time of Charlemagne.)

Before Service.

O GOD, the Creator and Ruler of the world, favorably give heed to the prayers which I humbly offer; and as Thou hast granted me, Thy servant, not on the ground of any desert of mine, but out of the bounty of Thine infinite goodness, to serve the heavenly mysteries, so make me a worthy minister of Thy sacred altar; through Jesus Christ our Lord.

LEONINE SACRAMENTARY.

For the Priest.

O MY God, Heavenly Father, Thou Lord of Hosts, I thank Thee for this exceeding grace, that I dare to serve Thee, this day, at Thine altar; and that, prostrate at Thy feet, I may, for my sins and ignorance, and for the sins and ignorance of the people, supplicate Thy mercy. Hear, then, my humble prayer, and with Thy saints, whose memory we do here celebrate to Thy glory, keep me pure in Thy service; and grant me power of Thy holy and hallowing Spirit, that, by its mediation, with a conscience free from sin I may glorify Thee, and call upon Thee in all my ways, and that Thou mayest be gracious to me according to the fulness of Thy mercy. *Amen.*

St. Chrysostom. (A. D. 344-407.
Translated by L. G. Ware.)

From an Ancient Greek Liturgy.

Thanksgiving after the Communion.

O GOD of my Fathers, Thou our God, who art powerful, faithful, and true, and without deceit in Thy promises, who didst send upon earth Jesus Christ Thy Son to converse with men, as a man, to take away error by the roots; do Thou, even now, through him, be mindful of this Thy Holy Church, which Thou hast purchased with the precious blood of Thy Christ, and deliver it from all evil, and perfect it in Thy love and Thy truth, and gather us all together into Thy Kingdom which Thou hast prepared. *Amen.*

BUNSEN'S HIPPOLYTUS.

The Priest.

WHO can be worthy of this office, unless he is first fitted for it by Thy preventing grace and compassion? Since, then, it is of Thy gift, not of our merit, Thou must also interpose Thy guidance, that it may not prove the everlasting punishment of our negligence, but rather become in due order the cause of an eternal reward for our having discharged it; through Jesus Christ our Lord.

LEONINE SACRAMENTARY.

The Priest.

O GOD, who providest for Thy people with tenderness, and rulest over them in love, give the spirit of wisdom to those to whom Thou hast given the authority of government; that from the well-being of the holy sheep may proceed the eternal joy of the pastors; through Jesus Christ our Lord.

GREGORIAN SACRAMENTARY.

The Priest.

O GOD, who, passing over the sins of human frailty, dost vouchsafe to unworthy men the dignity of the Priesthood; and not only pardonest sins, but also art pleased to justify the sinners themselves; of whose gift it cometh that things which are not should receive a beginning, — having begun, should receive nourishment, — being nourished, should bear fruit, — and being fruitful, should be able to continue; who hast created me when I was not, — having created me, hast endued me with steadfast faith, and given to me, being one of the faithful, although defiled by sin, the dignity of the Priesthood; I humbly beseech Thine Almighty goodness to cleanse me from my past sins, to strengthen me in good works during my passage through this world, and to confirm me in unwavering perseverance. And make me so to serve Thine altars, that I may be able to attain the fellowship of those priests who have been pleasing unto Thee. And may my prayer be acceptable to Thee through Him who offered up Himself to Thee as a sacrifice, who is the Maker of all things, and the only High Priest without spot of sin, Jesus Christ our Lord.

GREGORIAN SACRAMENTARY.

The Priest.

O MOST merciful God, incline Thy loving ears to my prayers, and illuminate my heart with the grace of the Holy Spirit, that I may be enabled worthily to minister to Thy mysteries, and to love Thee with an everlasting love, and to attain everlasting joys through Jesus Christ our Lord.

ANCIENT MISSAL. (Bright.)

Opening of Service.

LORD our God, great, eternal, wonderful, in glory, who keepest covenant and promises for those that love Thee with their whole heart; who art the Life of all, the Help of those that flee unto Thee, the Hope of those who cry unto Thee; cleanse us from our sins, secret and open, and from every thought displeasing to Thy goodness,—cleanse our bodies and souls, our hearts and consciences, that with a pure heart and a clear soul, with perfect love and calm hope, we may venture confidently and fearlessly to pray unto Thee.

COPTIC LITURGY OF ST. BASIL.

For Wisdom.

WE beseech Thee, O Lord, to look upon Thy servants, whom Thou hast enabled to put their trust in Thee; and grant them both to ask such things as shall please Thee, and also to obtain what they ask; through Jesus Christ our Lord.

LEONINE SACRAMENTARY.

For the Spirit of Prayer.

O God of hope, the true Light of faithful souls, and perfect Brightness of the blessed, who art verily the Light of the Church, grant that our hearts may both render Thee a worthy prayer, and always glorify Thee with the offering of praises; through Jesus Christ our Lord.

GELASIAN SACRAMENTARY.

After Service.

O GOD, the Life of the faithful, the Bliss of the righteous, mercifully receive the prayers of Thy suppliants, that the souls which thirst for Thy promises may evermore be filled from Thine abundance; through Jesus Christ our Lord.

GELASIAN.

For Pastors.

LORD God of Powers, do Thou sanctify the Pastors and Prelates of Thy sheep; that our adversary the Devil, overcome by their faith and holiness, may not dare to touch or violate the flock of the Lord; through the same our Lord Jesus Christ.

GOTHIC MISSAL.

For Trust in God.

O MOST loving Father, who willest us to give thanks for all things, to dread nothing but the loss of Thee, and to cast all our care on Thee who carest for us; preserve us from faithless fears and worldly anxieties, and grant that no clouds of this mortal life may hide from us the light of that Love which is immortal, and which Thou hast manifested unto us in Thy Son, Jesus Christ our Lord.

MODERN, — BRIGHT'S COLLECTS.

The Priest.

ALMIGHTY and everlasting God, the Source and Perfection of all virtues, grant us, we beseech Thee, both to do what is right and to preach what is true; that both by action and teaching we may afford to Thy faithful people the instruction which is of Thy grace; through Jesus Christ our Lord.

SACRAMENTARY OF LEO. (Fifth Century.)

The Priest.

ALMIGHTY and merciful God, who art pleased to use the ministry of priests for the rendering of service and prayer to Thee, we implore Thy boundless mercy, that whatever we now visit Thou wouldst visit, whatever we bless Thou wouldst bless, and that at Thy humble servants' entrance evil spirits may flee away, and the Angel of peace may come in; through Jesus Christ our Lord.

GREGORIAN SACRAMENTARY. (590–604.)

For Patience and Peace.

O LORD and Saviour Christ, who camest not to strive nor cry, but to let Thy words fall as the drops that water the earth, grant all who contend for the Faith once delivered, never to injure it by clamor and impatience; but speaking Thy precious Truth in love, so to present it that it may be loved, and that men may see in it Thy goodness and Thy beauty; who livest, &c.

MODERN, — BRIGHT'S COLLECTS.

For Pure Hearts.

ALMIGHTY God, unto whom all hearts are open, all desires known, and from whom no secrets are hid, cleanse the thoughts of our hearts by the inspiration of Thy Holy Spirit; that we may perfectly love Thee, and worthily magnify Thy holy name, through Christ our Lord. *Amen.*

ENGLISH SERVICE BOOK. (1789.)

For the Grace of Charity.

O LORD, who hast taught us that all our doings without charity are nothing worth, send Thy Holy Ghost, and pour into our hearts that most excellent gift of charity, the very bond of peace, and of all virtues; without which, whosoever liveth is counted dead before Thee: grant this for Thine only Son Jesus Christ's sake. *Amen.*

EPISCOPAL SERVICE. (1789.)

For Peace.

O GOD, who art the author of peace and lover of concord, in knowledge of whom standeth our eternal life, whose service is perfect freedom, defend us, Thy humble servants, in all assaults of our enemies; that we, surely trusting in Thy defence, may not fear the power of any adversaries, through the might of Jesus Christ our Lord. *Amen.*

At Morning.

O LORD, our Heavenly Father, almighty and everlasting God, who hast safely brought us to the beginning of this day, defend us in the same with Thy mighty power, and grant that this day we fall into no sin, neither run into any kind of danger; but that all our doings, being ordered by Thy governance, may be righteous in Thy sight, through Jesus Christ our Lord. *Amen.*

At Evening.

O LORD, our Heavenly Father, by whose almighty power we have been preserved this day, by Thy great mercy defend us from all perils and dangers of this night, for the love of Thy only Son our Saviour, Jesus Christ. *Amen.*

For Peace.

O GOD, from whom all holy desires, all good counsels, and all just works do proceed, give unto Thy servants that peace which the world cannot give; that our hearts may be set to obey Thy commandments, and also that by Thee, we, being defended from the fear of our enemies, may pass our time in rest and quietness, through the merits of Jesus Christ our Saviour. *Amen.*

PART XIII.

TIMES AND SEASONS.

Morning Prayer.

WHEN first thy eies unveil, give thy soul leave
To do the like; our bodies but forerun
The spirit's duty. True hearts spread and heave
Unto their God, as flow'rs do to the sun.
Give him thy first thoughts, then; so shalt thou keep
Him company all day, and in Him sleep.

Yet never sleep the sun up. Prayer should
Dawn with the day. There are set, awful hours
'Twixt heaven and us. The manna was not good
After sun-rising; far day sullies flowers.
Rise to prevent the sun; sleep doth sins glut,
And heaven's gate opens when this world's is shut.

Walk with thy fellow-creatures: note the hush
And whispers amongst them. There 's not a spring
Or leafe but hath his morning hymn. Each bush
And oak doth know I am. Canst thou not sing?
O leave thy cares and follies! go this way,
And thou art sure to prosper all the day.

Serve God before the world; let Him not go,
Until thou hast a blessing; then resigne
The whole unto Him; and remember who
Prevailed by wrestling ere the sun did shine.
  Poure oyle upon the stones; weep for thy sin;
  Then journey on, and have an eie to heav'n.

HENRY VAUGHAN. (A. D. 1621–1695.)

Awaking in the morning, say:

O MY God, my only good, the author of my being, and my last end, I offer Thee my heart. Praise, honor, and glory be to Thee for ever and ever. *Amen.*

At the up-rising, say:

I will rise from this bed of sleep to adore my God, and to labor for the salvation of my soul. O, may I arise on the last day to life everlasting!

While clothing yourself, say:

O my God, clothe my soul with the nuptial robe of charity, and grant that I may carry it pure and undefiled before Thy judgment-seat.

When clothed, kneel and say:

Come, O Holy Ghost, take possession of my heart, and enkindle therein the fire of Thy divine love.

Attend seriously to the presence of God; return Him thanks for his benefits; and offer yourself to Him without reserve.

MANUAL OF CATHOLIC PIETY.

Morning Hymn of the Early Church.

GLORY be to God on high, and on earth Peace Good Will among men. We praise Thee, we bless Thee, we worship Thee: we give thanks to Thee for Thy great glory; O Lord, Heavenly King, God the Father Almighty! O Lord, the only-begotten Son Jesus Christ; and the Holy Ghost, O Lord God! O Lamb of God! Son of the Father, that takest away the sins of the world, have mercy upon us. Thou that takest away the sins of the world, have mercy upon us, receive our Prayer. Thou that sittest at the right hand of God the Father, have mercy upon us. For Thou only art holy: Thou only the Lord, Jesus Christ, to the glory of God the Father. *Amen.*

ALEXANDRIAN MS.

Preparation for Prayer.

DEARLY beloved brethren, the Heavenly Father in whose presence we must stand is always more ready to hear than we to pray: nor does anything hide Him from us but the veil of our impure and earthly mind. And since the preparations of even the willing heart are not without Him, let us inwardly pray for the grace of a humble and holy spirit: that for a little while we may be alone with Him; and, as His beloved Son went up into the mountain to pray, so we may rise above the haste and press of life, and commune with Him in spirit and in truth.

J. MARTINEAU.

For the Opening of Service.

MINISTER. Glory be to God, all glory be to Him who did, as on this day, create the light, and command it to shine on the face of the deep! How much more glorious is that light which shines in upon our minds, by the example of patriarchs, the revelations of prophets, the sweet solace of holy psalms, the instruction of wise proverbs, the profit and experience of faithful histories!

People. Blessed be His name for this light which no darkness ever overspreads, this sun which never goes down.

Minister. God is the Lord who hath showed us such light.

People. His mercy is everlasting, and his truth endureth from generation to generation.

MARTINEAU'S SERVICE BOOK.

At Morning.

GOD, our Heavenly Father, quicken in us, we beseech Thee, every good and pure thought, and strengthen us in our devout resolves this day. Let no unhallowèd words pollute the tongues which Thou hast made to praise and bless Thee; no evil action defile the sanctuaries which Thou hast, in Thy wondrous mercy, chosen for Thyself. Remove whatever in us may be a hindrance to holy living, or a stumbling-block in another's way. May our trust in Thee, and our kindness to one another, never fail. May we bring to Thee, not only a humble spirit of obedience, but also great love. O Lord God, make us what Thou wouldest have us to be, and may we do what Thou wouldest have us to do: only be Thou ever with us to cleanse and renew, to teach, rule, and sustain us; till at last we come to Thee, to dwell forever with Thee and Thy saints in light. *Amen.*

MARTINEAU'S SERVICE BOOK.

An Horology.

O THOU, that hast put in Thine Own Power
the times and the seasons,
give us grace that we may pray to Thee
in a convenient and opportune season;
and deliver us.
Thou, that for us men and for our salvation,
wast born in the depth of night,
grant us to be renewed daily by the Holy Ghost,
until Christ Himself be formed in us,
to a perfect man;
and deliver us.
Thou, that very early in the morning,
at the rising of the sun,
didst rise again from the dead,
raise us also daily to newness of life,
suggesting to us, for Thou knowest them,
methods of penitence;
and deliver us.
Thou, that at the third hour didst send down

Thy Holy Ghost
on the Apostles,
take not that same Holy Spirit from us,
but renew Him every day in our hearts;
and deliver us.
Thou, that at the sixth hour of the sixth day
didst nail together with Thyself on the Cross
the sins of the world,
blot out the handwriting of our sins
that is against us,
and, taking it away, deliver us.
Thou, that at the sixth hour didst let down
a great sheet from Heaven to earth,
the symbol of Thy Church,
receive into it us sinners of the Gentiles,
and with it receive us into Heaven;
and deliver us.
Thou, that at the ninth hour for us sinners
and for our sins,
didst taste of death,
mortify our members which are upon earth,
and whatsoever is contrary to Thy Will;
and deliver us.
Thou, that didst will the ninth hour to be
the hour of prayer,
hear us while we pray at the hour of prayer,
and grant unto us that which we pray for and desire;
and deliver us.
Thou, that at eventide wast pleased to be taken down
from the Cross,

and laid in the grave,
take away from us and bury in Thy sepulchre
our sins,
covering whatever evil we have committed
with good works;
and deliver us.
Thou, that late in the night, by breathing
on Thine Apostles,
didst bestow on them the power
of the remission and retention of sins,
give unto us to experience that power
for their remission, O Lord, not for their retention;
and deliver us.
Thou, that at midnight didst raise David Thy Prophet,
and Paul Thine Apostle, that they should praise Thee,
give us also songs in the night,
and to be mindful of Thee upon our beds;
and deliver us.
Thou, that with Thine own mouth hast declared,
at midnight the Bridegroom shall come,
grant that the cry may ever sound in our ears,
Behold! the Bridegroom cometh!
that we may never be unprepared to go forth
and meet Him;
and deliver us.
Thou, that by the crowing of the cock didst
admonish Thine Apostle,
and didst cause him to return to repentance,
grant that we, at the same warning, may follow
his example,—

may go forth and weep bitterly,
for the things in which we have sinned against Thee;
and deliver us.
Thou, that at the seventh hour didst command the fever to leave the nobleman's son,
if there be any fever in our hearts,
if any sickness, remove it from us also;
and deliver us.
Thou, that at the tenth hour didst grant unto Thine Apostle
to discover Thy Son,
and to cry out with great gladness we have found the Messiah,
grant unto us also, in like manner, to find the same Messiah,
and having found Him, to rejoice in like manner;
and deliver us.
Thou, that didst, even at the eleventh hour of the day,
of Thy goodness send into Thy vineyard
those that had stood all the day idle,
promising them a reward,
give us the like grace,
and though it be late, even as it were about the eleventh hour,
favorably receive us who return unto Thee;
and deliver us.
Thou, that at the sacred hour of the Supper,
wert pleased to institute
the Mysteries of Thy Body and Blood,
render us mindful and partakers of the same,

yet never to condemnation, but to the remission of
sin, and to the acquiring the promises
of the New Testament;
and deliver us.
Thou, that hast foretold Thy coming to judgment
in a day when we think not, and in an hour
when we are not aware,
grant that every day and every hour
we may be prepared, and waiting Thy advent;
and deliver us.
Thou, that sendest forth the light, and
createst the morning,
and makest Thy sun to rise upon the evil
and the good,
illuminate the blindness of our minds by the
knowledge of truth,
lift Thou up the light of Thy countenance upon us,
that in Thy light we may see light,
and at length in the light of Grace the light of Glory.
Thou, that givest food to all flesh,
that feedest the young ravens when they call
upon Thee,
and hast led us from our youth up until now,
fill our hearts with food and gladness,
and stablish our souls by Thy grace.
Thou, that hast made the evening the end
of the day,
so that Thou mightest bring the evening of life
to our minds,
grant us always to reflect

that our life passeth away like a day:
to remember the days of darkness,
that they are many;
that the night cometh
wherein no man can work;
by good works to prevent the darkness,
lest we be cast out into outer darkness;
and continually to cry unto Thee.
Tarry with us, O Lord,
for it draweth towards evening, and the day of
our life is now far spent.
The work of the Creator is Justice;
of the Redeemer, pity;
of the Holy Ghost, holy inspiration;
(Who is) the other Comforter;
the Unction;
the Seal;
the Earnest.

BISHOP ANDREWES'S DEVOTIONS.

Before a Journey.

GO before Thy servant this day;
if Thou Thyself go not forth with me,
carry me not up hence.
Thou, who didst guide the Israelites by an Angel,
the wise men by a star;
who didst preserve Peter in the waves,
and Paul in the shipwreck;
be present with me, O Lord, and dispose my way;
go with me, and lead me out, and lead me back,

BISHOP ANDREWES.

I COMMEND to Thee, Lord,
my impulses, and my startings,
my intentions, and my attempts,
my going out, and my coming in,
my sitting down, and my rising up.

IBID.

Morning.

FROM the night our spirit awaketh unto Thee, O God, for Thy precepts are a light unto us. Teach us, O God, Thy righteousness, Thy commandments, and Thy judgments. Enlighten the eyes of our mind, that we sleep not in sins unto death. Drive away all darkness from our hearts. Vouchsafe us the Sun of Righteousness. Guard our life from all reproach by the seal of Thy Holy Spirit. Guide our steps into the way of peace. Grant us to behold the dawn and the day with joyfulness, that we may send up to Thee our prayers at eventide.

DAY-BREAK OFFICE OF EASTERN CHURCH.
(Translated by Bright.)

At Vespers.

IN the evening, and morning, and noonday, we praise Thee, we bless Thee, we thank Thee, and pray Thee, Master of all, to direct our prayer as incense before Thee; and let not our hearts turn away to words or thoughts of wickedness; but rescue us from all things that hurt our souls. For to Thee, Lord, Lord, our eyes look up, and our hope is in Thee. Confound us not, O our God.

VESPERS OF EASTERN CHURCH. (Bright.)

At Evening.

O LORD God, the Life of mortals, the Light of the faithful, the Strength of those who labor, and the Repose of the dead, grant us a tranquil night free from all disturbance; that after an interval of quiet sleep, we may, by Thy bounty, at the return of light, be endued with activity from the Holy Spirit, and enabled in security to render thanks to Thee.

MOZARABIC SACRAMENTARY. (About 700. Bright.)

Morning Prayer.

O GOD, who art the unsearchable abyss of peace, the ineffable sea of love, the fountain of blessings, and the bestower of affection, who sendest peace to those that receive it, open to us this day the sea of Thy love, and water us with plenteous streams from the riches of Thy grace, and from the most sweet springs of Thy benignity. Make us children of quietness and heirs of peace. Enkindle in us the fire of Thy love; sow in us Thy fear; strengthen our weakness by Thy power; bind us closely to Thee and to each other in one firm and indissoluble bond of unity.

SYRIAN CLEMENTINE LITURGY.

For Morning.

O GOD, who givest us not only the day for labor, and the night for rest, but also the peace of this blessed day, grant, we beseech Thee, that this season of holy quiet may be profitable to us in heavenly things, and refresh and strengthen us to finish the work which Thou hast given us to do. *Amen.*

MARTINEAU'S SERVICE BOOK.

For Evening.

O BLESSED God, who neither slumberest nor sleepest, take us into Thy gracious keeping for this night, and make us mindful of that night where the noise of this busy world shall be heard by us no more. O Lord, in whom we trust, help us by Thy grace so to live, that we may never be afraid to die, and grant that at the last as now our even-song may be: I will lay me down in peace and sleep, for Thou, Lord, makest me dwell in safety. *Amen.*

IBID.

For Morning.

ALMIGHTY God, our Father and Preserver, who hast watched over us during the darkness, and made us glad with the light of this day, grant that we may employ it in Thy most holy service; and even as Thou sheddest now the beams of the sun upon the earth, to give light unto our bodies, so illumine our souls with the brightness of Thy Spirit, to guide us in the paths of Thy righteousness. *Amen.*

MARTINEAU'S SERVICE BOOK.

Collects. For Sunday Morning.

MOST Gracious God, who strengthenest the weak and renewest the weary, and givest to Thy faithful servants a peace which the world can neither give nor take away, may this season of heavenly rest be entirely free from sin, as from labor and worldly care; and let Thy grace abound in our hearts that we may be in the spirit on this Lord's Day. *Amen.*

MARTINEAU.

Another.

AS rest is sweet to the weary, and the cooling stream to him that is athirst, so in this Thy day and Thy house be rest sweet unto us, and Thy word a fountain of living water. As the hart desireth the water-brooks, so may our souls thirst after Thee, and our hearts and our flesh rejoice in the living God. *Amen.*

MARTINEAU.

For Grace.

GRANT, we beseech Thee, Almighty God, that the words which we have heard this day with our outward ears, may, through Thy grace, be so grafted inwardly in our hearts, that they may bring forth in us the fruit of good living; to the honor and praise of Thy name, through Jesus Christ our Lord. *Amen.*

For True Needs.

ALMIGHTY God, the fountain of all wisdom, who knowest our necessities before we ask, and our ignorance in asking, we beseech Thee to have compassion upon our infirmities; and those things which for our unworthiness we dare not, and for our blindness we cannot ask, vouchsafe to give us, for the worthiness of Thy Son Jesus Christ our Lord. *Amen.*

A Prayer of St. Chrysostom.

ALMIGHTY God, who hast given us grace at this time, with one accord to make our common supplications unto Thee; and dost promise that when two or three are gathered together in Thy name, Thou wilt grant their requests, fulfil now, O Lord, the desires and petitions of Thy servants, as may be most expedient for them; granting us in this world knowledge of Thy truth, and in the world to come life everlasting. *Amen.*

(344-407.)

Morning Prayer.

Communion with God.

O THOU, whose form the eye seeth not, whose voice the ear heareth not, whom outward sense discerneth not, so near, so inward art Thou to us. The heart pure from sin evermore seeth Thee; the soul alive in love and obedience heareth Thy voice in its depths; the mind exercised to discern between good and evil perceives Thee, with whom evil cannot dwell, Supreme Good, Parent and Centre of All Good. Open our hearts to behold the unseen presence. Open our ears to hear Thine everlasting word. Open our whole souls to take in the breath of Thy love. Creator of all, with the return of day come new tokens of Thy power and providence. Amidst the darkness and the deep silence, Thy Spirit hath encircled and filled nature and man; Thine the sleep which hath relieved our cares, and soothed our hearts, and repaired us with fresh strength. Thine is the morning which we welcome now; Thine the sun calling us forth to work, and to rejoice in its light; Thine are the hours rising over us with their invitations to action, and society, and rest. Thine, O God, this great nature which embosoms us in its changing beauty forever. May we love Thee; may we live in Thee.

Father, reveal the deeper mystery of Thy presence in our souls. Those secret aspirations, those silent visions, those living attractions which draw us toward Thee, and which seek communion with all pure and holy beings, we confess Thee, only Thee, their source and their end, ourselves Thy children, asking to dwell in Thy bosom whence we came. Father, reveal Thy love within us; we have nothing else to seek.

We bow before Thee now, confessing our weakness, our ignorance, our sin. Amidst the world shining with Thy beauty, silent and benignant voices sounding to us through heaven and earth, we have yet forgotten Thee many times, and disobeyed Thy sweet and holy laws. Among Thy children we have lived so long we have failed to do for them the services which we owe from Thee. May the remembrance of our errors check all pride, and keep us in sincere lowliness. May the sense of our need forever urge us to Thee; that in Thy power we may have strength, that from Thy wisdom we may receive knowledge, that by Thy Spirit we may be consecrated to holiness of heart and deed. Quicken us with Thy life; imbue us with Thy love; discover to us the heavenly vision, and help us to obey its teaching. Our Maker, draw us into harmony with Thine infinite order. Our Father, unite us to Thyself and Thy great family in heaven and on earth.

ALTAR AT HOME.

Morning Prayer.

For God's Continual Presence.

OUR Father in Heaven, we thank Thee for the return of this morning, and for the renewal of our daily blessings. We love to feel that we are always surrounded by Thee, and that the blessings of each day are the gifts of Thy providence. We love to feel that Thou art coming to us in the joy and freshness of the morning, in the serenity and peace of the evening, in the love of our loved ones, in the happiness of our home, in the discipline of daily experience, and in all things which make us glad, and strong, and heavenly-minded. And now, before entering upon the labors and trials of this day, we meet together that we may think how real and earnest life should be; how innocently and actively we should enter into it, and how much we need Thy guidance, even when we cannot think of Thee. O Lord, how often have we felt that we would be more obedient to all Thy commands! How often have we said within ourselves, "This day we will not sin; we will be kind, and just, and patient, and affectionate all day, and lie down at night without a regretful memory!" But alas! as the excitements of duty or pleasure come upon us, we grow anxious and restless, or forgetful and frivolous, and find at the close of the day that we are careful and troubled about many things, and that we have not yet found that "good part" which cannot thus be taken away from us. Our Heavenly Father, we now come to Thee with no confidence in our own strength, and pray that Thou wilt help us. Let Thy grace be sufficient for us. Come to us many times this day, in holy thought and reverent feeling, and thus keep us near Thee, even in our forgetfulness. May all that is beautiful remind us of Thee, the Infinite Beauty. May all that is lovely remind us of Thee, the One altogether lovely. May all that is true lead us to Thee, the Source of all truth. O send us not from Thy presence unblessed; but breathe Thy loving Spirit upon us all before we take up the burden of our daily duty, that we may go on our way rejoicing, and the words of our mouths and the meditations of our hearts may be acceptable in Thy sight, O Lord, our Strength and our Redeemer. *Amen.*

ALTAR AT HOME.

Morning Prayer. Filial Trust.

OUR Father, we thank Thee for Thy protection during the night that is past, and ask Thy blessing on the day that is to come.

Grant us the sense of Thy presence to cheer, and Thy light to direct us, and give us strength for Thy service. And yet more, Father, give us Thine own help and blessing in our sorrows, our faintness, our failure and sin. Thou knowest that we cannot bear our burdens alone. We are only little children, and the world seems very dark to us, and our path very hard if we are alone. But we are Thy little children; and so we know we can come to our Father, to ask Thee to help us, and enliven us, and strengthen us, and give us hope. We are not ashamed of our tears, for our Lord has wept with us. We do not ask Thee to take away our sorrow, for He was made perfect through suffering;

but we do ask Thee to be with us as thou wert with Him, our Father, close to Thy little ones, even as He has promised us. *Amen.*

ALTAR AT HOME.

A Daily Oblation.

MY God and my all! I most earnestly desire, by my every breath, every thought, every word, every desire, every movement of body and soul; I desire to tell Thee a thousand times I love Thee more than life, or anything in this world, and offer and dedicate myself to Thee; renewing my baptismal vows, together with the promises and resolutions of my life past. And this without will, wish, or desire, but those solely of pleasing Thee, loving Thee, living for Thee, and dying for Thee. I am Thine, my God and my all. O make me so entirely and eternally; above all, take my heart; extirpate from it all other affections, and fill it, for the future, with purest flames of the most ardent love for Thee.

MANUAL OF CATHOLIC PIETY.

Morning Prayer.

ALMIGHTY God! I humbly adore Thy sacred Majesty, and with all the force and powers of my soul exalt and praise Thy holy name. I thank Thee for Thy gracious protection from the dangers of the past night, and for bringing me safely to the beginning of this day. Continue, O Lord, Thy mercy to me, and as Thou hast awakened my body from sleep, so raise my soul from sin, that I may walk soberly and chastely as in the day, in all holy obedience before Thy face.

Deliver me, O merciful God, from the evils of this day, and guide my feet in the ways of peace. Strengthen my resolutions to embrace with gladness all opportunities of doing good, and carefully to avoid all occasions of sin, especially those which I have found by experience to be most dangerous to my soul; and when, through frailty, I forget Thee, do Thou in Thy mercy remember me; that as I often fall by the evil inclination of my nature, I may instantly rise again by the assistance of Thy grace. Make me diligent in the duties of my calling and state of life, and not too solicitous for the success of my affairs; but in all the miscarriages and crosses of this world, absolutely submit to Thy divine pleasure, and wholly rely on Thy merciful providence. Let Thy blessing be upon my actions, and Thy grace direct my intentions; that the whole course of my life, and the principal design of my heart, may always tend to the advancement of Thy glory, the good of others, and the eternal salvation of my own soul, through Jesus Christ our Lord and Saviour.

Give me grace, O Lord, to do what Thou commandest, and command what Thou pleasest.

Give me grace to suffer what Thou permittest, and permit what Thou pleasest.

The blessing of God Almighty, Father, Son, and Holy Ghost, descend upon me, and dwell in my heart forever. *Amen.*

KEY OF HEAVEN.

Morning Prayer.

ALMIGHTY God, by whose will we were created, and by whose providence we have been sustained, by whose mercy we have been called to the knowledge of our Redeemer, and by whose grace whatever we have thought or done, which hath been acceptable to Thee, hath been inspired and directed, — vouchsafe unto us, this day, Thy blessing. Strengthen us for the performance of the duties now before us. And, since Thou hast ordained labor to be the lot of man, and knowest the wants and necessities of all Thy creatures, bless, from time to time our several endeavors and employments. Give us, this day, our daily bread. Feed us with food convenient for us. If it be Thy pleasure to cause us to abound with the good things of this life, give us a compassionate spirit, that we may be ready to relieve the wants of others; but let neither riches nor poverty estrange our hearts from Thee, nor cause us to become negligent of those treasures in heaven which can never be taken from us. And, into whatever circumstances of life we may be brought, teach us to be cheerful and content. In our affliction, let us remember how often we have been succored; and, in our prosperity, may we acknowledge from whose hand our blessings are received.

And do Thou dispose us all, most merciful God, so to remember our sins, that we may be brought to a true repentance, and unfeigned sorrow, and contrition of soul. Strengthen our faith in Jesus Christ our Lord; and grant, that through the gracious help of Thy Holy Spirit, we may obtain that peace which the world cannot give, and may be enabled to pass the residue of our lives in humble resignation and willing obedience. We acknowledge, O God, that every day is Thy gift, and ought to be used according to Thy command. O Thou, in whose hands are life and death, and by whose mercy we are spared, help us so to improve the time that we may every day become more holy in Thy sight; and when it shall please Thee to call us from this mortal state, may we resign our souls into Thy hands with confidence and hope; and may we finally find mercy, and obtain a joyful resurrection to eternal life, through Jesus Christ our Lord.

We commend to Thy fatherly goodness all our relations and friends, especially those who are the most closely united to us. We beseech Thee to look mercifully upon them; and grant them whatever may most promote their present and eternal joy.

Bless the President of the United States, and all in authority. Extend Thy goodness to our whole native land. Pity the sorrows and relieve the necessities of all mankind. And let Thy kingdom come, and Thy will be done in earth, as it is in heaven.

O Lord, hear our prayers, for Jesus Christ's sake, to whom, with Thee and the Holy Ghost, be all honor and glory, world without end. *Amen.*

HENRY THORNTON.

Penitence. Evening Prayer.

O LORD! watch over me, lest I sleep the sleep of death. Alas! this day, has it not been void of good works? In it we might have gained everlasting life, and we have lost it in vain pleasures. Perhaps it may be the last of a life undeserving of Thy mercy. O fool! perhaps this very night Jesus may come to demand of thee thy soul, the image of the great God, which thou hast disfigured by sin.

O Lord! grant that whilst I sleep Thy love may watch over me, and keep guard around my heart. I am the prodigal son; I have wandered far away into a strange land, where I have lost all my inheritance. I am starving, and a beggar: but I know what I will do; I will return to my Father; I will say to Him, O my Father, I have sinned against heaven and against Thee. Art Thou not the good shepherd who leaves his flock to go into the desert after a single wandering sheep? Hast Thou not declared that there is joy in heaven over a single sinner who repents? Thou wilt not then despise an humble and contrite heart.

O Lord! watch over my spirit while I wake, and my body while I sleep, that I may sleep in peace and awake in Jesus. Pity my weakness. Send Thy holy angels, spirits of light, that they may keep far from me the spirit of evil that is ever around me. Grant that I may resist it with the courage of faith. Give penitence to sinners, perseverance to the just, and peace to the dead. Let my evening prayer rise to Thee, O Lord; and let Thy blessing descend upon me.

FÉNELON. (1651-1715.)

Evening Prayer.

Hid with Christ in God.

O GOD, Fountain of all life, we thank Thee for Thy good gift of the waters of life through another day. We bless Thee that we live and move and have our being IN Thee. The world presses hard upon us, and we might faint and die if we were alone; but we are not alone, for the Father is with us. Not one moment in all our life is passed without Thee; Thou wilt never leave us; no place is without Thee; Thou wilt never forsake us. Thou hast made us for life, Thou hast kept us in life. When our last night in this world shall close about us, Thy love will fold us to sleep, and when we awake in the life to come, we shall be still with Thee, for in Thy love we shall live forever. Our sun shall be turned into darkness, this earth shall pass away from our sight, the body shall return to the dust as it was, but the Sun that lights the sun shall shine forever. The hand in which the earth is but a speck of dust abides. Thou art the same; Thy years shall not fail; and we are the sons of God. Not our will, but Thy will made us; not our will, but Thine, has kept us this day. O God, our Father, help us to a deeper trust in the life everlasting, from the lesson of this one day. May we *feel* that this love which is now, ever shall be; this robe of the flesh is Thy gift to Thy child, and when it is worn out Thou wilt clothe him again; this work of life is the work Thou hast given us to do, and when it is done Thou wilt give us more; this love, that makes all our life so glad, flows out of the deep fountain of God, for God is love, and we shall love forever. O, set these lessons deep in our hearts; help us to feel how, day by day, we see some dim shadow of the eternal day that will break upon us at the last. May the Gospel of Thy Son, the whisper of Thy Spirit, unite to make our faith in the life to come solid and clear; then shall we be glad when Thou shalt call us, and enter into Thy glory in Jesus Christ. *Amen.*

ALTAR AT HOME.

As it is in Heaven.

O GOD, Unsearchable; why are we so blind to Thee, who besettest us behind and before?

In the daylight of Thy constant mercy, we scarcely lift our eye to the infinite heaven whence it flows. Now screen us with Thy hand, O Lord, that we may not wait for the night of sorrow, but here, under the shade of holy thought, may learn in what a world we live. Here let us rest from the weary shows of life, and converse with Thee, the Only True. And though Thou receivest higher praise than ours, from natures that know Thee more and serve Thee better, yet tune our spirits and join our voices with theirs; and unite us with the faithful and saintly, there and here, in one light of faith, one beauty of holiness, one repose on Thee. *Amen.*

MARTINEAU'S SERVICE BOOK.

Litany.

GLORY be to Thee, O Lord, glory to Thee.
Glory to Thee who givest me sleep
to recruit my weakness,
and to remit the toils
of this fretful flesh.
To this day and all days
a perfect, holy, peaceful, healthy, sinless course,
vouchsafe, O Lord.

The Angel of peace, a faithful guide,
guardian of souls and bodies,
to encamp around me,
and ever to prompt what is salutary,
vouchsafe, O Lord.

Pardon and remission
of all sins and of all offences
vouchsafe, O Lord.

To our souls what is good and convenient,
and peace to the world,
vouchsafe, O Lord.

Repentance and strictness
for the residue of our life,
and health and peace to the end,
vouchsafe, O Lord.

Whatever is true, whatever is honest,
whatever just, whatever pure,
whatever lovely, whatever of good report,
if there be any virtue, if any praise,
such thoughts, such deeds,
vouchsafe, O Lord.

A Christian close,
without sin, without shame,
and, should it please Thee, without pain,
and a good answer
at the dreadful and fearful judgment-seat
of Jesus Christ our Lord,
vouchsafe, O Lord.

BISHOP ANDREWES'S DEVOTIONS.

Conclusion, which may be read with great Profit every Sunday.

AS Christians it would be very profitable for us to reflect, every morning, that we have on that day a God to glorify, a Saviour to imitate, our souls to save, our bodies to mortify, virtues to acquire, sins to satisfy for, heaven to seek after, hell to avoid, eternity to meditate on, time to improve, temptation to overcome, the Devil to resist, our neighbor to edify, our passions to subdue, the world to guard against, and, perhaps, death and judgment to undergo. Reflect seriously on all these important truths, and they will not only incite you to begin the day well, but also, in the course thereof, to make the affair of your eternal salvation your principal study.

FROM THE FRENCH OF REV. F. BOHOURS.

Daily Striving.

HE that desires to make any progress in the service of God, must begin every day with fresh ardor; he must, as much as possible, keep himself in the presence of God, and, in all his actions, have no other object in view but that of promoting the Divine honor.

ST. C. BORROMEUS.

Particular objects in Prayer.

WHENEVER you go to communion have always in your mind some particular intention, —

such as the acquiring of some virtue; overcoming such a temptation; the knowledge of God's will with regard to yourself; the relief of the souls of the faithful departed; the conversion of infidels, heretics, and of sinners in general; for nothing is more capable of exciting fervor in devotion than some particular end to which it is referred.

CATHOLIC MANUAL.

Rules and Lessons.

TO meales when thou doest come give Him the praise
 Whose arm supply'd thee; take what may suffice,
And then be thankful; O admire His ways
Who fils the world's unempty'd granaries!
 A thankless feeder is a thief, his feast
 A very robbery, and himself no guest.

When night comes, list thy deeds; make plain the way
'Twixt heaven and thee; block it not with delays;
But perfect all before thou sleep'st: then say,
"Ther 's one sun more strung on my bead of days."
 What 's good score up for joy; the bad well scann'd
 Wash off with tears, and get thy Master's hand.

Being laid, and drest for sleep, close not thy eyes
Up with thy curtains; give thy soul the wing
In some good thoughts; so when the day shall rise,
And thou unrak'st thy fire, those sparks will bring
 New flames; besides where these lodge, vain heats mourn
 And die; that bush, where God is shall not burn.

Briefly, doe as thou would'st be done unto,
Love God, and love thy neighbour; watch and pray.
These are the words and works of life; this do,
And live; who doth not thus hath lost heav'n's way.
  O lose it not! look up, wilt change those lights
  For chains and darknes and eternal nights?

HENRY VAUGHAN.

PART XIV.

WORKING PRAYERS.

—♦—

The Student's Prayer.

INEFFABLY wise and good Creator, illustrious Original, true fountain of light and wisdom, vouchsafe to infuse into my understanding some ray of Thy brightness, thereby removing that two-fold darkness under which I was born, of sin and ignorance. Thou that makest the tongues of infants eloquent, instruct, I pray Thee, my tongue likewise; and pour upon my lips the grace of Thy benediction. Give me quickness to comprehend and memory to retain; give me happiness in expounding and a facility in learning, and copious eloquence in speaking. Prepare my entrance on the road of science, direct me in my journey, and bring me safely to the end of it, even happiness and glory, in Thine eternal kingdom, through Jesus Christ our Lord. *Amen.*

THOMAS AQUINAS. (1224–1274.
His customary prayer before study.)

The Student's Prayer.

TO God the Father, God the Word, God the Spirit, we now pour forth most humble and hearty supplications; that He, remembering the calamities of mankind, and the pilgrimage of this our life, in which we wear out days few and evil, would please to open to us new refreshments out of the fountain of His goodness, for the alleviating of our miseries.

This also we humbly and earnestly beg, that human things may not prejudice such as are divine; neither that from the unlocking of the gates of sense, and the kindling of a greater natural light, anything of incredulity, or intellectual night, may arise in our minds towards divine mysteries. But, rather, that by our mind thoroughly cleansed and purged from fancy and vanities, and yet subject and perfectly given up to the divine oracles, there may be given unto faith the things that are faith's. *Amen.*

LORD BACON. (1561-1626.)

The Writer's Prayer.

THOU, O Father, who gavest the visible light as the first-born of Thy creatures, and didst pour into man the intellectual light as the top and consummation of Thy workmanship, be pleased to protect and govern this work, which coming from Thy goodness, returneth to Thy glory. Thou, after

Thou hadst reviewed the works which Thy hands had made, beheldest that everything was very good, and Thou didst rest with complacency in them. But man, reflecting on the works which he had made, saw that all was vanity and vexation of spirit, and could by no means acquiesce in them. Wherefore, if we labor in Thy works with the sweat of our brows, Thou wilt make us partakers of Thy vision and Thy Sabbath. We humbly beg that this mind may be steadfastly in us; and that Thou, by our hands, and also by the hands of others on whom Thou shalt bestow the same spirit, wilt please to convey a largess of new alms to Thy family of mankind. These things we commend to Thy everlasting love, by our Jesus, Thy Christ, God with us. *Amen.*

LORD BACON.

For Guidance.

O GOD of light, Father of life, Author of grace, who givest, to those who are poor in spirit and put their trust in Thee, a knowledge of such things as the very angels desire to look into; who hast brought us out of darkness into light, from death to life, from bondage into liberty; even now, O Lord, do Thou enlighten our understandings by Thy Holy Spirit, and thoroughly sanctify us in body and in soul, through Thy beloved Son. *Amen.*

MARTINEAU'S SERVICE BOOK.

Instant in Season.

ETERNAL God, who committest to us the swift and solemn trust of life, since we know not what a day may bring forth, but only that the hour for serving Thee is always present, may we wake to the instant claims of Thy holy will; not waiting for to-morrow, but yielding to-day. Lay to rest, by the persuasion of Thy Spirit, the resistance of our passion, indolence, or fear. Consecrate with Thy presence the way our feet may go; and the humblest work will shine, and the roughest places be made plain. Lift us above unrighteous anger and mistrust into faith and hope and charity, by a simple and steadfast reliance on Thy sure will: and so may we be modest in our time of wealth, patient under disappointment, ready for danger, serene in death. In all things, draw us to the mind of Christ, that Thy lost image may be traced again, and Thou may'st own us at one with Him and Thee. *Amen.*

MARTINEAU'S SERVICE BOOK.

A Teacher's Prayer for Strength.

GUIDE and strengthen and enkindle me, O Lord, inspire me with zeal, and guide me with wisdom, that Thy name may be known to those committed to my care, and that they may be made and kept always Thine.

O Lord, save me from idle words, and grant that

my heart may be truly cleansed and filled with Thy Holy Spirit, and that I may arise to serve Thee, and lie down in entire confidence in Thee, and submission to Thy will, ready for life or for death. Let me live for the day, not overcharged with worldly cares, but feeling that my treasure is not here.

What is it to live unto God? May God open my eyes to see Him by faith, in and through His Son Jesus Christ: may He draw me to Him, and keep me with Him, making His will my will, His love my love, His strength my strength: and may He make me feel that pretended strength, not derived from Him, is no strength, but the worst weakness. May His strength be perfected in my weakness.

DR. ARNOLD OF RUGBY.

In School.

GIVE Thy blessing, we pray Thee, to this our daily work, that we may do it in faith and heartily as to the Lord, and not unto men. All our powers of body and mind are Thine, and we would fain devote them to Thy service. Sanctify them and the work in which they are engaged; let us not be slothful, but fervent in spirit, and do Thou, O Lord, so bless our efforts, that they may bring forth in us the fruits of true wisdom. Strengthen the faculties of our minds, and dispose us to exert them, but let us always remember to exert them for Thy glory, and for the furtherance of Thy kingdom, and save us from all pride, and vanity, and reliance upon our own power or wisdom.

Give us this day Thy Holy Spirit, that we may be Thine, in body and spirit, in all our work and all our refreshments, through Jesus Christ Thy Son, our Lord. *Amen.*

DR. ARNOLD OF RUGBY. (Memoirs.)

For Strength.

GRACIOUS Father, keep me now through Thy Holy Spirit; keep my heart soft and tender now in health and amidst the bustle of the world; keep the thought of Thyself present to me as my Father in Jesus Christ; and keep alive in me a spirit of love and meekness to all men, that I may be at once gentle, and active, and firm.

O strengthen me to bear sickness or pain or danger, or whatever Thou shalt be pleased to lay upon me, as Christ's soldier and servant; and let my faith overcome the world daily. Strengthen my faith, that I may realize to my mind the things eternal, — death, and things after death, and Thyself.

How much of good have I received at God's hand, and shall I not also receive evil? Only, O Lord, strengthen me to bear it, whether it visit me in body, in mind, or in estate. Strengthen me with the grace which Thou didst vouchsafe to Thy martyrs, and let me not fall from Thee in any trial.

O Lord, let me cherish a sober mind, to be ready

to bear evenly and not sullenly. Reveal to me Thyself in Christ Jesus, which knowledge will make all suffering and all trials easy.

DR. ARNOLD OF RUGBY. (1795-1842.)

Prayer of an Author.

O ETERNAL Wisdom! I am not a light unto myself, and the bodies which surround me cannot illuminate me; the superior intelligences themselves, seeing that they contain not in themselves the Reason which makes them wise, cannot communicate that reason to my mind.

Thou alone art the light of Angels and of men; Thou alone art the Universal Reason to all minds. Thou art the very wisdom of the Father.

Wisdom Eternal, unchangeable, necessary. O Thou, my true and only Master, show Thyself to me, cause me to see Light in Thy Light!

I appeal only to Thee, I would consult none but Thee. Speak, Thou Eternal Word, the word of the Father that has always been uttered, that utters itself now, that will utter itself forever. O speak, and so loudly, that I may hear Thee through all the confused noises which my senses and my passions are continually making in my soul!

But, O Jesus! I beseech Thee to speak only in me for Thy glory, and to make me know only Thy greatness; for in Thee are hidden all the treasures of the wisdom and knowledge of God. He who knoweth Thee knoweth the Father, and he who knoweth Thee and the Father is perfectly blessed.

Cause me then to know, O Jesus, what Thou art, and how all things subsist in Thee. Penetrate my mind with the brightness of Thy glory. Consume my heart with the fire of Thy love. Grant me in this work, which I compose only for Thy glory, expressions worthy of Thee, and such as shall increase in me, and in those who share my meditations, the knowledge of Thy greatness, the sense of Thv mercies.

MALEBRANCHE. (1638–1715.)

Prayer before Work.

O ETERNAL God, who has made all things for man and man for Thy glory, sanctify my body and soul, my thoughts, and my intentions, my words and actions, that whatsoever I shall think, or speak, or do, may be by me designed to the glorification of Thy name; and by Thy blessing it may be effective and successful in the work of God, according as it can be capable.

Lord, turn my necessities into virtue; the works of nature into the works of grace, by making them orderly, regular, temperate, subordinate, and profitable to ends beyond their own proper efficacy; and let no pride or self-seeking, no covetousness or revenge, no impure mixture or unhandsome purposes, no little ends and low imaginations, pollute my spirit, and unhallow any of my words and actions; but let my body be a servant to my spirit, and both body and spirit servants of Jesus; that doing all things for Thy glory here, I may be partaker of Thy glory hereafter; through Jesus Christ our Lord. *Amen.*

JEREMY TAYLOR.

The Prayer of Oberlin, and his wife Madeline.

HOLY Spirit! descend into our hearts: assist us to pray with fervor from our inmost souls. Permit Thy children, O gracious Father, to present themselves before Thee, in order to ask of Thee what is necessary for them.

May we love each other only in Thee, and in our Saviour Jesus Christ, as being members of his body. Enable us, at all times, to look solely to Thee, to walk before Thee, and to be united together in Thee; that thus we may grow, daily, in the spiritual life.

Grant that we may be faithful in the exercise of our duties, that we may stimulate each other therein, warning each other of our faults, and seeking together for pardon in the blood of Jesus Christ. When we pray together (and may we pray much and frequently), be Thou, O Lord Jesus, with us; kindle our fervor, O Heavenly Father, and grant us, for the sake of Jesus Christ, whatsoever Thy Holy Spirit shall teach us to ask.

Seeing that, in this life, Thou hast placed the members of our household under our authority, give us wisdom and strength to guide them in a manner conformable to Thy will. May we always set them a good example, following that of Abraham, who commanded his children and his household after him, to keep the way of the Lord, in doing what is right. If Thou givest us children, and preservest them to us, O grant us grace to bring them up to Thy service, to teach them early to know, to fear, and to love Thee, and to pray to that God who has made a covenant with them, that, conformably to the engagement which will be undertaken for them at their baptism, they may remain faithful from the cradle to the grave.

O Heavenly Father, may we inculcate Thy word, according to Thy will, all our lives, with gentleness, love, and patience, both at our rising up and lying down, at home and abroad, and under all other possible circumstances; and do Thou render it meet for the children to whom Thou hast given life only as a means of coming to Thee.

And when we go together to the Holy Supper, O ever give us renewed grace, renewed strength, and renewed courage, for continuing to walk in the path to heaven; and, as we can only approach Thy table four times in the year, grant that in faith we may much more frequently be there, yes, every day, and every hour; that we may always keep death in view, and always be prepared for it; and, if we may be permitted to solicit of Thee, O grant that we may not long be separated from each other, but that the death of the one may be speedily, and very speedily, followed by that of the other.

JOHN FREDERIC OBERLIN. (1768.)

A sincere renewal of my Baptismal Covenant.

IN the name of the most sacred Trinity, and before the holy angels, I profess my desire to consecrate the remainder of my life to God, relying upon his assistance. But O, Lord Jesus, what have I promised? I am taking too much upon me, poor worm of the dust, — I, so cold in heart, so blind to the darkness around me and within me, I would consecrate myself to the service of God.

Yes, I would? Where man has no merit nor power of his own, there my Saviour delights to make known his name, to show forth his compassion and infinite love. Dear Saviour! I see nothing but evil in myself; and my condition is so much the worse, in that I am insensible to my disease.

Lo here, dear Saviour, my heart and my hands; I am Thine; with my husband and my dear children, I am Thine. My desire is that we may all be completely Thine in body and soul. Take and possess all that I have; make us ready and prepare our hearts, so that, relying upon Thy merits alone, we may always be worthy to appear in Thy holy presence.

Once again, my dearest Saviour, I give myself to Thee; grant me Thy Holy Spirit, to be my guide and ruler; give me a docile and obedient heart, and a faithful attention to Thy voice. Bestow upon me the spirit of childlike love towards Thee, and not of slavish fear. Give me living faith, that incredulity may not separate me from Thee. At the hour of my death, dear Saviour, remember Thy lowly servant, that Thy angels may present me before Thy throne; let me there hear again that voice of peace and grace, which says, "Come, ye blessed of my Father, inherit the Kingdom prepared for you from the foundation of the world." Lord God, Jesus Christ, my kind Saviour, answer this request in tenderness. Most holy Trinity, answer and grant my prayer.

MADELINE SALOMÉ OBERLIN.

A Caution before Preaching.

LET the preacher labor to be heard intelligently, willingly, obediently. And let him not doubt, that he will accomplish this rather by the piety of his prayers than the eloquence of his speech. By praying for himself, and those whom he is to address, let him be their beadsman before their teacher; and approaching God with devotion, let him first raise to Him a thirsting heart, before he speaks of Him with his tongue; that he may speak what he hath been taught, and pour out what hath been poured in.

I cease not, therefore, to ask from our Lord and Master, that He may, either by the communication of His Scriptures, or the conversations of my brethren, or the internal and sweeter doctrine of His Own Spirit, deign to teach me things so to be proposed and asserted, that I may ever hold me fast to the truth: from this very Truth I desire to be taught the many things I know not: I have received the few I know.

I beseech this Truth, that loving-kindness prevailing and following me, it would teach me the wholesome things that I know not; keep me in the true things I know; correct me, wherein I am (which is human) in error, confirm me wherein I waver; preserve me from false and noxious things, and make that to proceed from my mouth which as it shall be chiefly pleasing to the Truth itself, so it may be accepted by all the faithful, through *Jesus Christ our Lord. Amen.*

St. Fulgentius. (468?-533.)

The Clergyman's Prayer.

I BESEECH Thee, O God, for my brethren and for myself; that, in the exercise of our ministry, we may depend much upon Thee; that we may learn from Thee what we ought to speak concerning Thee; that we may constantly speak the truth, boldly rebuke vice, and patiently suffer for righteousness' sake; that we may live and act as in the place of Christ, doing nothing unbecoming that character; and that we may preserve an apostolical firmness of mind under the vexations and persecutions of this world. *Amen.*

Bishop Wilson. (Sacra Privata.)

The Pastor's Prayer.

THE good Shepherd giveth his life for his sheep. O Sovereign Pastor! who gavest Thy life for Thy sheep, grant that I may never sacrifice Thy flock, to my own ease, convenience, profit, or pleasure. But that I may employ my time, my substance, my care, my labors, my prayers, for their welfare continually, and thus, at least, give my life for my sheep.

I have given you an EXAMPLE, that ye should do as I have done.

O Lord, that I could say this to the flock over which Thou hast made me overseer. That I could say, Be ye devout, as ye see me devout; do ye forgive one another, as ye see me ready to forgive; despise the world as ye see me do it.

Let me seriously consider that I am not only answerable for my own personal offences; I sin every time I cause others to sin by my example. What reparation can be made, what answer can be given, when Christ requires our flock at our hand?

Lord, suffer me not to follow my own will; reform me, that I may reform others; give me light to discover, and grace to amend, where I have done amiss. *Amen.*

BISHOP WILSON.

The Preacher's Prayer.

O GOD, the fountain of all wisdom, I most humbly beseech Thee to enlighten my mind, that

I myself may see, and be able to teach others the wonders of Thy Law; that I may learn from Thee what I ought to think and speak concerning Thee; and that whatever in Thy holy Word I shall profitably learn, I may indeed fulfil the same. Without which I shall disquiet myself in vain.

Direct and bless all my labors, without which I shall disquiet myself in vain. Give me a discerning spirit, a sound judgment, and an honest and a religious heart, that in all my studies, my first aim may be, to set forth Thy glory, by setting forward the salvation of men.

And if, by my ministry, Thy kingdom shall be enlarged, which God grant, let me, in all humility, ascribe the success not to myself, but unto Thy good Spirit, which enables us both *to will* and *to do* what is acceptable to Thee through Jesus Christ our Lord. *Amen.*

BISHOP WILSON.

Dedication of a Sermon.

O HOLY Spirit, be Thou present, and from heaven shed down Thy consolations on those that expect Thee; sanctify the temple of our body, and consecrate it a habitation to Thyself. Make the souls that desire Thee joyful with Thy presence. Make the house fit for Thee, the inhabitant; adorn Thy chamber and surround the place of Thy rest with all virtues; strew the pavement with jewels; let Thy mansion shine with the brightness of carbuncles and precious stones; and let the odors of all Thy gifts inwardly discover themselves; let Thy fragrant balsam perfume Thy residence, and expel whatever is noisome and the spring of corruption; do Thou make this our joy stable and lasting; and this renovation of Thy creature do Thou continue forever in unfading beauty.

CYPRIAN. (Third Century.)

A Prayer before Sermon.

O ALMIGHTY and Ever-living God! Majesty, and Power, and Brightness, and Glory! How shall we dare to appear before Thy face, who are contrary to Thee in all we call Thee? For we are darkness, and weakness, and filthiness, and shame. Misery and sin fill our days. Yet Thou art our Creator, and we Thy work. Thy hands both made us, and also made us lords of all Thy creatures; giving us one world in ourselves, and another to serve us. Then didst Thou place us in Paradise, and wert proceeding still on in Thy favors until we interrupted Thy counsels, disappointed Thy purposes, and sold our God, — our glorious, our gracious God, — for an apple. O, write it, O brand it in our foreheads forever! For an apple once we lost our God, and still lose Him for no more; for money, for meat, for diet. But Thou, Lord, art patience, and pity, and sweetness, and love; therefore we sons of men are not consumed. Thou hast exalted Thy mercy above all things, and hast made our salvation, not our punishment, Thy glory; so that there, where sin abounded, not death, but grace superabounded. Accordingly, where we had sinned beyond any help in heaven or earth, then Thou saidst, "Lo, I come!" Then did the Lord of life, unable of Himself to die, contrive to do it. He took flesh, He wept, He died; for His enemies He died; even for those that derided Him then, and still despise Him. Blessed Saviour! many waters could not quench Thy love, nor no pit overwhelm it. But, though the streams of Thy blood were current through darkness, grave, and hell, yet by these Thy conflicts, and seemingly hazards, didst Thou arise triumphant, and therein madest us victorious.

Neither doth Thy love yet stay here. For this word of Thy rich peace and reconciliation Thou hast committed, not to thunder or angels, but to silly and sinful men, even to me, pardoning my sins, and bidding me go feed the people of Thy love.

Blessed be the God of heaven and earth, who only doth wondrous things. Awake, therefore, my lute and my viol! awake all my powers to glorify Thee! We praise Thee, we bless Thee, we magnify Thee forever. And now, O Lord, in the power of Thy victories, and in the ways of Thine ordinances, and in the truth of Thy love, lo! we stand here, beseeching Thee to bless Thy word wherever spoken this day throughout the universal church.

O, make it a word of power and peace, to convert those who are not yet Thine, and to confirm those that are. Particularly bless it in this Thine own kingdom, which Thou hast made a land of light, a storehouse of Thy treasures and mercies. O, let not our foolish and unworthy hearts rob us of the continuance of this Thy sweet love; but pardon our sins, and perfect what Thou hast begun. Ride on, Lord, because of the word of truth, and meekness, and righteousness; and Thy right hand shall teach Thee terrible things. Especially bless this portion here assembled together, with Thy unworthy servant speaking unto them. Lord Jesu, teach Thou me, that I may teach them. Sanctify and enable all my powers, that in their full strength they may deliver Thy message reverently, readily, faithfully, and fruitfully. O, make Thy word a swift word, passing from the ear to the heart, from the heart to the lip and conversation; that, as the rain returns not empty, so neither may Thy word, but accomplish that for which it is given.

O Lord, hear; O Lord, forgive; O Lord, hearken, and do so for Thy blessed Son's sake: in whose sweet and pleasing words we say, Our Father, &c.

George Herbert. (1593-1634.)

A Prayer after Sermon.

BLESSED be God and the Father of all mercy, who continueth to pour his benefits upon us. Thou hast elected us, Thou hast called us, Thou hast justified us, sanctified, and glorified us. Thou wast born for us, and Thou livedst and diedst for us. Thou hast given us the blessings of this life, and of a better. O Lord! Thy blessings hang in clusters: they come trooping upon us; they break forth like mighty waters on every side. And now, Lord, Thou hast fed us with the bread of life. *So man did eat angels' food.* O Lord, bless it! O Lord, make it health and strength to us! — still striving and prospering so long within us, until our obedience reach the measure of Thy love, who hast done for us as much as may be. Grant this, dear Father, for Thy Son's sake, our only Saviour; to whom, with Thee and the Holy Ghost, — three persons, but one most glorious, incomprehensible God, — be ascribed all honor, and glory, and praise, ever. *Amen.*

George Herbert. (1593-1634.)

For Trust in Providence.

ALMIGHTY God, who beholdest Thy creatures encompassed with such darkness of ignorance that often they distrust Thy Providence, thinking themselves forsaken when Thou dost not immediately relieve them, O grant that with uplifted minds we may contemplate those things which Thy holy Word reveals; not doubting that Thou lookest upon us, and givest Thine angels charge to keep us, to bear us up in their hands, and to guide us in all difficulties. So may we wholly commit ourselves to Thy fatherly care; and while we press forward to the mark of the prize of our high calling in Jesus Christ, do Thou ever draw and direct us in the ways of Thine appointment, until at length we be gathered into our rest. *Amen.*

MARTINEAU'S SERVICE BOOK.

For Strength to endure Suffering for Conscience' Sake.

TO all those who may be ordained to suffer for Thy sake, impart, O merciful God, such plentiful succor of Thy Holy Spirit, pour into their hearts such contempt of pain and death, kindle within them such love of Thee and zeal for Thy truth, fill them with such an animating hope of immortality, give them so much of the spirit of Him who died on the cross, that, after the example of the blessed saints and martyrs of the primitive ages, they may steadfastly confess Thee before men, and, having by their sufferings glorified Thy name upon earth, may attain the everlasting crown of righteousness in Thy kingdom, with Him who loved us and gave Himself for us. *Amen.*

MARTINEAU'S SERVICE BOOK.

Prayer of a Missionary.

O HOW is every hour lost that is not spent in the love and contemplation of God, my God. O send Thy light and Thy truth, that I may live always sincerely, always affectionately, towards God.

May my soul, in prayer, never rest satisfied without the enjoyment of God! May all my thoughts be fixed on Him! May I sit so loose to every employment here, that I may be able at a moment's warning to take my departure for another world! May I be taught to remember that all other studies are merely subservient to the great work of ministering holy things to immortal souls! May the most holy works of the ministry, and those which require most devotedness of soul, be the most dear to my heart!

O, what shall separate us from the love of Christ! neither death nor life, I am persuaded. O, let me feel my security, that I may be, as it were, already in Heaven, that I may do all my work as the angels do theirs, and O, let me be ready for every work! be ready to leave this delightful solitude, or remain in it, to go out or go in, to stay or depart, just as the Lord shall appoint. Lord, let me have no will of my own; or consider my true happiness as depending, in the smallest degree, on anything that can befall the outward man, but as consisting altogether in conformity to God's will. May I have Christ here with me in this world, not substituting imagination in the place of faith; but seeing outward things as they really are, and thus obtaining a radical conviction of their vanity.

HENRY MARTYN. (1781-1812.)

Prayer made by a Plantation Negro at Norfolk, Va.

The Sunday after the Assassination of President Lincoln.

O LORD, we come to Thee holding up our souls as empty pitchers, to be filled from the fountains of Thy love. Did n't you tell us, Lord, if we were hungry you would feed us? Did n't you tell us, Lord, if we were thirsty you would give us drink from the waters of salvation? Did n't you tell us, Lord, if we were poor and weak, Come unto me, all ye feeble, and weary, and heavy-laden, and I will give you rest? Did n't you tell us, Lord, if we would be patient and wait, you would bring us out of all our troubles? And when the hour was come, as you raised up Moses to break the power of Pharaoh and let the people go, so you have sent us a deliverer, to lead us out of slavery: and while the good shepherd was with us, he led us over the wilderness, and toted the little ones in his arms, and gave us to browse in the green pastures.

But now, Lord, when his work was done, you saw it was done, and took him up higher, and gave him a seat among the archangels, and clothed him in white robes; and he pleads for us. When any of us are worthy, we shall see him where he is, and embrace him. And the Lord will say, "Who be these?" And Abraham will answer, "These are they whom I brought out with much tribulation and anguish, from the house of bondage, and for whom I was killed."

The Queen's Prayer.

STRETCH forth, O Lord most mightie, Thy right hand over me, and defend me from mine enemys, that they never prevayle against me. Give me, O Lord, the assistance of Thy Spiritt, and comfort of Thy grace, truly to know Thee, intirely to love Thee, and assuredly to trust in Thee. And as I do acknowledge to have received the government of this Church and Kingdom at Thy hand, and to hold the same of Thee, so grant me grace, O Lord, that in the end I may render up and present the same unto Thee, a peaceable, quiett, and well-ordered State and Kingdome, as also a perfect reformed Church, to the furtherance of Thy glory. And to my subjects, O Lord God, grant, I beseech Thee, faithful and obedient hearts, willingly to submit themselves to the obedience of Thy word and commandments, that we altogether being thankfull unto Thee for Thy benefitts received, may laud and magnifie Thy Holy Name world without end. Grant this, O merciful Father, for Jesus Christ's sake, our only Mediator and Advocate. *Amen.*

QUEEN ELIZABETH. (1574.)

PART XV.

PATER-NOSTER, LITURGICAL, &c.

The Lord's Prayer Paraphrased.

OUR Father which art in Heaven.

In whom we live and move and have our being, grant that I and all Christians may live worthy of this glorious relation, and that we may not sin, knowing that we are accounted Thine.

We are Thine by adoption; O make us Thine by the choice of our will.

Hallowed be Thy name.

O God, whose name is great, wonderful, and holy, grant that I and all Thy children may glorify Thee, not only with our lips but in our lives; that others, seeing our good works, may glorify our Father which is in Heaven.

Thy Kingdom come.

May the Kingdoms of this world become the Kingdoms of the Lord and of his Christ. And may all that own Thee for their King become Thy faithful subjects and obey Thy laws. Dethrone, O God, and destroy Satan and his Kingdom; and enlarge the Kingdom of grace.

Thy will be done on earth as it is in Heaven.

We adore Thy goodness, O God, in making Thy will known to us in Thy holy Word. May this Thy Word be the rule of our will, of our desires, of our lives and actions. May we ever sacrifice our will to Thine; be pleased with all Thy choices for ourselves and others, and adore Thy providence in the government of the world.

Give us this day our daily bread.

O Heavenly Father, who knowest what we have need of, give us the necessaries and comforts of this life with Thy blessing; but above all, give us the bread that nourisheth unto eternal life.

O God, who givest to all life and health and all things, give us grace to impart to such as are in want, of what Thou hast given more than our daily bread.

And forgive us our trespasses, as we forgive them that trespass against us.

Make us truly sensible of Thy goodness and mercy and patience towards us, that we may from our hearts forgive every one his brother their trespasses. May my enemies ever have place in my prayers, and in Thy mercy.

And lead us not into temptation.

Support us, O Heavenly Father, under all our saving trials, and grant that they may yield us the peaceable fruits of righteousness.

But deliver us from evil.

From all sin and wickedness, from our ghostly enemy, and from everlasting death, good Lord deliver us!

Deliver us from the evil of sin, and from the evil of punishment.

Deliver us, O Heavenly Father, from the temptations and snares of this world, and from falling again into the sins we have repented of.

For Thine is the kingdom, and the power, and the glory, for ever and ever. Amen.

By Thy almighty power, O King of Heaven, for the glory of Thy name, and for the love of a Father, grant us all these blessings which Thy Son has taught us to pray for.

Thine infinite power, wisdom, goodness, faithfulness, and truth are the only foundation on which we may surely depend. O, give us a firm faith in these Thy glorious perfections.

Unto Him that is able to do for us abundantly more than we can ask or think, unto Him be glory in the Church by Christ Jesus, through all ages, world without end. *Amen.*

BISHOP WILSON. (1663-1755.)

Pater-Noster.

FATHER! almighty art Thou in Thy Work and in Thy works. Blessed in Thy Love, and in the fulness of Thy Grace!

Our Father Thou art! Father art Thou of all

men and of all souls and of all created things; the Preserver of them too!

Who art in Heaven! Ah, there Thou reignest in Thy great Excellency; but still art Thyself the Heaven of angels and of saints, the Heaven of all the hearts of Thy faithful ones still following their pilgrimage here below.

Hallowed be Thy name! Yes, so shall it hallowed be, to be and to abide the dearest comfort on our lips, a song of transport in our ears, and in our hearts a psalm sweet and jubilant.

Thy kingdom come! proven to us a Joy without sorrow, Peace without alarms, one sure and endless Rest.

Thy will be done in earth as it is done in Heaven! and in our work shall it be fulfilled; to love what Thou lovest, to hate what Thou hatest, and, in smallest as in greatest things, to do what is bidden in Thy holy commandment.

Give us, this day, our daily bread! Give us, this day, not only what the body needs, but, and much rather, that which is most needful to the soul, — Thy wholesome Truth divine, and the Heavenly Bread of the Sacrament from the altar!

And forgive us our trespasses as we also forgive those who trespass against us! O, pardon us all our sins, which against Thee and our neighbor and ourselves we have committed: gladly will we pardon them who sought to wrong us with an evil will, hard words, or careless deeds, who have done us harm in body or soul, or in our earthly goods!

And lead us not into temptation! For, verily, enough for us the danger which threatens out of the allurements of the world, the flesh, and the Evil One!

But deliver us from evil! From evil now present, and that which is past and that to come, be Thou our Deliverer!

Amen! From Thee and through Thee may it all come to pass in all men, and in me! *Amen.*

St. Bernard. (Translated by Rev. L. G. Ware.)

A General Thanksgiving for God's Goodness.

O ETERNAL Essence, Lord God, Father Almighty, maker of all things in heaven and earth; it is a good thing to give thanks to Thee, O Lord, and to pay to Thee all reverence, worship, and devotion, from a clean and prepared heart, and with an humble spirit to present a living and reasonable sacrifice to Thy holiness and majesty; for Thou hast given unto us the knowledge of Thy truth; and who is able to declare Thy greatness, and to recount all Thy marvellous works which Thou hast done in all the generations of the world?

O great Lord and Governor of all things, Lord and Creator of all things visible and invisible, who sittest upon the throne of Thy glory, and beholdest the secrets of the lowest abyss and darkness, Thou art without beginning, uncircumscribed, incomprehensible, unalterable, and seated forever immovable in Thy own essential happiness and tranquillity;

Thou art the Father of our Lord Jesus Christ, who is our dearest and most gracious Saviour, our hope, the wisdom of the Father, the image of Thy goodness, the word eternal, and the brightness of Thy person, the power of God from eternal ages, the true light that lighteneth every man that cometh into the world, the redemption of man, and the sanctification of our spirits.

By whom the Holy Ghost descended upon the church; the Holy Spirit of truth, the seal of adoption; the earnest of the inheritance of the saints; the first fruits of everlasting felicity; the life-giving power; the fountain of sanctification; the comfort of the Church, the ease of the afflicted, the support of the weak, the wealth of the poor, the teacher of the doubtful, scrupulous, and ignorant; the anchor of the fearful; the infinite reward of all faithful souls, by whom all reasonable and understanding creatures serve thee, and send up a never-ceasing and never-rejected sacrifice of prayer, and praises, and adoration.

All angels and archangels, all thrones and dominions, all principalities and powers, the cherubim with many eyes, and the seraphim covered with wings from the terror and amazement of Thy brightest glory; these, and all the powers of heaven, do perpetually sing praises and never-ceasing hymns and eternal anthems to the glory of the Eternal God, the Almighty Father of men and angels.

Holy is our God; holy is the Almighty; holy is

the Immortal; holy, holy, holy, Lord God of Sabaoth, heaven and earth are full of the majesty of Thy glory. *Amen.* With these holy and blessed spirits I also, Thy servant, O Thou great lover of souls, though I be unworthy to offer praise to such a majesty; yet, out of my bounden duty, humbly offer up my heart and voice to join in this blessed choir, and confess the glories of the Lord. For Thou art holy, and of Thy greatness there is no end; and in Thy justice and goodness Thou hast measured out to us all Thy works.

(Here follows an enumeration of God's general benefits to man from the beginning of the world.)

O that men would therefore praise the Lord for his goodness, and declare the wonders that he hath done for the children of men.

O give thanks unto the Lord, for he is gracious, and his mercy endureth forever.

O all ye angels of the Lord, praise ye the Lord; praise him and magnify him forever.

O ye spirits and souls of the righteous, praise ye the Lord; praise him and magnify him forever.

And now, O Lord God, what shall I render to Thy Divine Majesty for all the benefits Thou hast done unto Thy servant in my personal capacity?

Thou art my Creator and my Father, my Protector and my Guardian; Thou hast brought me from my mother's womb; Thou hast told all my joints, and in Thy book were all my members written; Thou hast given me a comely body, Christian and careful parents, holy education; Thou hast been my guide and my teacher all my days; Thou hast given me ready faculties, an unloosed tongue, a cheerful spirit, straight limbs, a good reputation, and liberty of person, a quiet life, and a tender conscience (a loving wife or husband, and hopeful children). Thou wert my hope from my youth, through Thee have I been holden up ever since I was born. Thou hast clothed me and fed me, given me friends and blessed them; given me many days of comfort and health, free from those sad infirmities with which many of Thy saints and dearest servants are afflicted. Thou hast sent Thy angel to snatch me from the violence of fire and of water, to prevent precipices, fracture of bones, to rescue me from thunder and lightning, plague and pestilential diseases, murder and robbery, violence of chance and enemies, and all the spirits of darkness; and in the days of sorrow Thou hast refreshed me; in the destitution of provisions Thou hast taken care of me, and Thou hast said unto me, "I will never leave Thee, nor forsake Thee."

I will give thanks unto the Lord with my whole heart, secretly among the faithful, and in the congregation.

Thou, O my dearest Lord and Father, hast taken care of my soul, hast pitied my miseries, sustained my infirmities, relieved and instructed my ignorances; and though I have broken Thy righteous laws and commandments, run passionately after vanities, and was in love with death, and was dead in sin, and was exposed to thousands of temptations, and fell foully, and continued in it, and loved to have it so, and hated to be reformed; yet Thou didst call me with the checks of conscience, with daily sermons and precepts of holiness, with fear and shame, with benefits and the admonitions of Thy most Holy Spirit, by the counsel of my friends, by the example of good persons, with holy books and thousands of excellent acts, and would not suffer me to perish in my folly, but didst force me to attend to Thy gracious calling, and hast put me into a state of repentance, and possibilities of pardon, being infinitely desirous I should live, and recover, and make use of Thy grace, and partake of Thy glories.

I will give thanks unto the Lord with my whole heart, secretly among the faithful and in the congregation. For salvation belongeth unto the Lord, and Thy blessing is upon Thy servant. But as for me, I will come into Thy house in the multitude of Thy mercies, and in Thy fear will I worship toward Thy holy temple. For of Thee, and in Thee, and through and for Thee, are all things. Blessed be the name of God, from generation to generation. *Amen.*

LITURGY OF ST. BASIL. (Fourth Century.)

For all Conditions of Men.

WE most earnestly beseech Thee, O Thou lover of mankind, to be mindful of the one holy

Catholic and Apostolic Church, which is spread over the face of the whole earth: be mindful, O Lord, of all Thy people, the flocks of Thy fold.

Send down from heaven into our hearts that peace which the world cannot give, and that of this world also.

Guide in peace the King, the armies, the commanders, the councils, the people, the neighborhood, our coming in, and our going out.

O King of Peace, give us Thy peace; keep us in love and charity; be our God, for we know none besides Thee; we call upon Thy name: grant unto our souls the life of righteousness, that the death of sin may not prevail against us, or any of Thy people.

Visit, O Lord, and heal those who are sick, according to Thy pity and compassion; turn from them and from us all sickness and diseases; restore them to, and confirm them in, their strength. Raise up those who have lingered under long and tedious indispositions; succor those who are vexed with unclean spirits. Relieve those who are in prisons or in the mines, under accusations or condemnations, in exile or in slavery, or loaded with grievous tribute; deliver them all, for Thou art our God who loosest those who are in bonds, and raisest up those who are oppressed; the hope of the hopeless, the helper of the helpless, the lifter up of those who are fallen, the haven of those who are shipwrecked, the avenger of those who are injured.

Give Thy pity, pardon, and refreshment to every Christian soul, whether in affliction or in error. And, O Lord, Thou physician of soul and body, heal all our infirmities both of soul and body: O Thou, who art the overseer of all flesh, watch over us and heal us by Thy saving health. Be a guide at all times, and in all places, to our brethren who are travelling or about to travel, whether by land or by water; whatever way they pursue their journey, bring them all to a quiet and safe port: be with them in their voyages and on their road, restore them to their friends, and let them receive each other in joy and health. Preserve us also, O Lord, in our pilgrimage through this life from hurt and danger. Send rain out of Thy treasures upon those places which stand in need of it; renew and make glad the face of the earth by its descent, that, bringing forth, it may rejoice in the drops thereof. Raise the waters of the river to their just height; renew and make glad the face of the earth by the ascent of them, water its furrows, and increase its produce. Bless, O Lord, the fruits of the earth, and preserve them incorrupt for our use, that we may sow and reap from them. Bless also, O Lord, and crown the year with the riches of Thy goodness, for the sake of the poor, the widow, the fatherless, and the stranger; for the sake of all of us, who put our trust in Thee, and call upon Thy holy name: for the eyes of all wait upon Thee, O Lord, and Thou givest them their meat in due season. O Thou that givest food to all flesh, fill our hearts with joy and gladness; give us always what is sufficient for the relief of our necessities, that we may abound in every good work in Jesus Christ our Lord.

Give rest, O Lord our God, to the souls of our fathers and brethren, who are departed in the faith of Christ: be mindful of our forefathers from the beginning of the world, of the patriarchs, prophets, apostles, martyrs, confessors, bishops, saints, just men, and the soul of every one who is gone before us in the faith of Christ.

Give rest to the souls of all these, O Lord our God, in the tabernacles of Thy saints; dispense unto them in Thy Kingdom those good things which Thou hast promised, which eye hath not seen, nor ear heard, neither have entered into the heart of man, which Thou hast prepared, O God, for those who love Thy holy name. Give rest to their souls, and vouchsafe them the kingdom of heaven: but grant unto us that we may finish our lives as Christians, well pleasing to Thee, and free from sin, and that we may have our portion and lot with all Thy saints. Receive, O God, unto Thy holy heaven and to Thy intellectual altar in the heaven of heavens, by the ministry of archangels, the eucharistical praises of those that offer sacrifices and oblations to Thee; of those who would offer much or little, privately or openly, but have it not to offer; of those who have this day brought their offerings.

Receive them as Thou didst the gifts of Thy righteous Abel, the sacrifice of our father Abraham, the incense of Zacharias, the alms of Cornelius, and the widow's mite. Receive their offerings of praise and thanksgiving, and for their earthly things give them heavenly, for their temporal, eternal.

ALEXANDRIAN LITURGY. (175-254.)

"THAT beautiful prayer of the second Alexandrian Liturgy may be considered as the perfection to which liturgical composition attained in the ancient Church. It may be considered, on the whole, as perfect, — if we assume, as I believe, that it was intended rather as a model than as a literal formulary."

BUNSEN'S HIPPOLYTUS.

THE END.

Cambridge: Electrotyped and Printed by Welch, Bigelow, & Co.

www.ingramcontent.com/pod-product-compliance
Lightning Source LLC
LaVergne TN
LVHW010159110826
845151LV00002B/559